Dual Labor Markets

Dual Labor Markets:

A Macroeconomic Perspective

Gilles Saint-Paul

The MIT Press
Cambridge, Massachusetts
London, England

This book was set in Palatino by Asco Trade Typesetting Ltd., Hong Kong.

Printed and bound in the United States of America.

Library of Congress Cataloging-in-Publication Data

Saint-Paul, Gilles.
  Dual labor markets : a macroeconomic perspective / Gilles, Saint-Paul.
    p.   cm.
  Includes bibliographical references and index.
  ISBN 0-262-19376-0 (hc : alk. paper)
  1. Labor market—United States. 2. Skilled labor—United States.
3. Subsistance economy—United States. 4. Labor market—Europe.
5. Skilled labor—Europe. 6. Subsistence economy—Europe.
I. Title.
  HD5724.S182   1996
  331.12'094—dc20   96-24366
                                             CIP

Nox nocti indicat scientiam

Contents

Foreword

This book brings together research that I have done on dual labor markets and macroeconomics over the last six years. I started studying this topic when I was a graduate student in the Department of Economics at MIT from 1987 to 1990. I found that there was enough unity in this theme to bring all the research together in a book. I hope that this book will shed some light on the issue of labor market flexibility in both Europe and the United States.

My work has greatly benefited from discussions with Olivier Blanchard and Michael Piore, as well as from my joint work with Samuel Bentolila, who also very kindly made comments on an earlier draft of the book. I am also grateful to an anonymous reviewer for very constructive comments.

Dual Labor Markets

1   Introduction

"There is a fact, a big unmistakable unsubtle fact: Essentially everywhere in the modern industrial capitalist world, unemployment rates are much higher than they used to be two or three decades ago. Why is that? If macroeconomics is good for anything, it ought to be able to understand and explain that fact."

—Robert M. Solow (1986).

Macroeconomists have undoubtedly taken the challenge of explaining rising unemployment, as evidenced by the large number of books and articles that have been published on the topic. How successful they have been is a matter of debate. In this book I bring together various theoretical models of the labor market that are often ignored by macroeconomists. These models are representative of my research on that topic over the past few years. I use these models to analyze macroeconomic policy issues such as the level and persistence of unemployment, real wages, the unskilled unemployment problem, human capital accumulation, and the political viability of labor market reform.

As Solow has stated in the quote above, the increase in unemployment is not confined to Europe; it is very much a transatlantic problem—and this would be even more evident if we were to lump so-called bad jobs with unemployment. Accordingly this book takes both a U.S. and a European perspective and analyzes bad jobs as much as it analyzes unemployment. The "dual labor markets" of the title refers to the coexistence of good and bad jobs within the same economy, and often within the same firms. This dualism will be given a more precise meaning in the course of the book.

It would be a caricature to think of the United States as having mainly a bad jobs problem and Europe mainly an unemployment problem. First, unemployment is high in the United States by the standards of the 1960s, particularly for the unskilled labor market. This suggests that rigidities and labor market institutions, which play an important role in my analysis, cannot take the sole blame for the rise in unemployment in Europe. To put it another way, the rigidities are not only due to regulation, they can also arise from market imperfections, so deregulation cannot eliminate them altogether. Second, so-called bad jobs are increasingly perceived in Europe as the price to pay for full employment. In particular, many of the reforms that have been enacted in the 1980s, by increasing flexibility "at the margin," have contributed to creating a two-tier labor market that bears some similarity to the U.S. dual labor market. Workers with fixed-term contracts (bad jobs) coexist with workers with permanent contracts (good jobs). In the United States this dual structure arises from imperfections in the labor market, and we have to understand why. In Europe it is intimately linked with regulation, which may have important policy implications.

I will begin by connecting the contents of the book with the underlying debates about dual labor markets in the United States and flexibility in Europe.

1.1   The U.S. Debate on Dual Labor Markets

The theory of dual labor markets was developed in the United States in the context of the debate on poverty and discrimination, in particular, by Michael Piore (see Doeringer and Piore 1971; Piore 1980; Berger and Piore 1980). It is based on a two-tier picture of the labor market. In the upper tier of the labor market (or primary sector) workers enjoy high wages, high fringe benefits, high employment security, and often the protection of unions. In the lower tier (or secondary sector) all is the contrary. Blacks and women are more often found in the lower than in the upper tier. Workers in the lower tier have lower attachment to work force participation and enjoy more frequent spells of unemployment. Another characteristic of dual labor markets is that the labor market is *internal* in the primary sector, meaning that many job positions are not filled by posting vacancies in the market but by internal promotion; by contrast, the market is the main source of recruitment in the secondary sector.

At the time this theory was developed, it was perceived as a departure from mainstream, neoclassical theory because no mention was made of the link between labor income and the marginal product of labor and of the tendency of competition to equalize welfare across workers with identical marginal products (see Cain 1976 for a critical survey of the literature and the issues).

More recently, however, it has been shown, in particular, by Bulow and Summers (1986) that one may provide within a neoclassical framework explicit deviations from market clearing that would account for such dualism. The Bulow and Summers idea is based on the efficiency wage model pioneered by Solow (1979) and Salop (1979) and developed in Shapiro and Stiglitz (1984).[1] In the Shapiro-Stiglitz model firms have an interest in paying wages above market clearing because of costly monitoring and bounded penalties. The mechanism is simple: Since the highest penalty that may be inflicted upon the worker is job loss, the cost to the worker of this loss is made higher by increasing wages so that he will work harder. If the market cleared, the cost of job loss would be zero; the worker would instantaneously find another job at the same wage and not provide work effort. Shapiro and Stiglitz thus show that there must be unemployment in equilibrium and that this unemployment must be involuntary: Unemployed workers are strictly worse off than employed workers but are unable to underbid them, since the employer knows that they would shirk if paid below the existing wage level.[2]

Bulow and Summers extend the Shapiro-Stiglitz model to show how it can explain dualism: Suppose that there are now two sectors in the economy, one with monitoring costs (IBM), the other without monitoring costs (MacDonald's). Then the sector without monitoring costs will pay competitive wages. From the point of view of workers, working in that sector or being unemployed would just be equivalent.[3] We here have an equilibrium where sector 1 pays more than sector 2 for workers with identical productivity. Jobs in sector 1 are rationed, while jobs in sector 2 are not. More generally, we could consider models with several sectors all paying different wages, depending on how high their monitoring cost is. Furthermore wages are correlated with some observable characteristic of the workers that may have nothing to do with productivity. It can be shown, in the context of the Shapiro-Stiglitz model, that workers with a higher turnover are more costly to employ. This is because they lose less from being fired, since they expected to leave anyway. Hence they must be

---

1. More recent studies include Akerlof and Yellen (1987) and Weiss (1991).

2. Rebitzer (1987a) provides direct evidence that unemployment positively affects productivity growth, which is in the spirit of the Shapiro-Stiglitz model.

3. If working in the secondary sector is strictly preferable to being unemployed, then there is full employment. In that case it is still correct to say that being unemployed and working in the secondary sector are equivalent because, if a worker becomes unemployed, he finds a job instantaneously in the secondary sector. That is, while unemployment is equal to zero, the value of being unemployed is still defined and is equal to the value of working in the secondary sector.

paid more to be prevented from shirking. Therefore it is more likely that these workers will end up in sectors with low monitoring cost, which means the low-paying, lower tier of the labor market. Observable characteristics correlated with high turnover will result in lower wages. This may explain why women, blacks, and young people are paid less.

The recent literature has also provided empirical evidence on the extent of labor market segmentation; such evidence comes from *earning functions*, which traditionally relate income to some individual characteristics such as age, experience, and schooling, and from looking at interindustry wages differentials. The bottom line is that there are many wage differentials in the economy that are not explained by productivity differentials or compensating differentials but instead come from competitive failures in the labor market. I discuss this literature in chapter 5. There is also considerable heterogeneity in turnover rates. In a well-known paper, Hall (1982) has documented how workers in the United States had very high turnover at the start of their careers and then settled into jobs that lasted a very long time.

All this is very interesting, but what does it have to do with macroeconomics? The macroeconomy played an important role for early proponents of the dual labor market theory. The secondary labor market was thought of as providing flexibility to the economy. These workers were used to adjust to fluctuations in labor demand, including those induced by the business cycle. Indeed, for Piore (1980), dual labor markets often arose *within* the same firm: The firm was using a core of primary workers along with a periphery of secondary workers who were fired in case of a slump (figure 1.1). Even where the two tiers did not coexist within the same firm, the same outcome could be achieved by using subcontractors (in the European context collective bargaining often prevents large firms from having a two-tier labor force). Therefore an essential ingredient in curing discrimination was countercyclical stabilization policy.

In chapters 3 and 4 I provide foundations for this intuition, using the same efficiency wage model as Bulow and Summers and Shapiro and Stiglitz. The key idea is that there are costs to *adjusting* the primary labor force, though not the secondary one. Firms will therefore prefer to hire primary workers (paying efficiency wages) provided these firms do not expect to change employment too often. When they expect wider demand fluctuations, they are more likely to use secondary workers. By using secondary workers on the *margin of adjustment*, they can *insulate* primary workers from these fluctuations. The secondary work force therefore allows firms to employ a primary work force and to avoid paying the

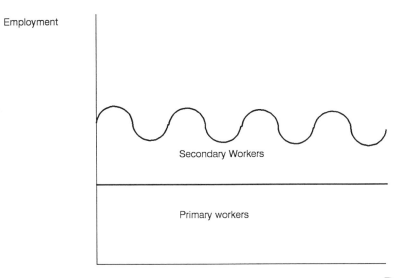

Employment

Secondary Workers

Primary workers

Time

Figure 1.1
Demand for primary and secondary workers over the cycle

associated adjustment costs. Hence dualism endogenously arises within firms as a response to demand fluctuations, and under plausible conditions, reducing these fluctuations reduces the share of secondary workers.

Where do these adjustment costs come from? The efficiency wage model is again sufficient to get these costs. We have seen that one of its predictions is that workers with higher turnover are more costly. This is equally true if they expect to lose their jobs, not for individual reasons but because the firm is laying off employees. The firm can therefore *save money by granting its primary employees employment security*. This is just what big firms such as IBM are traditionally thought to do. But this precisely means that it is costly for the firm to change its primary labor force. The firm will rather use secondary workers to deal with demand fluctuations.

Therefore the same rationalization of dual labor market theory that was used by Bulow and Summers to justify segmentation across sectors can be used to account for the internal aspect of dualism and its connection to volatility. The key mechanism is that efficiency wages also act as a *firing cost*. This is an implication not only of the "shirking" model, which is the focus in this book, but of many other models of noncompetitive wage formation. Hence firms would like to grant employment security to some workers, but not all. In many European countries, however, they do not have much choice over the amount of job security they can grant to workers.

1.2   The European Debate over Labor Market Flexibility

While in the United States the unemployment rate fluctuates around some natural rate, in Europe it does not seem to go down after an adverse shock has increased it, seeming to drift hopelessly upward (figure 1.2). This impression has been confirmed by numerous empirical analyses (see Blanchard and Summers 1986; Alogoskoufis and Manning 1988).

It is customary to blame labor market rigidities for European unemployment; high firing costs, strong unions, generous unemployment benefits, minimum wages, plague many European countries. Yet theoretical and empirical research has not been successful in building a strong case against these rigidities. A comparison of the U.S. and European experience suggests that altogether labor market rigidities account for at most three to four percentage points of unemployment.

To illustrate the ambiguous theoretical predictions about the effect of rigidities, let us consider the case of job protection on which this book is focused. Suppose that regulation imposes such a firing cost F for all workers. Consider the simplest two period model. In each $t = 1, 2$ the firm pays

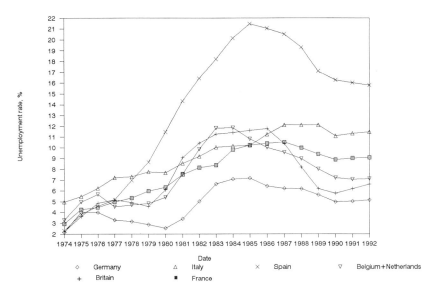

Figure 1.2
Unemployment in Europe, 1974–92 (Source: OECD)

a fixed wage w. The discount rate is zero. In period 1 the firm's revenue if it employs l_1 workers is $f(l_1)$. In period 2 there is a demand shock θ so that revenue is $\theta f(l_2)$. Downward adjustment of the work force in period 2 is associated with a firing cost equal to F per worker laid off. The firm's expected present discounted profits at $t = 1$ are thus equal to

$$f(l_1) - wl_1 + E_1(\theta f(l_2) - wl_2 - F\max(l_1 - l_2, 0)), \tag{1.1}$$

where E_1 is expectations conditional on the information available at $t = 1$. Consider, first, how employment is determined in period 2. The firm inherits l_1 workers. For each additional worker it hires, its marginal product is $\theta f'(l_1)$, while its marginal cost is w. Consequently, if $\theta f'(l_1) > w$, the firm will hire up to the point where marginal product equals marginal cost, $\theta f'(l_2) = w$. Suppose now that the firm fires a marginal worker. It spares the wage w but has to pay the firing cost F and loses the marginal product $\theta f'(l_1)$. It will therefore fire if $\theta f'(l_1) < w - F$, and it will do so up to the employment level l_2 such that $\theta f'(l_2) = w - F$. In other words, the marginal cost of labor when the firm is firing is equal to $w - F$: It is lower than the wage, more so when F is higher. What happens, next, if $w - F < \theta f'(l_1) < w$? It is clear that it is optimal for the firm to neither fire nor hire. Therefore there exists a band of values of θ, $[\theta_m = (w - F)/f'(l_1), \theta_M = w/f'(l_1)]$, or *corridor*, where inaction is optimal.

Figure 1.3 summarizes the effect of the firing cost on employment in period 2: First, it creates a corridor of inaction. Second, it increases employment, relative to the no firing cost case, in all states of nature where the firm is firing, since it makes it more difficult to fire. Note that because of the linear nature of the adjustment cost, whenever the firm is adjusting its work force upward or downward, the final employment level does not depend on l_1. In other words, the marginal cost schedule has a step at the past employment level l_1, but its position on either side of this step does not depend on l_1.

These properties are true in all models of firing costs, regardless of the complexity of their dynamic structure, and they will appear again in chapters 3, 4, and 6. Adding hiring costs practically does not change the analysis, so the results apply to a general class of models with *linear* adjustment costs (see Oi 1962; Nickell 1986). One interesting implication of the corridor effect is *hysteresis*, whereby temporary shocks may have permanent effects on employment. The hysteresis result is more formally derived in chapter 3. In the context of the two-period model above, it simply means that the firing cost makes employment dependent on past

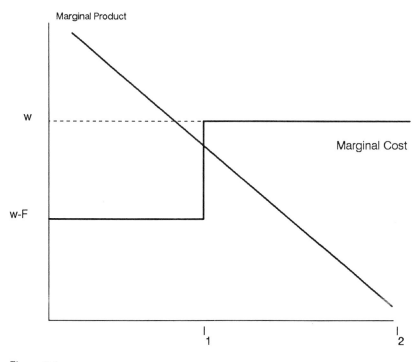

Figure 1.3
Employment determination in period 2

employment (if θ is within the corridor, it is then *equal* to past employment), even though the current distribution of shocks does not depend on the past.

Let us return now to period 1. Suppose that there is a marginal increase in l_1. This generates a gain equal to the current marginal value of labor, $f'(l_1)$, a loss equal to the wage w; it also generates losses in period 2: In all states of nature where the firm is firing, it starts with a higher work force (it has one more worker) and therefore has to be rid of more people (exactly one more worker, since its employment level does not depend on l_1). The loss in all these states of nature is thus equal to F. Furthermore, in all states of nature where inaction prevails, the marginal revenue of labor is $\theta f'(l_2) = \theta f'(l_1) < w$: The firm is facing losses on each additional worker. Hiring an additional worker therefore entails a loss of $w - f'(l_1)$ in all these states of nature. In the end the net expected present-discounted marginal benefit in period 1 is

$$f'(l_1) - w - F \cdot G(\theta_m) - \int_{\theta_m}^{\theta_M} (w - \theta f'(l_1)) g(\theta) d\theta,$$

where g (resp. G) is the density (resp. cumulative density) of θ. In period 1 firms will hire up to the point where the above expression becomes equal to zero, implying that

$$f'(l_1) = w + F \cdot G(\theta_m) + \int_{\theta_m}^{\theta_M} (w - \theta f'(l_1)) g(\theta) d\theta. \tag{1.2}$$

The right-hand side of (1.2) is the *shadow cost of labor* in period 1, and it is higher than the wage because the firm expects to either fire or improductively retain the worker in some future states of nature.

To summarize, firing costs make employment more persistent and dampen its fluctuations by increasing the marginal cost of labor when the firm is hiring and reducing it when it is firing. They may therefore account for the above-mentioned fact that unemployment is more persistent in Europe than in the United States. But it is not clear whether firing costs increase or reduce average labor demand: Their net effect on employment is the average of the positive effects on firing firms and the negative effects on hiring firms. In a celebrated paper Bentolila and Bertola (1990) found that the direct effect on firing dominates, so firing costs slightly increase employment. This is also my finding in the model developed in chapter 6. But the net result is very sensitive to assumptions about the stochastic process driving demand shocks. In Bentolila and Saint-Paul (1994), for example, using the model of chapter 3 with a linear-quadratic specification, voluntary quits and a nonnegativity constraint on employment, we found that firing costs first lower and then raise employment as they increase. In Saint-Paul (1995) I show that firing costs can generate multiple equilibria. In one equilibrium they do not matter very much because voluntary quits generate high labor turnover; firms do not fire people to reduce their labor force, rather they lay them off. In the other equilibrium labor turnover is low, so firms who want to get rid of their workers have to wait a long time or to pay the firing cost. For that reason labor demand is low, which validates the high unemployment and low quit levels.

So far we have only considered the direct effect of firing costs on labor demand in partial equilibrium. There are other reasons to believe that a reduction in firing costs may be desirable.[4] First, by reducing the value of the firm, they lower the incentive for entry and capital accumulation. If new technology is brought by new firms, then this lower entry rate may

---

4. See Bertola (1991) and Hopenhayn and Rogerson (1993).

have adverse effects on growth. Second, they increase the bargaining power of insiders by making it more expensive to replace them by outsiders (see Lindbeck and Snower 1988).[5] Third, society may care more about the duration of unemployment than its level. Duration is considerably longer in Europe than in the United States.[6] A reduction in firing costs will typically increase both job creation and job destruction. Although unemployment may rise or fall, unemployment duration is almost certain to fall. Indeed, in chapter 11, I show that the unemployed may support a reduction in firing costs that actually increases the equilibrium rate of unemployment—because it increases their probability of finding a job.

In the 1980s many European countries attempted to reduce firing costs. But these reductions were not very large and, quite interestingly, were done in a way that favored a two-tier labor market. While we have seen that even in the absence of regulatory firing costs there is a tendency for dualism to endogenously arise within the labor market, in Europe dualism ended up being embodied in the law through the coexistence of "rigid," permanent contracts with high firing costs and "flexible," temporary contracts with low firing costs. At the time the reform was introduced, the rights of incumbent employees were preserved. Furthermore temporary contracts were prevented from eventually replacing all permanent contracts by clauses that limited their use and the number of times they could be renewed. In chapters 6 and 7, I study the impact of these reforms on average employment, wage formation, and the cyclical response of employment. Among the various results that are derived, one is worth keeping in mind: overshooting. When flexible contracts are introduced, there is an employment boom, but employment eventually goes down to a lower level. The mechanism behind that is simple: Firms that want to increase their labor force will do so instantaneously by hiring many temporary workers, while firms that want to downsize will only do so progressively

---

5. In efficient bargaining models legally mandated severance payments may be entirely offset by payments from workers to firms, a point made by Lazear (1990). This extreme neutrality result is clearly a mere theoretical possibility. Part of the firing cost is in the form of legal procedures and is therefore paid to a third party (e.g., see Burda 1992). Second, firing costs may affect outside options in bargaining (as in Millard and Mortensen 1995) and thus how the surplus of the match is split. In this case separations will remain privately efficient, but job creation will be inefficient. Third, other assumptions about wage formation may also generate privately inefficient separations as an outcome of severance payments (see Saint-Paul 1995).

6. Descriptions of the anatomy of unemployment can be found in Layard et al. (1991) or Alogoskoufis et al. (1995).

to avoid paying high firing costs. The benefits of the reform in terms of employment are therefore front-loaded, while its costs are spread over the future. Another important effect of temporary contracts is that they will affect wage formation for workers who hold permanent contracts; these workers will ask for different wages because both their bargaining power and employment security has changed. The effect of temporary contracts on wage formation is studied in chapter 7.

Chapter 11 studies these reforms from a very different point of view, namely a political one. There it is argued that policy design is shaped by the conflicting interests of the employed and the unemployed. Reducing firing costs benefits the unemployed by increasing hirings but harms the employed by increasing firings. The two-tier system is a way to reconcile these conflicting interests; since only newly hired employees will have lower firing costs, the incumbent employed workers will support the reform. I show that under certain conditions there will be unanimity on the reform. However, incumbent workers anticipate that the growing mass of workers under flexible contracts will alter the balance of power in the future. The consequences of that for the reform's political viability are also studied in chapter 11. One interesting result is that increasing labor market flexibility by means of a two-tier system is more viable when the employed's exposure to unemployment is higher.[7] As a corollary, it is easier to reduce firing costs when they are not too high to begin with. Otherwise, the employed are so protected against unemployment that they benefit very little from the reform. The economy is then locked in a "rigid" equilibrium with no political support for flexibility.

1.3   Are Rigidities That Bad? The Debate on Labor Market Flows and "Renovating Economies"

An important question is whether unemployment is the result of some undesirable disequilibrium or whether it is the sign of large labor reallocation from declining to growing sectors. Recent literature has shed light on these issues by looking at gross labor market flows.[8] In Europe this literature has come to the surprising conclusion that despite large firing costs and other usual suspects for eurosclerosis, many jobs are created each year. The order of magnitude is 10% a year, which is about as many jobs as

---

7. This is not the case in an across-the-board reduction in firing costs.
8. See, for example, Lilien (1982), Abraham and Katz (1986), Blanchard and Diamond (1990), Davis and Haltiwanger (1990, 1992), and Burda and Wyplosz (1994).

unemployed workers. Of course, about the same number is destroyed every year. It is also true that in recessions job creation only moderately falls. What sense does it make, then, to talk about firing restrictions and insufficient mobility in an economy where the annual flow from employment to unemployment is around 10% of employment, and the opposite flow around 100% of unemployment?

In chapter 8 I study how a dual vision of the labor market may help to reconcile the evidence on flows with a role for rigidities. I argue that high turnover may be concentrated in the "flexible," secondary tier, while (relatively) high-job creation in recessions may be the outcome of a higher flow of secondary jobs as greater uncertainty induces firms to substitute secondary jobs for primary jobs.

1.4   Unemployment and Skills

Most of the analysis in this book is concerned with a dual labor market with identical workers. Dualism arises in the same fashion as unemployment does: Primary jobs are rationed, and firms want to offer both types of jobs in order to achieve flexibility. There are, however, some important aspects of the labor market that cannot be addressed with the assumption of identical workers: Unemployment falls more on the less educated; they have a higher probability of losing their jobs, longer unemployment spells, and are more likely to be fired in a slump. It is also true that the employability of the unskilled relative to the skilled has deteriorated in the late 1970s and in the 1980s.

In chapter 9 I develop a model where, in some sense, the secondary labor market is made of unskilled workers, while the primary one is made of skilled workers.[9] The argument is as follows: Skilled and unskilled workers are substitutes in that they perform the same tasks, but the skilled are more efficient. Firms would, everything else equal, prefer to employ skilled rather than unskilled workers. Search and recruiting are costly, however. If skilled workers are too scarce (meaning the skilled labor market is too tight), firms will employ unskilled ones. An equilibrium emerges where the unskilled unemployment rate is higher than the skilled one. If firing costs are very high, the economy is in a *rigid* or *one-tier* regime where the unskilled, although they have a lower probability of finding a job when unemployed, have the same probability of losing their job when

9. Brunello (1993) has studied aspects of internal labor markets for a similar type of model.

employed. If firing costs are not so high, the economy is in a *flexible* or *two-tier* regime, where the unskilled have a higher turnover rate because they are temporarily employed until the firm has found a skilled worker to fill the job. Firms post vacancies in the skilled labor market for jobs temporarily filled with unskilled workers.

An interesting aspect of the results derived in chapter 9 is the role of the supply of skilled workers. When the proportion of skilled workers in the labor force is higher, the unskilled employability deteriorates because the skilled are more easily found: The economy moves along a locus where both the unskilled and skilled unemployment rates increase, and the former typically more than the latter.

A very commonly held view is that the unskilled's employment prospects have deteriorated because technical progress has made them useless.[10] In the United States this has generated a fall in their relative wage; in Europe real wage rigidity has prevented that from happening and their unemployment rate has risen instead.[11] In chapter 9, I study how this phenomenon is exacerbated when firing restrictions create an option value of leaving a vacancy idle until a skilled worker is found, rather than filling it with an unskilled one. Chapter 9 also suggests that the rise in the proportion of skilled workers decreases the employment opportunities of unskilled workers. This is important because a shortcoming of the common "relative demand shift" view is that it does not explain why both the skilled and unskilled unemployment rates have increased and why they generally move together.[12]

Another question I tackle in this book is the interaction between labor market institutions and long-run growth. This is discussed in chapter 10, with a particular focus on the effect of firing costs on the returns to education. The two most interesting results are that (1) firing costs increase the returns to education by lowering the employability of the unskilled so that people want to acquire more skills to escape unemployment and (2) because of the option value effect, there may be increasing returns to education. An increase in the proportion of skilled workers may depress the demand for unskilled workers so much that the returns to becoming skilled increase. The economy can be either at a high-education, high-

---

10. See Bound and Johnson (1992), Katz and Murphy (1992), and Juhn, Murphy, and Pierce (1993).
11. See Drèze and Sneessens (1994) for the implications of those views for unemployment policy in Europe.
12. See, for example, Nickell and Bell (1994).

unskilled unemployment equilibrium or at a low-education, low-unskilled unemployment equilibrium.

1.5   Required Technical Background

With the exception of dynamic programming and the notion of a "matching function," the book uses elementary techniques throughout. For readers unfamiliar with these techniques, they are introduced in the next chapter. Others can directly proceed to chapter 3.

2   Some Technical Background

This chapter introduces the matching function and dynamic programming. Those readers who already know these techniques can proceed to the next chapter. For a more thorough introduction to dynamic programming, the reader can refer to Lucas and Stokey (1989) or Dixit (1976). For matching functions, see Pissarides (1990) and the references therein.

2.1   An Introduction to Dynamic Programming

Figure 2.1 depicts a simple optimization problem: finding a path that goes from A to H that yields the highest payoff. The payoff is the sum of the values of all the arrows that have been used. For example, $ABGH$ yields a payoff of 5.

There are several ways to approach this problem. One is to compute all the possible paths from A to H and pick the one with the highest payoff. Hence the values are $ABGH$, 5; $ABFH$, 8; $ACFH$, 5; $ACEH$, 7; and $ACDH$, 6. The best path is therefore $ABFH$. Note that we do not know whether it is better to go from A to C or A to B until all the paths are computed.

The idea behind dynamic programming is to compute the optimal path starting from the endpoint. Each node is associated with a value that gives the maximum payoff that can be obtained from that node to the end. The values can be computed recursively starting from the end: I can compute the value of one node by maximizing the sum of the value of an arrow and the value of the next node.

In the example of Figure 2.1, the value of the last node is set to $V(H) = 0$. There is a single arrow going from D, E , F , and G to H. The payoffs from those nodes to the end are therefore equal to $V(D) = 2$, $V(E) = 1$, $V(F) = 2$, and $V(G) = 0$, respectively. Consider now the value of C. There are three arrows, leading to D, E, and F. The values of these arrows are 1, 3, and 0, respectively. The associated payoffs to the end are

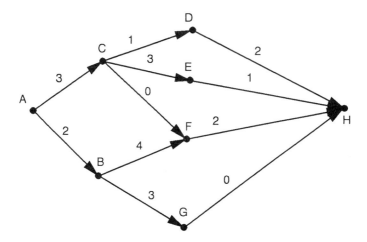

Figure 2.1
A simple dynamic programming problem

therefore $1 + V(D) = 2$, $3 + V(E) = 4$, and $0 + V(F) = 2$. From C the best route is therefore to go to E. This gives us the value of node C, $V(C) = 4$. Similarly from B one either goes to F, which yields $4 + V(F) = 6$, or G, which yields $3 + V(G) = 3$. Hence from B the optimal strategy is to go to F, and one has $V(B) = 6$.

Then, knowing the values of being at nodes B and C, we go one step backward to compute the optimal strategy at node A. If we go to B, the total payoff is $2 + V(B) = 8$. If we go to C, it is $3 + V(C) = 7$. Therefore the optimal choice is to go to B.

This example illustrates the two key concepts of dynamic programming, the value function and the policy function. The value function gives us the maximum payoff we can achieve as a function of the current state. Here our state is the node where we are located; in other examples it will be a (vector of) state variable(s) such as employment, the capital stock, or wealth. The policy function gives us our optimal decision as a function of our state. If I know the value function for all states at stage $n + 1$, I can compute both the value function and the policy function at stage n. For this I just have to know how my policy choice today will affect my state tomorrow, and to pick the choice that leads to the highest payoff. In the above example, the value function $V(\cdot)$ is given by $V(H) = 0$, $V(D) = 2$, $V(E) = 1$, $V(F) = 2$, $V(G) = 0$, $V(C) = 4$, $V(B) = 6$, $V(A) = 8$. The policy function—call it $P(\cdot)$—is $P(D) = DH$, $P(E) = EH$, $P(F) = FH$, $P(G) = GH$, $P(C) = CE$, $P(B) = BF$, $P(A) = AB$, where XY means the arrow going from X to Y.

Dynamic programming is particularly useful in infinite horizon problems and stochastic problems. Let us consider the following consumption example: A consumer lives from $t = 0$ to $t = T$. In each period he owns a capital stock k_t, which generates an income equal to $y_t = \theta_t k_t$. θ_t is an independently and identically distributed (i.i.d.) shock. The consumer can either consume or invest. If i_t is investment at date t, capital evolves as

$$k_{t+1} = (1 - \delta)(k_t + i_t), \qquad 0 \leq \delta \leq 1.$$

Consumption is then equal to $c_t = y_t - i_t$. In the last period consumption equals income plus remaining capital: $c_T = y_T + k_T$. The consumer maximizes

$$E_0 \sum_{t=0}^{T} u(c_t)\gamma^t, \tag{2.1}$$

where $\gamma \in \,]0, 1[$ is the discount factor and E_t the expectation operator conditional on the information available at date 0. Maximization takes place over all the sequences of contingent consumption paths $(c_0, \ldots, c_T)$, where c_t depends on the current and past realizations of the shock θ.

Let us solve this problem using dynamic programming. We define the value function $V(t, k_t, \theta_t)$ as the maximum payoff discounted as of t, between t and T if capital is equal to k_t and the current shock to θ_t. The "state" is therefore defined by calendar time, the capital stock, and the current value of the shock. This is all the relevant information needed. $V(t, k_t, \theta_t)$ is simply the maximum value of $E_t \sum_{s=t}^{T} u(c_s)\gamma^s$ if we start from that state.

Dynamic programming tells us that V is recursively defined as

$$V(t, k_t, \theta_t) = \max_{i_t} u(\theta_t k_t - i_t) + \gamma E V(t + 1, (1 - \delta)(k_t + i_t), \theta_{t+1}). \tag{2.2}$$

Equation (2.2) can be solved starting from $V(T, k_T, y_T)$. We know that in the last period all is consumed, so we have $V(T, k_T, \theta_T) = u(k_T(1 + \theta_T))$. This allows us to compute $V(T - 1, \cdot, \cdot)$, $V(T - 2, \cdot, \cdot)$, and so on. In the process we get the policy function $i(t, k_t, \theta_t)$ which gives us i_t as a function of the current state. It is the solution to the first-order condition

$$u'(\theta_t k_t - i_t) = \gamma(1 - \delta)E_{t+1} \frac{\partial V(t + 1, (1 - \delta)(k_t + i_t), \theta_{t+1})}{\partial k}. \tag{2.3}$$

What happens when the horizon becomes infinite? The problem becomes stationary: If capital and income are the same at two different dates, the situation will be the same from the consumer's point of view; hence the value and policy functions will be the same. In other words, time is no longer an argument in equations (2.2) and (2.3), which become

$$V(k_t, \theta_t) = \max_{i_t} u(y_t - i_t) + \gamma EV((1 - \delta)(k_t + i_t), \theta_{t+1}), \tag{2.4}$$

$$u'(\theta_t k_t - i_t) = \gamma(1 - \delta)E_{t+1}\frac{\partial V((1 - \delta)(k_t + i_t), \theta_{t+1})}{\partial k}. \tag{2.5}$$

To solve the problem, we need to find two functions $V(k_t, \theta_t)$ and $i(k_t, \theta_t)$ (the value and policy functions) that are a solution to the two functional equations (2.4) and (2.5). Lucas and Stokey (1989) provide some mathematical results that guarantee the existence of a unique solution to these equations. For example, the Blackwell (1965) theorem allows us to prove the existence of a unique solution by proving that the mapping T defined by

$$T(V)(k_t, \theta_t) = \max_{i_t} u(y_t + i_t) + \gamma EV((1 - \delta)(k_t + i_t), \theta_{t+1})$$

is a contraction. The first step, following Blackwell, is to prove that T is monotonous, that $T(W) \geq T(V)$ for $W \geq V$, and that there exists $\beta \in {]}0, 1{[}$ such that $T(V + k) = T(V) + \beta k$ for any *constant* k. The theorem implies that if these two conditions hold, then T is a contraction mapping, implying existence and uniqueness of a fixed point and thus of the policy and value functions. These conditions are trivially satisfied for the above defined transformation.

It is generally impossible to find an explicit solution, but it is possible to prove some results using these functions and the equations that they satisfy, or to solve (2.4) and (2.5) numerically. Another useful tool is to use the envelope theorem[1] to compute the derivative of the value function with respect to a state variable in (2.4). For example, we know that $\partial V(k_t, \theta_t)/\partial \theta_t = u'(\theta_t k_t - i_t) \cdot k_t$.

In the example above, it is possible to find an explicit solution in the case where $u(c) = \log(c)$. We can check that the solution is

$$V(k_t, \theta_t) = \frac{\log k_t + \log(\theta_t + 1)}{1 - \gamma} + C,$$

$$i(k_t, \theta_t) = \gamma\theta_t k_t - (1 - \gamma)k_t,$$

---

1. The envelope theorem states that in an optimization problem, when differentiating the objective function with respect to some exogenous parameter (here k), we can take the partial derivative of that function with respect to that parameter and disregard the fact that the endogenous policy variables (here i) will change.

with $C = \gamma \log(1 - \delta)/(1 - \gamma)^2 + \log(1 - \gamma)/(1 - \gamma) + \gamma \log(\gamma)/(1 - \gamma)^2$
$+ \gamma E(\log(1 + \theta))/(1 - \gamma)^2$.

The technique can be extended to a continuous time framework. The best approach is simply to consider each period as a very small time interval of length dt; the corresponding discount factor is $1 - rdt$, where r is the appropriate discount rate. Powers of dt greater than one are then neglected.

Let us consider a continuous time version of the above problem. The consumer now maximizes, instead of (2.1),

$$\int_0^{+\infty} u(c_t)e^{-rt}dt. \tag{2.6}$$

Capital accumulation is now given by

$$\frac{dk_t}{dt} = i_t - \delta k_t. \tag{2.7}$$

We can assume that instead of being i.i.d., the shock θ follows a Poisson process with two states θ_H and θ_L and transition probabilities α and β. This means that if $\theta_t = \theta_H$, it shifts to θ_L with probability α per unit of time. At date $t + dt$, θ_{t+dt} is equal to θ_H with probability $1 - \alpha dt$ and θ_L with probability αdt. Note that since α is a *flow* probability, it can take any value between zero and infinity. It does not have to be below one. The probabilities are αdt and $1 - \alpha dt$, which, given that dt is very small, are between 0 and 1. Similarly there is a probability β per unit of time of switching from θ_L to θ_H.

To find the equivalent of (2.4) and (2.5), we look for a value function $V(k_t, \theta_t)$ where $\theta_t \in \{\theta_H, \theta_L\}$ is the current value of the shock. Equation (2.4) can simply be rewritten between date t and date $t + dt$, where we have replaced $t + 1$ by $t + dt$ and γ by the discount factor between t and $t + dt$ which is simply $1 - rdt$. Hence

$$V(k_t, \theta_t) = \max_{i_t} u(\theta_t k_t - i_t)dt + (1 - rdt)E_t V(k_t - \delta k_t dt + i_t dt, \theta_{t+dt}).$$
$$\tag{2.8}$$

Note in equation (2.8) that the contribution of the current flow of utility to the value function is now infinitesimal (it is multiplied by dt), since the length of the period is infinitesimal. Similarly the discount factor is almost equal to 1, and tomorrow's capital stock is equal to today's capital stock, plus the infinitesimal contribution of investment, minus the infinitesimal contribution of depreciation.

The second step is to note that if $\theta_t = \theta_H$,

$$E_t V(k_t - \delta k_t dt + i_t dt, \theta_{t+dt}) = (1 - \alpha dt) V(k_t - \delta k_t dt + i_t dt, \theta_H)$$

$$+ \alpha dt \cdot V(k_t - \delta k_t dt + i_t dt, \theta_L), \qquad (2.9)$$

it is then possible to derive a *differential equation* for $V(k_t, \theta_H)$ by plugging (2.9) into (2.8), using a Taylor expansion and neglecting the terms of order 2 or higher in dt. We obtain, after some simplification,

$$0 = u(\theta_H k_t - i_t) - rV(k_t, \theta_H) + (i_t - \delta k_t)\frac{\partial V(k_t, \theta_H)}{\partial k}$$

$$+ \alpha[V(k_t, \theta_L) - V(k_t, \theta_H)]. \qquad (2.10)$$

The optimal policy $i(k_t, \theta_H)$ is found by straightforward differentiation of (2.8) with respect to i_t. Neglecting second-order terms, we find the equivalent of (2.5) as

$$u'(\theta_H k_t - i_t) = \frac{\partial V(k_t, \theta_H)}{\partial k}. \qquad (2.11)$$

Two other equations can be derived for the L state, with H (resp. L) replaced by L (resp. H) and α by β in (2.10) and (2.11).

Equations (2.10) and (2.11), and their counterparts for the L state, are four differential equations in the four functions $V(k, \theta_H)$, $i(k, \theta_H)$, $V(k, \theta_L)$, and $i(k, \theta_L)$. After solving these equations, we have the solution to the consumer's optimization problem.

An interesting interpretation of (2.10) is in terms of asset value. $V(k_t, \theta_H)$ is the value of an asset, which is "being in state H with a capital stock equal to k_t". The rate of return on this asset must be equal to the discount rate r. If, on the other hand, we compute this rate of return between t and $t + dt$, it must be equal to dividends (here, utility), plus expected capital gains, divided by the value of the asset. Dividends are equal to $u(\theta_H k_t - i_t)dt$, while expected capital gains are equal to $[dV(k_t, \theta_H)/dt + \alpha(V(k_t, \theta_L) - V(k_t, \theta_H))]dt$. The first term is the time variation in V in the H state, and it is also equal to $(i_t - \delta k_t)\partial V(k_t, \theta_H)/\partial k dt$. The second term is the expected capital gain from shifting to the L state (which may be negative). When we compute the rate of return this way, we must find that it is equal to the discount rate r. This is what (2.10) says. It can be rewritten

$$r = \frac{u(\theta_t k_t - i_t) + (i_t - \delta k_t)\partial V(k_t, \theta_H)/\partial k + \alpha[V(k_t, \theta_L) - V(k_t, \theta_H)]}{V(k_t, \theta_H)},$$

or

$$\text{Rate of return} = \frac{\text{Dividends} + \text{Expected capital gains}}{\text{Value}}.$$

2.2   The Matching Function

In chapter 9, I use the matching function that tells us how the *flow* of hirings (i.e., the number of hirings per unit of time) relates to the *stocks* of vacancies and unemployment (i.e., the amount of search on both sides of the market). The matching function is generally used in continuous time search models (see Diamond 1982; Pissarides 1990; Blanchard and Diamond 1990). In our case, formally, we have

$$h_t = m(u_t, v_t), \qquad (2.12)$$

where h_t is the level of hirings at date t, u_t the stock of unemployment, and v_t the stock of vacancies. The matching process is assimilated with a production process, where matches (hires) are produced with the search inputs (u and v) of the two sides of the market. The m function is typically thought to have constant returns to scale, as is the production function. This hypothesis is generally not rejected empirically (e.g., see Blanchard and Diamond 1989, who find that a Cobb-Douglas specification $m(u, v) = Au^\alpha v^{1-\alpha}$ matches the data well).

The evolution of aggregate employment is driven by

$$\frac{dl_t}{dt} = h_t - s_t = m(u_t, v_t) - s_t, \qquad (2.13)$$

where s_t is the flow of job separations. For s_t proportional to employment, $s_t = s(n - u_t)$, where n is total labor force. Equation (2.13) then defines a steady state locus in the (u, v) plane called the "Beveridge curve" (figure 2.2). The Beveridge curve is a decreasing relationship between unemployment and vacancies. In steady state the economy ends up at some point on the Beveridge curve, which is farther to the right, the lower labor demand. Also, if there are constant returns in the matching function, the Beveridge curve is *convex*: This means that when the labor market is tighter, increasingly more vacancies are needed to generate a given reduction in unemployment. Convexity of the Beveridge curve is due to decreasing marginal returns to any input in the matching function.

To close the model, we need to determine the position of the economy on the (u, v) plane. Pissarides (1990) closes the model by assuming that

Figure 2.2
The Beveridge curve

firms will supply vacancies up to the point where the present discounted value of a new vacancy is zero (this is not the assumption I make in chapter 9). Otherwise, firms would go on creating new vacancies. Implicit in this assumption is that there are no costs to changing the level of vacancies, implying that it is a "jump" or nonpredetermined variable.

Thus, at any point in time, the value of a vacancy must be equal to zero. Assuming a cost c per unit of time of maintaining a vacancy, the value of a vacancy satisfies:

$$rV_t = -c + q_t(J_t - V_t) + \frac{dV_t}{dt},\qquad(2.14)$$

where r is the interest rate, V is the PDV (present discounted value) of a vacancy, q_t the probability per unit of time of filling a vacancy, and J_t the value to the firm of a job. This equation is similar to (2.10), but here $-c$ is the dividend and expected capital gains are $q_t(J_t - V_t)$ (the gain made if the vacancy is filled) and dV_t/dt (the gain made if it is not filled). Plugging

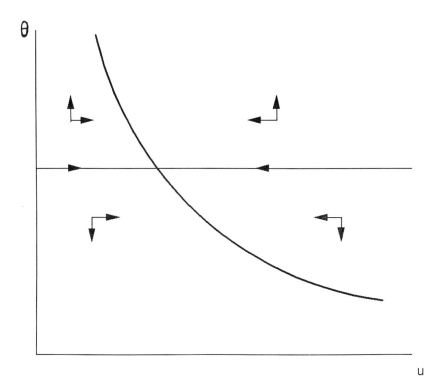

Figure 2.3
Convergence toward steady state

$V_t = 0$ into (2.14), we simply get

$$J_t = \frac{c}{q_t}. \tag{2.15}$$

Now q_t must be equal to the number of matches per unit of time divided by the stock of vacancies: $q_t = m(u_t, v_t)/v_t$. Under constant returns to the matching function, this can simply be rewritten $q_t = q(\theta_t)$, $q' < 0$, with $\theta_t = v_t/u_t$. The ratio of vacancies over unemployment, θ_t, is the appropriate indicator of labor market tightness. Note that (2.13) can be rewritten, using constant returns, in terms of unemployment and θ:

$$\frac{du_t}{dt} = s(n - u_t) - u_t \theta_t q(\theta_t). \tag{2.16}$$

We determine J_t by assuming constant returns to production, where the productivity of a match is m. Let w_t be the wage at t. Then

$$rJ_t = m - w_t + s(V_t - J_t) + \frac{dJ_t}{dt}. \tag{2.17}$$

To fix the idea, let us assume that workers earn a fraction φ of the match's output: $w_t = \varphi m$. Then, plugging this into (2.17) and making use of $V = 0$ and $J = c/q(\theta)$, we get an evolution equation for θ:

$$\frac{rc}{q(\theta)} = (1 - \varphi)m - \frac{sc}{q(\theta)} - \frac{cq'}{q(\theta)^2} \frac{d\theta}{dt}. \tag{2.18}$$

The evolution of the system in the (u, θ) plane is given by (2.16) and (2.18) (figure 2.3). The state variable is u, and the nonpredetermined variable θ. A key property is that u does not enter (2.18). Accordingly the unique non-explosive saddle path is such that θ is constant. This property, which I use in chapter 11, is due to the assumption of constant returns in the matching and production functions and to the fact that vacancies are a jump variable. In richer models of wage formation, they imply a dependence of w on θ and possibly $\dot{\theta}$, but not on the state variable u, which, because of constant returns, is irrelevant to the probabilities of finding a job or filling a vacancy.

3   The Dynamic Efficiency
       Wage Model

Two central features of dual labor markets are that workers in the secondary sector are not able to underbid those in the primary sector, and that firms find it more difficult to adjust their labor force in the primary sector than in the secondary sector. The dynamic efficiency wage model which I present in this chapter provides microeconomic foundations for both features.[1]

The literature on efficiency wages, which was pioneered by Solow (1979), Salop (1979), and Shapiro and Stiglitz (1984), with important contributions by Akerlof (1982) and Akerlof and Yellen (1990), is based on the idea that firms will prevent real wages from falling in response to unemployment because they recognize that lower real wages are associated with lower productivity. There are many ways to get such effects. Here I concentrate on the Shapiro and Stiglitz "shirking model" where work effort is imperfectly monitored and where firing is the highest penalty that the firm can inflict upon a worker.

This chapter explores a dynamic extension of that model. The main result of interest is that the cost of labor increases when the firm is expected to lay off workers. The intuition is that when a firm's employment is expected to shrink, workers have a greater incentive to shirk. To prevent workers from doing so, the firm has to raise future wages.[2] Efficiency wages are therefore equivalent to the existence of costs of adjusting the labor force. This has two important implications. First, efficiency wages are a channel of persistence for macroeconomic shocks. Firms do not want to adjust fully to these shocks because that would be costly in terms of incentives. As shown below, the efficiency wage model generates *linear* adjustment costs. The structure of adjustment costs generated by the incentive problem is thus very similar to the one generated by

---

1. This chapter elaborates on Saint-Paul (1995a).
2. For a related model, see Strand (1992).

a constant firing or hiring cost per worker. That is, effort inducement generates a cost function that is kinked at the current level of employment, implying *corridor effects* in the same fashion as is obtained in models with linear adjustment costs. Hence, as we will see, small shocks have no effects on employment, while big shocks have *permanent* effects. Most of an adjustment to the labor force tends to be front-loaded at the time the shock occurs. This is usually considered a realistic characteristic of labor demand (see Hamermesh 1992). By contrast, the more standard convex adjustment cost model predicts adjustment to be complete and spread over the whole future. Therefore shocks have no permanent effects, and there is no qualitative difference between the response to a large shock and the response to a small shock.

The second implication, which is further discussed in chapter 4, is that provided they can do so, firms will have an incentive to set up a dual structure within their labor force. By reducing its workers' probability of being fired, the firm will manage to improve incentives and therefore get lower wages. One way to do so is to shift the burden of adjustment to a "secondary tier" of workers who, for some reason, are not paid an efficiency wage. For example, they may be monitored at some cost. Turnover then has no impact on labor costs for the secondary tier. By splitting its work force in two, the firm manages to reduce its costs.

3.1 Presentation of the Model

Let us consider an infinite-horizon firm that is subject to shocks to its product demand and must pay workers efficiency wages in order to avoid shirking. In each period, for a given level of employment l_t, the total revenue of the firm is

$$R_t = \theta_t f(l_t).$$

This formula can be interpreted in a competitive fashion; θ_t is then just the price of the firm's good in period t and f is the production function. It can also be interpreted as the total revenue of an imperfectly competitive firm facing a downward-sloping demand curve. In any case, f is a concave, increasing function and θ_t is a random variable with a cumulative density function $G(\theta)$, $G' = g$. We assume that the θs are i.i.d. Hence the firm faces only temporary shocks.

We assume that the value of the shock in period $t + 1$ is known at time t by both the firm and its employees. Hence l_{t+1} is known one period ahead. This assumption will allow us to translate the intuition into a very simple form for the labor cost function, but the results do not rest crucially on the setup of the model.

We first derive the equation describing wage behavior. We assume that if people shirk, they can be caught with some probability, that people are never caught erroneously, and that anyone caught shirking is fired. Because the penalty from being caught shirking is losing one's job, employed people must enjoy rents compared to the unemployed. Otherwise, the penalty from shirking would be equal to zero, and people would not work. This prevents the unemployed from credibly underbidding the employed, thereby generating equilibrium involuntary unemployment.

Although this assumption sounds quite natural and realistic, it is surprisingly controversial. In particular, it has been argued that workers should post a bond when hired, on which they would earn some annuity while employed, and that they would forfeit the money if caught shirking. Bonding would thus allow employers to make the loss from shirking large enough to induce effort without the need for a wage increase beyond the reservation wage. Hence involuntary unemployment would be eliminated. This argument is not very convincing. First, as Katz (1986) argues, bonding is never observed in practice and subject to severe legal limitations. Second, the firm would have an incentive to pretend that the worker has shirked in order to collect the bond. This problem could be solved with the intervention of a third party. However, it is clear that such a contract would be costly to enforce, subject to frequent litigations, with the risk of collusion between the firm (or the worker) and the third party. Paying efficiency wages may well be a preferable alternative.[3] Another critique that has been made is that firms would use a wage profile that increases with experience in order to induce incentives.[4] While this may be true, in the absence of bonding it certainly does not surrender the worker's rent: As long as workers caught shirking cannot be made worse off than the unemployed, a rent must be paid to workers in order to prevent shirking.[5] The argument of this chapter only rests on the existence of such a rent, not on the timing of payments from the firm to the worker.

Once bonding is ruled out, it is clear that firing in case of shirking is the best alternative at least in this chapter's model. This is because it imposes

---

3. The microeconomic aspects of efficiency wage models are discussed, for example, by Carmichael (1985) and McLeod and Malcomson (1990). Ritter and Taylor (1994) have formalized the idea that bonding cannot arise in equilibrium when some of the firm's characteristics are unobservable to the workers.

4. See Lazear (1979, 1990).

5. See, for example, Akerlof and Katz (1989).

the highest possible punishment on a worker but not any costs on the firm. (In a more complex model, for example, with match-specific investment and the possibility of erroneous detection of shirking, other punishment schemes might be preferable for the firm.)

Workers have an infinite horizon.[6] In any period t a worker's instantaneous utility is equal to the difference between his wage and his effort:

$$u_t = w_t - e_t$$

If the employed worker "shirks," $e_t = 0$; if he does not shirk, $e_t = 1$. Let U_t (resp. V_t) be the present discounted utility of an unemployed (resp. employed) person at time t. Let w_t be the wage paid in period t.

Suppose that a worker who does not shirk loses his job with probability p_t at the end of period t, whereas a worker who shirks losses his job with probability $q_t > p_t$. If γ is the discount factor, then the worker who shirks in period t has an expected utility

$$V_{st} = w_t + \gamma[(1 - q_t)E_t V_{t+1} + q_t E_t U_{t+1}],$$

where E_t is the expectations operator conditional on information available in period t, which includes θ_{t+1}.

The worker who does not shirk has an expected utility

$$V_{nt} = w_t - 1 + \gamma[(1 - p_t)E_t V_{t+1} + p_t E_t U_{t+1}]. \tag{3.1}$$

To prevent workers from shirking in period t, the firm must set wages in such a way that

$$V_{nt} \geq V_{st} \tag{3.2}$$

We know that workers who are paid efficiency wages typically enjoy rents. This implies that there are queues for those jobs (in the Shapiro-Stiglitz model, there is involuntary unemployment). Therefore the firm can lower wages down to the point where (3.2) is satisfied with equality while being still able to attract workers. The condition $V_{nt} = V_{st} = V_t$ can be written

$$E_t V_{t+1} = E_t U_{t+1} + \frac{1}{\gamma(q_t - p_t)}. \tag{3.3}$$

Equation (3.3) is the *no-shirking condition* expressed in terms of present discounted values. It states that in discounted terms, employed workers must earn a rent over unemployed workers to be discouraged from

---

6. The standard dynamic programming techniques that I use are described in chapter 2.

shirking. This rent is equal to the last term in the right-hand side of (3.3). The current wage plays no role in this equation, however. What is relevant for incentives is the cost of getting fired, which consists of forgone *future* wages embodied in V_{t+1}. Only future wages determine the worker's current effort.

Suppose now that there is a monitoring process such that people who shirk are caught with probability x while they can lose their jobs for other reasons with probability p_t, the two events being independent. Then

$$q_t = p_t + x - xp_t. \qquad (3.4)$$

Using (3.4), (3.3) can be rewritten

$$E_t V_{t+1} = E_t U_{t+1} + \frac{1}{\gamma x(1 - p_t)}. \qquad (3.5)$$

The rent is therefore decreasing in the probability of being caught but increasing in the probability of losing one's job for other reasons. When p_t is higher, workers discount future wages paid by their current employer at higher rates. This reduces the loss incurred from being caught. The rent must therefore rise to prevent shirking.

If (3.5) is satisfied, then workers will not shirk, and $V_t = V_{nt}$ in every period. Using this condition and equations (3.1) and (3.5), we get

$$E_{t-1} w_t = (E_{t-1} U_t - \gamma E_{t-1} U_{t+1}) + \left(1 - \frac{1}{x}\right) + \frac{1}{\gamma x(1 - p_{t-1})}. \qquad (3.6)$$

In this expression for the "no-shirking condition," the present discounted value of future wages paid by the employer has disappeared. $E_{t-1}(U_t - \gamma U_{t+1}) + 1$ is the alternative wage, and the remaining term is the rent. Given that future wages, not current wages, matter for current incentives, it is the expectation of the wage, rather than the wage itself, that enters the no-shirking condition. However, given that the shock and the employment level are known one period in advance, the firm can simply set w_t at date $t - 1$ and make it equal to the right-hand side of (3.6).

Let us assume then that w_t is not random.[7] For simplicity and to focus on the effect of incentives on the cost structure, let us restrict ourselves to the case where $E_{t-1} U_t - \gamma E_{t-1} U_{t+1}$ is somewhat constant. We can therefore neglect the effect of aggregate employment changes on an

---

7. One could arbitrarily add a white noise term to the right-hand side of (3.6). But, since l_t is known at time $t - 1$, the cost of labor is linear in the noise term. Therefore expected labor costs are unchanged.

unemployed person's expected utility. This assumption can be taken as an approximation, meaning that $E_{t-1}U_t - \gamma E_{t-1}U_{t+1}$ does not fluctuate much.[8] Alternatively, it can be taken as a partial equilibrium analysis.[9] Equation (3.6) can therefore be rewritten as

$$w_t = a + \frac{b}{1 - p_{t-1}},\tag{3.7}$$

where $a = E_{t-1}U_t - \gamma E_{t-1}U_{t+1} + 1 - 1/x$ and $b = 1/\gamma x$. This equation implies that the higher the probability that a worker be fired at the end of period $t - 1$, the higher his wage at t must be in order to induce him to work during period $t - 1$.[10]

3.2   The Cost of Labor

Let us now consider the total cost of labor for a firm whose workers must be paid according to equation (3.7). I first show that this cost depends only on the total labor force l_t and not on the distribution of firing probabilities p_t across workers.

The Irrelevance of Firing Rules

The firm can choose any firing rule it wants. It may decide that some people will have a high probability of being fired, and others a low probability. But all the rules that achieve a given level of employment imply the same total cost. To see this, consider two rules A and B. Assume that

---

8. This is exactly the case if we assume that unemployment compensation is adjusted each period so as to keep U_t constant. This reflects the general tendency of unemployment benefits to be adjusted upward when joblessness becomes higher.

9. In Saint-Paul (1995a), I study the feedback effect of employment on alternative wages and its implications for the model's predictions about the persistence of unemployment and the cyclical behavior of real wages.

10. How good is the assumption that employment is known one period ahead by workers? One might think that the firm has private information about future profits and that it has no incentive to reveal it to the workers. However, the efficiency wage model provides such an incentive. Suppose that the firm knows that good times are coming. Then it can make an extra profit by announcing it to the workers in a credible way. This is because it will lower the worker's subjective probability of losing his job, and hence wages, according to equation (2.7). Now, if the firm does not make such an announcement, then workers will infer that relatively bad times are coming, which will imply higher wages and higher firing probability. But again, among those relatively bad times, some are relatively good, and the firm can again make extra profits by announcing them, and so on. In the limit, the firm will eventually always reveal its information. (I present this argument more formally in Saint-Paul 1990.)

rule A implies that half of the workers are fired with probability p_1 and the other half with probability p_2. The corresponding probabilities for rule B are p_1' and p_2'. Suppose that the labor force is large enough for the law of large numbers to hold. Total employment is therefore equal to expected employment. We will see that if the two rules achieve the same level of total employment, they have the same cost. Expected employment has to be the same under both rules, implying that

$$(1 - p_1) + (1 - p_2) = (1 - p_1') + (1 - p_2').$$

The expected cost of labor under rule A is

$$(1 - p_1)\left(a + \frac{b}{1 - p_1}\right) + (1 - p_2)\left(a + \frac{b}{1 - p_2}\right) = 2b + a(2 - p_1 - p_2)$$

$$= 2b + a(2 - p_1' - p_2'),$$

which is equal to the cost of labor under rule B. Hence all rules for achieving a given level of employment are equivalent from the point of view of the firm (this simple proof is generalized in the appendix). We can assume that the firm will choose a uniform rule, with everyone facing the same probability of being fired. Thus each worker has the probability

$$p_t = \max\left\{\frac{l_t - l_{t+1}}{l_t}, 0\right\}$$

of being fired at the end of period t. For this reason the firm offers the same wage to all workers in period $t + 1$, which, according to (3.7), is equal to

$$w_{t+1} = a + b\max\left\{\frac{l_t}{l_{t+1}}, 1\right\}.$$

The cost of employing l_{t+1} workers at date $t + 1$ is then

$$c(l_{t+1}, l_t) = w_{t+1}l_{t+1} = al_{t+1} + b\max\{l_t, l_{t+1}\}. \tag{3.8}$$

Properties of the Cost Function (3.8)

Figure 3.1 depicts the cost of employing l_{t+1} workers in period $t + 1$. We can see that there is a kink at $l_{t+1} = l_t$. The marginal cost of labor is lower for $l_{t+1} < l_t$ than for $l_{t+1} \geq l_t$. That is to say, the marginal cost of *not firing* an additional worker is less than the marginal cost of *hiring* an additional worker. Hence the model is formally similar to a model of labor demand

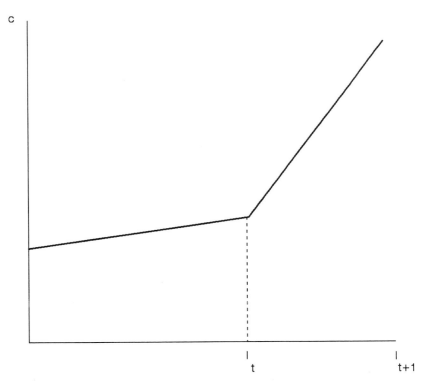

Figure 3.1
The cost of labor

with linear adjustment costs (see chapter 1). Efficiency wages introduce an adjustment cost because the expectation of being fired raises the wage that must be paid to the worker in order to prevent him from shirking.

The fact that the kink is at the *current* level of employment implies that this level will influence the future levels of employments, even though no pure adjustment costs are embodied in the firm's optimization program. Furthermore, because of this discontinuity, small shocks will have no effect on the level of employment.

The next section studies the dynamic optimization program of a firm that is subject to shocks and whose labor cost function is described by (3.8).

3.3   The Dynamics of Labor Demand

This section studies the behavior of a firm whose labor cost function is described by equation (3.8). Let $V(l_t, \theta_{t+1})$ be the expected discounted value of the firm's profit at the end of period t, with δ the discount factor. Then

$$V(l_t, \theta_{t+1}) = \max_{l_{t+1}} \theta_{t+1} f(l_{t+1}) - c(l_{t+1}, l_t) + \delta \cdot E_t V(l_{t+1}, \theta_{t+2})$$

$$= \max \theta_{t+1} f(l_{t+1}) - a l_{t+1} - b \cdot \max\{l_t, l_{t+1}\}$$

$$+ \delta \cdot E_t V(l_{t+1}, \theta_{t+2}), \tag{3.9}$$

where E_t denotes expectations at the end of period t. Notice that profits and wages are omitted in period t, since they are determined in period $t - 1$.

Since θ_{t+2} is independent of θ_{t+1}, we can write

$$E_t V(l_{t+1}, \theta_{t+2}) = H(l_{t+1}).$$

At the beginning of time t, the firm chooses l_{t+1} in order to solve equation (3.9). This problem is formally equivalent to a stochastic labor demand problem with linear adjustment costs as treated, for example, in Bentolila and Saint-Paul (1994). We can distinguish three cases:

1. The optimal solution satisfies $l_{t+1} < l_t$. The first-order condition can be written

$$\theta_{t+1} f'(l_{t+1}) + \delta \cdot h(l_{t+1}) = a, \tag{3.10}$$

where $h = H'$. This will happen whenever θ_{t+1} is lower than the so-called firing point:

$$\theta_m(l_t) = \frac{a - \delta h(l_t)}{f'(l_t)}. \tag{3.11}$$

2. The optimal solution satisfies $l_{t+1} > l_t$. The first-order condition is then

$$\theta_{t+1} f'(l_{t+1}) + \delta \cdot h(l_{t+1}) = a + b. \tag{3.12}$$

This happens if θ_{t+1} is higher than the hiring point:

$$\theta_M(l_t) = \frac{a + b - \delta h(l_t)}{f'(l_t)}. \tag{3.13}$$

3. If $\theta_m \leq \theta_{t+1} \leq \theta_M$, then $l_{t+1} = l_t$. The firm is inside the "corridor" and stays inactive.

Equations (3.10) and (3.12) can be easily interpreted. The left-hand side is the marginal value of labor. The right-hand side is its marginal cost, which is $a + b$ when the firm is expanding but only a when the firm is contracting. When the marginal value of labor at $l_{t+1} = l_t$ is between a and $a + b$, it is profitable not to alter the labor force (case 3).

The marginal cost of labor is lower when the firm is downsizing than when it is expanding. This is because in a contraction, by refraining from firing an additional worker, the firm lowers their perceived probability of losing their jobs, thus improving incentives and reducing labor costs.

Furthermore, it is shown in the appendix that h is negative and decreasing and that it satisfies the following equation:

$$h(l) = -f'(l) \cdot \int_{\theta_m(l)}^{\theta_M(l)} G(\theta)d\theta. \tag{3.14}$$

Combining equation (3.14) with equations (3.11) and (3.13), we can solve for the $h(l)$ function. We can also use (3.14) to check that the marginal value of labor $MV(l) = \theta f'(l) + \delta h(l)$ is decreasing in l. Since h is negative, the marginal value of labor is lower than its marginal product in the current period. This is due to the fact that each additional worker increases the potential losses that the firm would incur if it were to layoff (or unprofitably retain) workers in the future.[11]

Both the corridor and the gap between the marginal value of labor and its marginal product are generated by a *shadow firing cost* equal to b. That is, labor demand is the same as if wages were equal to a and firing costs equal to b. Note that b is decreasing in x: The better the monitoring is, the lower will be the shadow firing cost—and the narrower will be the corridor and the gap between marginal product and marginal value. In the absence of monitoring problems, b would collapse to zero, the corridor would disappear, and the marginal product of labor would be equal to the opportunity cost of labor in each period.[12]

Figure 3.2 shows that l_{t+1} is determined by the intersection of the MV schedule and the marginal cost schedule MC derived from equation (3.8). Depending on where the MV schedule is located, we can distinguish three cases, shown in panels a, b, and c of figure 3.2. They are the geometric counterpart to the three cases studied above.

---

11. Equivalently $\delta h(l)$ can be subtracted from the cost of labor, rather than added to its marginal product. That would increase the shadow cost of labor rather than reduce its marginal value. But it is a matter of convention.

12. In this discrete time model, the monitoring problem cannot disappear because even if workers are caught with probability one, firing only comes into effect in the next period, after workers have reaped the benefit from shirking. Eliminating the incentive problem is thus equivalent to letting x goes to infinity, not one. This can be more clearly seen in a continuous time model such as in Saint-Paul (1995b).

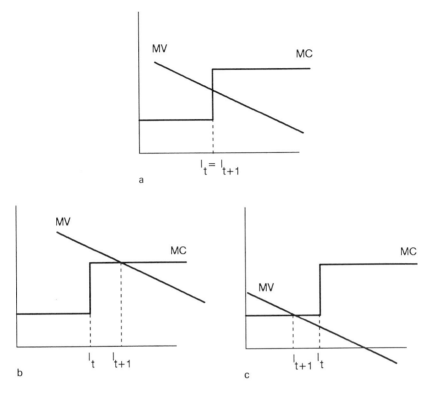

Figure 3.2
Employment determination in the three regimes

Now suppose that panel a of figure 3.2 shows how the economy is operating normally, say if θ is equal to its expected value $E\theta$. Suppose that there is a small shock (i.e., $\theta_{t+1} \neq E\theta$) that shifts the MV schedule. It is clear from figure 3.3 that if the shock is small enough, the size of the labor force remains unchanged. Hence a first implication of the model is that it exhibits corridor effects:

Small shocks have no effect on the level of employment.

Consider now the impact of a large shock, for instance, downsizing in period $t + 1$. Then, as is shown in figure 3.4, the MV schedule shifts downward, and this shift is large enough for employment in period $t + 1$ to be lower. But the relevant marginal cost schedule for period $t + 2$ will also shift, since it has now a step at the new level of employment, $l_{t+1} < l_t$. MC' is the new schedule.

Now assume that in period $t + 2$, θ is back to its normal value. Then the new level of employment is given by the intersection of the MV schedule

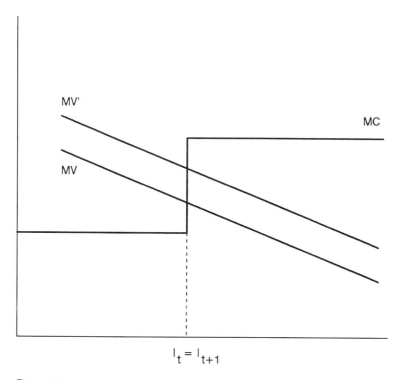

Figure 3.3
Effect of a small shock

and the MC' schedule. It is clear from figure 3.4 that $l_{t+2} = l_{t+1}$. In words, the level of unemployment does not return to its normal value, and it will never do so if θ stays at its normal value. If the MV schedule were steeper than that shown in the figure, employment would rise in period $t + 2$, though not enough to offset the drop in period $t + 1$. Hence at least some of the temporary shock persists forever.

Hence another implication of the model is that

Large transitory shocks have permanent effects on the level of employment

Notice, however, that this effect is smaller than the transitory effect that would be obtained if the firm was not paying efficiency wages (i.e., if the MC schedule were flat). Furthermore the effect of the shock will persist only until a new shock *changes* the labor force.

Therefore efficiency wages generate a cost function that is observationally equivalent to what one would obtain in the presence of linear adjustment cost (see chapter 1). They generate persistence of demand

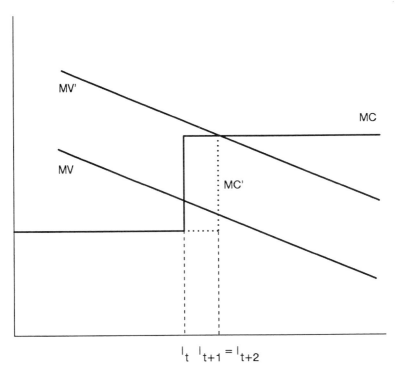

Figure 3.4
Effect of a large shock

shocks in the same way as linear adjustment costs do: There is a band of shock values within which the firm does not adjust. Because of this band small shocks have no effect, while large shocks have a permanent effect on the firm's labor force.

3.4   Aspects of Commitment

For the results discussed in the preceding section to hold, the firm must make a number of commitments to its workers.

First, it should be clear that the very idea of efficiency wages is based on some commitment on the firm's side to pay higher than equilibrium wages in the future. That is because, as we have seen, *future*, not *current* wages are those which determine *current* effort.

Second, for incentive problems to generate a cost function such as (3.8), the firm must demonstrate that it has some commitment to keeping its employees. In the model this is represented by the fact that employment at date $t + 1$ is set at date t. Again, *future* employment can influence *current* incentives by lowering the probability that one might lose his job between now and tomorrow. If future employment is expected to be lower than current employment, the firm can reduce its labor costs by making a commitment to raise future employment, which will lower the employed's expectation of being fired. In the absence of such commitment, past employment would be irrelevant when the firm sets current employment, since raising current employment will not lead to better enforcement of the current no-shirking condition. Therefore there would not be any persistence of demand shocks.

Third, expected changes in employment will have an impact on the probability of losing one's job only if those currently employed have more chance to be employed tomorrow than outsiders. This is a very natural assumption, but in a purely competitive, Walrasian model there would be a different labor market for each date: Being employed today in firm X would not imply being employed in firm X tomorrow. Each worker would expect to (almost surely) work in a different firm tomorrow, so the firm's employment policy would be irrelevant to the workers. It is the efficiency wage model that tells us why this does not happen in reality. It is efficient for firms to give priority to their current workers over tomorrow's employment because this reduces their turnover, thus allowing them to enforce the no-shirking condition at lower wages.

3.5 Introducing Dualism

The efficiency wage model is a natural microeconomic foundation for the study of dual labor markets for two reasons:

First, the model tells us that workers who are paid efficiency wages must enjoy rents. I have followed Shapiro and Stiglitz in assuming that the only alternative to working and being paid efficiency wages was unemployment. But we could equally assume that there exists a competitive sector where monitoring is not a major issue and workers are paid their opportunity cost. This is the route taken by Bulow and Summers (1986). In that case there would be a dual labor market, with a primary sector paying efficiency wages and a secondary sector paying competitive wages. Workers in the primary sector earn more than workers in the secondary sector, and secondary workers queue for primary jobs. This structure explains why firms can hire workers in both sectors without bothering about any sort of arbitrage condition between working in the primary sector versus working in the secondary sector. It also has natural implications for the pattern of mobility, which I study in chapter 8.

Second, the model generates the cost function defined in (3.8), which explains three other features of the dual labor market:

1. The primary sector is characterized by lower turnover and higher job protection.

2. Employment fluctuations are small and persistent in the primary sector.

3. Under some conditions, dualism endogenously arises *within* a firm because the secondary tier is used as a margin of adjustment to demand fluctuations, thus *insulating* primary workers from these demand fluctuations and allowing firms to enforce their effort at a lower cost.

Points 1 and 2 have been demonstrated above, they simply are the result that efficiency wages generate a form of labor adjustment cost. Point 3 is fully developed in the next chapter. Here I want to provide some basic intuition for its validity. To get that intuition, let us consider a very simplified case where there are only three periods: $t = 1, 2$, and 3. We can assume that employment at $t = 1$ is equal to 0, while employment at $t = 3$ is equal to some fixed, perfectly anticipated value l_3. How will the firm determine l_2? The total cost of labor is given by using (3.8) for all periods. Assuming a zero interest rate, to simplify, we see that the cost of labor is equal to

$$(a + b)l_2 + al_3 + b \cdot \max(l_2, l_3).$$

Figure 3.5 depicts the marginal cost of labor in period 2. When l_2 becomes larger than l_3, there is a jump in the marginal cost of labor from $a + b$ to $a + 2b$ because workers now consider that they have a positive probability of being fired and therefore require higher values of tomorrow's wages. In the above analysis that effect was present but embodied in the MV schedule which captured the effect of l_{t+1} on all future wages.

Assume now that the firm has the option of drawing from a pool of secondary workers at a constant unit cost s. These workers can be interpreted as being paid the level of unemployment insurance or any competitive wage and being monitored at some constant unit cost. Assume $a + b < s < a + 2b$. In figure 3.5 the marginal product of labor MP has been drawn along with the marginal cost s of secondary workers. The marginal cost of labor is now given by the lower envelope of the MC and SS schedule. When it is given by MC, the marginal worker is primary; when it is given by SS, the marginal worker is secondary. It is clear from figure 3.5 that if the marginal product of labor at $l_2 = l_3$ is greater than

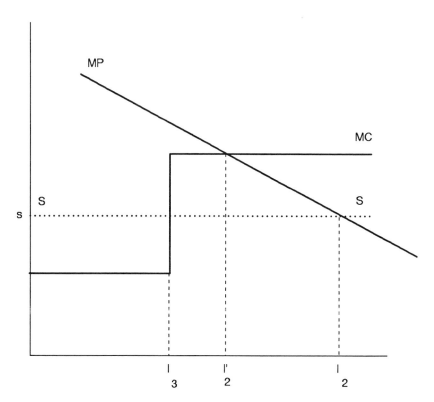

Figure 3.5
Employment determination in the dual case

s, the firm will have a dual structure as long as $l_2 > l_3$, hiring l_3 primary workers and $l_2 - l_3$ secondary workers. Note that all those secondary workers will be fired in period 3; precisely because of that, they are not paid efficiency wages. Note also that in the absence of secondary workers, the firm will hire l_2' primary workers. Total employment will be lower but total primary employment greater. Introducing internal dualism both reduces the size of the primary sector and increases that sector's employment security. The mechanism is simple: Primary workers who expect to be fired are more expensive than secondary workers, while primary workers who do not expect to be fired are cheaper than secondary workers. Accordingly the firm will determine the internal structure of its labor force in order to minimize the primary workers' probability of being fired. Internal dualism plays a twin role: First, by changing the nature of the marginal worker from primary to secondary, it reduces the marginal cost of labor as long as the marginal worker is fired. At the same time it reduces the inframarginal, primary worker's probability of being fired, thus insulating such workers from demand fluctuations and allowing the firm to pay them lower wages.

3.6 Conclusion

This chapter has illustrated that incentive problems can generate a cost of labor function that is very similar to what is obtained when there are linear adjustment costs such as firing or hiring costs. It has shown that the greater the monitoring problem, the greater is the "shadow adjustment cost" generated by imperfect monitoring. Therefore "rigidities" may not only be created by regulation but also by market imperfections. We have also seen that these costs can account for dualism. This explains why the dual structure of the labor market is widespread in both the United States and Europe. In the United States it is the outcome of a large volatility of product demand shocks. In Europe firing costs have long prevented the secondary sector to arise, but a two-tier labor market has emerged as flexibility has been increased at the margin by introducing temporary contracts with low firing costs while leaving existing contracts unaffected.

3.7 Appendix

A More General Proof of the Irrelevance of Firing Rules

Let $i \in [0, l_t]$ be an index for any infinitesimal employee in the firm's labor force at date t. Let us define a *firing assignment* as a mapping G from $[0, l_t]$ to $\{0, 1\}$ such that $G(i) = 1$ if the worker is fired and $G(i) = 0$ if the worker is not fired. Let us define a *firing rule* as a probability measure $d\varphi(G)$ over the space of all firing assignments. For any subset of the firm's labor force, the firing rule simply tells us the probability that those workers are the ones who will be fired. The firing rule is further defined as being *consistent* with l_{t+1} if it always yields an employment level equal to l_{t+1}. Formally, $d\varphi(G)$ is consistent with l_{t+1} if and only if

$$d\varphi(G) > 0 \Rightarrow \int_0^{l_t} (1 - G(i))di = l_{t+1} \qquad \forall G. \qquad (A3.1)$$

Let $d\varphi$ be any firing rule consistent with l_{t+1}. Then the probability that worker i will be fired is

$$p(i) = \int_G G(i)d\varphi(G). \tag{A3.2}$$

The firm's total cost of labor is the integral over all workers of the wage that will be paid to them times the probability that they remain within the firm:

$$c(l_t, l_{t+1}) = \int_0^{l_t} \left(a + \frac{b}{1 - p(i)} \right)(1 - p(i))di \tag{A3.3}$$

The term in (A3.3) is clearly linear in $p(i)$. Now, plugging (A3.2) into (A3.3), interverting integrals, and using A3.1, we see that the right-hand side of (A3.3) is simply equal to that of (3.8). ∎

Solution of the Firm's Optimization Problem

The problem is

$$V(l_t, \theta_{t+1}) = \max_{l_{t+1}} \theta_{t+1} f(l_{t+1}) - (al_{t+1} + b \cdot \max\{l_t, l_{t+1}\})$$

$$+ \delta \cdot E_t V(l_{t+1}, \theta_{t+2}). \tag{A3.4}$$

Since θ_{t+2} is independent of θ_{t+1}, let us define $E_t V(l_{t+1}, \theta_{t+2}) = H(l_{t+1})$, thus $E_t \partial V/\partial l(l_{t+1}, \theta_{t+2}) = h(l_{t+1}) = H'(l_{t+1})$.

It is clear that the solution must be of the following form:

1. For $\theta_{t+1} < \theta_m$, $l_{t+1} < l_t$.
2. For $\theta_m \le \theta_{t+1} \le \theta_M$, $l_{t+1} = l_t$.
3. For $\theta_M < \theta_{t+1}$, $l_{t+1} > l_t$.

To solve this problem, we must determine the critical values θ_m and θ_M and the value of l_{t+1} when it differs from l_t.

First, if $l_{t+1} < l_t$, the first-order condition (FOC) is

$$\theta_{t+1} f'(l_{t+1}) + \delta h(l_{t+1}) = a.$$

Then θ_m must be the value of θ such that this condition holds for $l_{t+1} = l_t$:

$$\theta_m(l_t) = \frac{a - \delta h(l_t)}{f'(l_t)}.$$

In this case thee envelope theorem gives us the value of $\partial V/\partial l(l_t, \theta_{t+1})$. Differentiating (A3.4) with respect to l_t under the assumption that $l_t > l_{t+1}$ yields

$$\frac{\partial V}{\partial l} = -b.$$

This expression simply means that when the firm is firing, each additional unit of past employment lowers the firm's present discounted value by the amount of the firing cost.

Second, if $l_{t+1} > l_t$, the FOC is

$$\theta_{t+1} f'(l_{t+1}) + \delta h(l_{t+1}) = a + b.$$

Then θ_M must be such that this condition is true for $l_{t+1} = l_t$:

$$\theta_M(l_t) = \frac{a + b - \delta h(l_t)}{f'(l_t)}.$$

The envelope theorem implies that in this case, since l_t no longer appears in (A3.4),

$$\frac{\partial V}{\partial l} = 0.$$

Third, suppose now that θ_{t+1} is between θ_m and θ_M. Then $l_{t+1} = l_t$. Since the firm's choice of l_{t+1} is at the kink of the total cost function, we cannot apply the envelope theorem, but we can compute directly $\partial V / \partial l_t$:

$$\frac{\partial V}{\partial l_t} = \theta_{t+1} f'(l_{t+1}) \frac{dl_{t+1}}{dl_t} - a \frac{dl_{t+1}}{dl_t} + b \frac{d}{dl_t} \max\{l_t, l_{t+1}\} + \delta h(l_{t+1}) \frac{dl_{t+1}}{dl_t}.$$

Since in this zone $l_{t+1} = l_t$, we have

$$\frac{dl_{t+1}}{dl_t} = 1,$$

$$\frac{d \max\{l_t, l_{t+1}\}}{dl_t} = 1.$$

Hence

$$\frac{\partial V}{\partial l_t} = \theta_{t+1} f'(l_{t+1}) - (a + b) + \delta h(l_{t+1})$$

$$= \theta_{t+1} f'(l_t) + \delta h(l_t) - (a + b),$$

which is between $-b$ and 0 if θ_{t+1} is between θ_m and θ_M.

Let us finally compute the h function. Let G be the cumulative density function of θ, $g = G'$. The above calculations can be rewritten

$$h(l_t) = E_{t-1} \frac{\partial V}{\partial l_t}(l_t, \theta_{t+1})$$

$$= -bG(\theta_m) + \int_{\theta_m}^{\theta_M} [\theta f'(l_t) + \delta h(l_t) - (a+b)]g(\theta)d\theta. \qquad (A3.5)$$

This expression implies that $h(l)$ is always lower than 0 and greater than $-bG(\theta_M)$. After integrating by parts, we get

$$h(l_t) = -f'(l_t) \int_{\theta_m(l_t)}^{\theta_M(l_t)} G(\theta)d\theta, \qquad (A3.6)$$

which is just (3.14).

4   The Dual Model

The efficiency wage model has been used to explain labor market segmentation and interindustry wage differentials. As an alternative to the classical theory of compensating differential (see Rosen 1986), the efficiency wage model attractively explains these phenomena. First, it relates wages to features unrelated to individual productivity (e.g., monitoring costs in the shirking model), and second, it generates rationing whereby people employed in unfavorable segments of the labor market cannot successfully underbid those employed in the high-wage sector.

4.1   Internal Dualism and Demand Volatility

In this chapter I insist on an alternative aspect of dual labor markets: They endogenously arise in response to (idiosyncratic or aggregate) product demand volatility, and the two tiers of the labor market can coexist within the same firm. Alternatively, the firm can use subcontractors to achieve flexibility, which is very similar to internal dualism. I thus extend the previous chapter's model to allow for internal dualism, in the way that it was sketched at the end of chapter 3.[1]

This chapter elaborates on Saint-Paul (1991).

1. Jacobsen and Schultz (1992) also find dualism arising endogenously within the firm. This is done within the context of a very different model. Teulings (1993) also generates dualism using an extension of the Shapiro-Stiglitz model, but dualism arises as the outcome of worker heterogeneity rather than differences in adjustment costs. The dualism that arises in this chapter is very different from the two-tier systems considered by Fehr and Kirchsteiger (1994), who argue that when the insiders of a firm set high wages, it is jointly optimal for them and the firm to hire secondary workers who are paid their opportunity cost, thus expanding membership beyond the union's employment. The problem with their approach is that a firm that would only hire the outsiders would make more money than a firm that would operate under a two-tier systems, so the former would eventually drive the latter out of business. In the current chapter secondary workers are actually more costly, on average, than primary workers, contrary to the Fehr and Kirchsteiger hypothesis. See also Rosén (1991) and MacLeod and Malcomson (1993).

Because secondary workers are fired and hired at a lower cost than in the primary sector, they will be used by firms to deal with the uncertain part of demand. I show that the dynamic version of the efficiency wage model that I have developed can capture these ideas. I do so by allowing the firm to monitor some of its workers at a cost. It is shown that it is in general optimal for the firm to have a dual structure, with a stable "primary" pool of workers who are paid efficiency wages and a fluctuating pool of secondary workers who are monitored (See figure 1.1). The main intuition behind this result is in fact the same as for the hysteresis result: the efficiency wage model generates a labor cost function which is analogous to a one with linear adjustment costs. A firm facing such a cost function will be averse to fluctuations in employment. If it has the opportunity to deal with these fluctuations with a pool of secondary workers which can be adjusted at a low cost, then it will do so. The fact that a kinked cost function comes from efficiency wages rather than linear adjustment costs implies that primary workers and secondary workers may be strictly identical, or differ by irrelevant characteristics, while in equilibrium the former are strictly better-off than the latter. It can be shown that under fairly general assumptions, an increase in the volatility of demand implies a shrink in the size of the primary labor force and an increase in the size of the secondary labor force.

4.2 Introducing Internal Dualism in the Dynamic Efficiency Wage Model

To capture these ideas, I use the model introduced in chapter 3. I therefore assume that the firm can hire primary workers (workers who are paid efficiency wages) and that the cost of these workers is given by equation (3.8), which is reproduced below:

$$c(l_t, l_{t+1}) = al_{t+1} + b \max(l_t, l_{t+1}). \qquad (3.8)$$

In addition I assume that the firm has the option of hiring a pool of secondary workers who are perfectly monitored at some cost and paid their alternative wage.[2] These workers are not different from primary workers, but they are typically paid less and must queue up for primary jobs. The probability of being fired does not influence the cost of employing these workers, since they cannot shirk. Before we derive the main results, three comments should be made:

---

2. Rebitzer and Taylor (1991) and Albrecht and Vroman (1992) have independently developed related models.

1. As in the standard literature, dualism arises here as a response to differences in monitoring technologies. However, these differences are themselves *endogenous* and determined by the structure of uncertainty. The secondary sector exists because demand is volatile. In my model, if demand were not volatile, the firm would only hire primary workers because primary workers are cheaper than secondary workers as long as enough employment security is granted to them. When demand is volatile, the primary workers will have an incentive to shirk when expecting a slump, and this increases their cost. Hence it will pay for the firm to use the monitoring technology for the pool of marginal workers which is adjusted in response to fluctuations in demand.

2. Dualism is not associated with any observable characteristics of the workers. Both the primary and the secondary sectors are defined as a set of jobs, not a set of workers. Workers could freely be reallocated from one sector to another. Informational problems prevent secondary workers from underbidding primary workers. Hence nothing prevents the employer from allocating people across primary and secondary jobs randomly or on the basis of discriminatory principles. In other words, the firm decides which share of the labor force will be monitored and which share will be paid efficiency wages. *Who* is allocated across these two sectors is irrelevant from the firm's point of view, although primary workers end up strictly better off than secondary workers.

That story would be complicated, however, if workers differed according to some observable characteristic that affects the terms of trade between monitoring them and paying efficiency wages. For example, workers with a higher propensity to quit would require higher wages in order not to shirk, so they would be more likely to work in the secondary market. Chapters 9 and 10 study what happens when workers have different skill levels—and there it can be shown that the unskilled are more likely to end up in the secondary tier.

3. As long as there is free entry into the secondary sector, the model is not consistent with involuntary unemployment. However, it is consistent with semi-involuntary unemployment where the marginal unemployed person is indifferent about getting a secondary job but would be strictly better off if he or she held a primary job.[3]

---

3. Jones (1987) shows that a binding minimum wage on the secondary sector will affect incentives in the primary sector: Employment and effort in the primary sector may well go up if the minimum wage depresses the utility of a worker outside the primary sector, thus having beneficial incentive effects.

To have a model where it is profitable to hire both primary and secondary workers, I must assume that the sum of the monitoring cost and the secondary wage is greater than the minimum efficiency wage. Let s be this sum. Then we must have $s > a + b$.

In any period t, let l_t^p be the primary labor force used by the firm and l_t^s its secondary labor force. As in the previous chapter, I assume that the firm's demand shocks are i.i.d. The cost of the primary labor force in period $t + 1$ will depend on l_t^p, whereas l_t^s will have no influence on the value of the firm at the beginning of period $t + 1$, since the secondary labor force can be adjusted costlessly. The only state variable is thus l_t^p. Therefore this value can be written as a function of l_t^p and θ_{t+1}, $V(l_t^p, \theta_{t+1})$. We have

$$V(l_t^p, \theta_{t+1}) = \max_{\substack{l_{t+1}^p \\ l_{t+1}^s}} \theta_{t+1} f(l_{t+1}^p + l_{t+1}^s) - c(l_{t+1}^p, l_t^p) - s l_{t+1}^s + \delta E_t V(l_{t+1}^p, \theta_{t+2}).$$

(4.1)

Equation (4.1) comes from the fact that since primary workers are paid efficiency wages, their cost is determined by equation (3.8) while each period the secondary workers have a constant unit cost of s.

We can readily write the first-order conditions of problem (4.1). Concerning the FOC with respect to l_{t+1}^s, we see that

$$\theta_{t+1} f'(l_{t+1}^p + l_{t+1}^s) = s \qquad \text{if } \theta_{t+1} f'(l_{t+1}^p) > s, \tag{4.2}$$

$$l_{t+1}^s = 0 \qquad \text{if } \theta_{t+1} f'(l_{t+1}^p) < s \tag{4.3}$$

The FOC with respect to l_{t+1}^p are similar to those corresponding to the primary case derived in chapter 3, with the exception that one now has to take the secondary tier into account:

$$\theta_{t+1} f'(l_{t+1}^p + l_{t+1}^s) + \delta k(l_{t+1}^p) = a + b \tag{4.4}$$

if

$$\theta_{t+1} f'(l_t^p + l_{t+1}^s) + \delta k(l_t^p) > a + b,$$

$$\theta_{t+1} f'(l_{t+1}^p + l_{t+1}^s) + \delta k(l_{t+1}^p) = a, \tag{4.5}$$

if

$$\theta_{t+1} f'(l_t^p + l_{t+1}^s) + \delta k(l_t^p) < a,$$

$$l_{t+1}^p = l_t^p, \tag{4.6}$$

if

$a \leq \theta_{t+1} f'(l_t^p + l_{t+1}^s) + \delta k(l_t^p) \leq a + b.$

In (4.4)–(4.6), k is the expected marginal value of an additional primary worker tomorrow:

$$k(l_{t+1}^p) = \frac{E_t \partial V(l_{t+1}^p, \theta_{t+2})}{\partial l_{t+1}^p}. \tag{4.7}$$

I now discuss the main properties of the solution. These are formally derived in the appendix.

1. There exists a number $\bar{l}$ such that the amount of primary labor employed by the firm will never exceed $\bar{l}$. The value of $\bar{l}$ is given by the equation

$$\delta k(\bar{l}) = a + b - s, \tag{4.8}$$

where k is defined by equation (4.7) and turns out to be equal to h (as defined in equation 3.14) at $l = \bar{l}$.

2. Whenever $l_{t+1}^p < \bar{l}$, $l_{t+1}^s = 0$. Therefore the firm will not start firing primary workers until it has fired all its secondary workers; it will not start hiring secondary workers until it has reached a number of $\bar{l}$ primary workers. When it has no secondary workers, the firm behaves as a "primary" firm studied in the previous chapter. In this case all the equations derived in that chapter hold. For instance, employment will decrease if and only if

$$\theta_{t+1} < \theta_m(l_t^p), \tag{4.9}$$

where the formula of θ_m is the same as in chapter 3.

3. When $l_{t+1}^p = \bar{l}$ and $l_{t+1}^s > 0$, the value of l_{t+1}^s is given by the equation

$$\theta_{t+1} f'(\bar{l} + l_{t+1}^s) = s. \tag{4.10}$$

Therefore the marginal product of a secondary worker is equal to its marginal (average) cost. There is no gap due to the possibility of future firing and no corridor effect. The firm will hire some secondary workers whenever

$$\theta_{t+1} > \frac{s}{f'(\bar{l})} = \underline{\theta}. \tag{4.11}$$

As long as the shock is greater than $\underline{\theta}$, the firm operates in a "dual zone" where it employs a constant amount $\bar{l}$ of primary workers and a fluctuating amount l_t^s of secondary workers. Secondary employment l_t^s is determined by the equalization of marginal product and marginal cost.

As long as θ is above $\underline{\theta}$, the dual firm responds smoothly and temporarily to temporary shocks by adjusting its secondary labor force in a way given by equation (4.11). Therefore the dynamics of labor demand in a secondary firm are very different from the primary firm studied in chapter 3.

When demand drops below $\underline{\theta}$, then the firm fires all its secondary workers. Equations (4.8), (4.9), and (3.11) tell us that the firm will start firing some primary workers when θ becomes lower than

$$\theta_m(\tilde{l}) = \underline{\theta} - \frac{b}{f'(\tilde{l})}.$$

In this case the dual firm becomes a primary firm and its behavior is as described in the previous chapter, with hysteresis and no effect of small shocks.

When a higher θ brings the firm back to the dual zone, there is no track of its trip in the primary zone. Therefore, if the firm is normally operating in the dual zone ($E\theta > \underline{\theta}$), temporary shocks have no permanent effects. Their effects are long-lasting only when demand is "unusually" low ($\theta < \underline{\theta}$), and that only persists as long as demand remains below $\underline{\theta}$. So, in some sense, negative shocks are more persistent than positive ones.

To understand the structure of the solution, note that (4.2) and (4.4) imply that whenever the firm is employing secondary workers, the marginal product of labor (the left-hand side of equation 4.2) is pinned down by the cost of these workers. It does not depend on the current value of the shock θ_{t+1}. A change in θ_{t+1} would be met by a change in total labor force, using secondary workers as an adjustment margin so as to maintain the marginal product of labor equal to s.

Consider now the firm's decision on how many primary workers to employ. Assume that it replaces one secondary worker with one primary worker. Then, given that the marginal cost of a primary worker in the hiring regime is $a + b$ while the marginal cost of a secondary worker is $s > a + b$, it makes a saving of $s - (a + b)$. This saving has to be weighted against expected future marginal losses from having to fire the primary worker in bad states of nature, $-\delta k(l_{t+1}^p)$. This quantity does not depend on the current value of the shock because θ is i.i.d. Furthermore this quantity is increasing in l_{t+1}^p because a larger primary labor force increases the likelihood that these workers will be fired in the future. Therefore there exists a unique value of l_{t+1}^p, $\tilde{l}$, that maximizes the firm's value, and it is independent of the current shock θ_{t+1}. Primary workers are

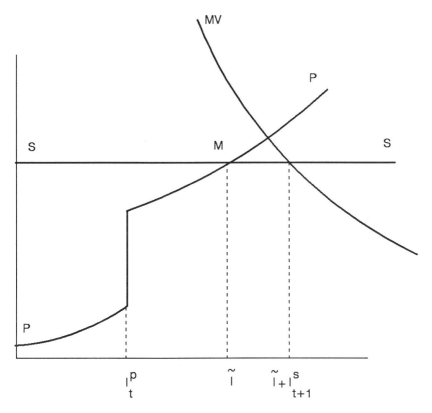

Figure 4.1
Employment determination in a dual firm

therefore insulated from demand fluctuations as long as secondary workers are used at the margin to adjust to product demand fluctuations.

The solution is graphically illustrated in figure 4.1, with employment on the x-axis. The MV schedule depicts the current marginal value of labor, $\theta_{t+1}f'(l)$. The horizontal line SS depicts the marginal cost of a secondary worker s. The broken line PP depicts the shadow marginal cost of a primary worker, $a - \delta k(l)$ if $l < l_t^p$, $a + b - \delta k(l)$ if $l > l_t^p$. The jump is at the current level of primary employment l_t^p, which was assumed to be lower than $\tilde{l}$ (implying that the previous shock was negative enough to put the firm off the dual zone). As shown in figure 4.1, the firm will hire primary workers as long as their shadow marginal cost is lower than that of secondary workers. The primary labor force is thus simply determined by the intersection M of SS and PP; it is equal to $\tilde{l}$ and, as long as MV is on the right of M, does not depend on the position of MV. Beyond $\tilde{l}$ the cost of secondary workers is lower than the cost of primary workers, so the firm uses them to complete its labor force up to point E where the marginal value of labor is equal to s.[4]

4. It can be shown (see the appendix) that $\bar{l}$ is given by the unique solution to the following equation:

$$a + b - s = -\delta f'(\bar{l}) \int_{(s-b)/f'(\bar{l})}^{s/f'(\bar{l})} G(\theta)\, d\theta. \tag{4.12}$$

Note that only the lower tail of the distribution of θ, truncated at $\theta = s/f'(\bar{l})$, enters the determination of $\bar{l}$. This is Bernanke's (1983) "bad news principle": The expected marginal cost of primary workers, and therefore the size of the primary labor force, only depends on the "bad news." This is because the firm will incur adjustment costs on its primary workers only if it is hit by a shock negative enough to prompt it to fire all its secondary workers. Therefore, while in the dual regime the primary labor force does not react to the current shock, it does depend on the distribution of shocks. A thicker lower tail for that distribution means that primary workers are fired more often. This raises their shadow marginal cost $-\delta k(l^p)$ and reduces the equilibrium value of $\bar{l}$.

5. Consider now the impact of the volatility of demand on the maximum number of primary workers $\bar{l}$. An increased volatility of demand may imply a higher future probability of firing a primary worker and hence, through equation (3.8), a higher cost of the primary labor force. Therefore it is reasonable to think that when the dispersion of $\underline{\theta}$ increases, $\bar{l}$ decreases.

Unfortunately, it is not possible to show that for any type of spread in the distribution of θ. In the appendix I show that a *median*-preserving spread of the type depicted in figure 4.2 will lower $\bar{l}$ for a firm that normally operates in the dual zone (i.e., θ is greater than $\underline{\theta}$ with probability greater than $\frac{1}{2}$). Also, since in the absence of uncertainty the firm will hire only primary workers, a mean-preserving spread in θ must then reduce the share of primary employment at least over some range.

---

4. The problem is analogous to the analysis of electric utilities. The primary labor force is the one with a high fixed cost and a low marginal cost. The secondary labor force is the one with no fixed cost and a high marginal cost. It is well-known from the analysis of electric utilities that the technology with a high marginal cost should be used on the margin, where demand is fluctuating, while the technology with a high fixed cost must be used to deal with inframarginal KWh in order to cover the fixed cost by using its capacity more often.

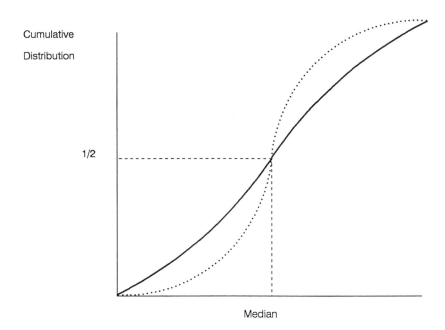

Figure 4.2
Median preserving spread

This result is quite natural if we think of secondary workers as being used for the fluctuating component of demand and primary workers for its certain component. When demand is more volatile, the number of secondary workers rises and the number of primary workers decreases.

4.3   Persistent Shocks

What happens if we assume that instead of being i.i.d., product demand shocks have some persistence? For example, we could assume that they follow an AR1 process:

$$\theta_t = \rho(\theta_{t-1} - \bar{\theta}) + \bar{\theta} + \varepsilon_t.$$

Then it is reasonable to speculate that the more persistent the shocks (the higher ρ), the more the firm will adjust using its primary labor force. In other words, the primary labor force will react to the permanent component of the shock, and the secondary labor force to its transitory component.

This intuition can be understood formally by looking at the impact of changes in the distribution of shocks $G(\theta)$. In (4.12) the distribution of shocks G should be understood as *tomorrow's* distribution. If shocks are i.i.d., it will actually be invariant to today's value of θ. If there is persistence, then it will depend on the current value of θ. A higher value of θ today means higher values of θ tomorrow, which is equivalent to lower values of $G(\theta)$. By differentiating the right-hand side of (4.12), we can easily check that a decline in $G(\cdot)$ is matched by an increase in $\tilde{l}$, meaning that higher values of the shock on average imply a higher value of $\tilde{l}$.[5]

4.4 Conclusion

In this chapter I have shown how labor market dualism may arise within a firm when two types of labor have different adjustment costs. The firm will use the segment of the labor market with a low adjustment cost at the margin do deal with fluctuations in demand. In the model we have studied, based on chapter 3, the segment with low adjustment costs is the "flexible" tier of workers who are monitored rather than paid efficiency wages. The analysis is however more general and applies to any source of discrepancy in adjustment costs between two types of labor. I have also shown that under certain conditions the secondary sector increases at the expense of the primary one when there is more volatility. This can be taken as a piece of argument in favor of the view that macroeconomic stabilization generates a higher primary sector and therefore "good jobs at good wages."

4.5 Appendix

Solution of the Dual Firm's Optimization Problem

The problem is

$$V(l_t^p, \theta_{t+1}) = \max_{\substack{l_{t+1}^p \\ l_{t+1}^s}} \theta_{t+1} f(l_{t+1}^p + l_{t+1}^s) - (al_{t+1}^p + b\max\{l_t^p, l_{t+1}^p\}) - sl_{t+1}^s$$

$$+ \delta E_t V(l_{t+1}^p, \theta_{t+2}),$$

where I assume that $s > a + b$. Let us define

$$K(l_{t+1}^p) = E_t V(l_{t+1}^p, \theta_{t+2}),$$

---

5. Remember that a cumulative distribution H dominates another distribution G in the first-order stochastic dominance sense if and only if $H(x) < G(x)$ for all x. This implies that the expectation of any increasing function of x is higher using H than G: $E_H f(x) > E_G f(x) \ \forall f$, $f' > 0$. An example is the horizontal translation, $H(x) = G(x - \mu)$, which simply adds a constant μ to the random variable defined by G.

$$k(l_{t+1}^p) = K'(l_{t+1}^p) = E_t \frac{\partial V}{\partial l}(l_{t+1}^p, \theta_{t+2}).$$

Since $\theta_{t+1}f(l_{t+1}^p + l_{t+1}^s) - (al_{t+1}^p + b\max\{l_t^p, l_{t+1}^p\}) - sl_{t+1}^s$ is concave in $(l_t^p, l_{t+1}^p, l_{t+1}^s)$, $V(l_t^p, \theta_{t+1})$ is concave in l_t^p. This implies that $k' < 0$. Furthermore, $\partial V/\partial l_t^p$ is always greater than $-b$. This is true because if l_t^p increases by dl_t^p and if the firm does not change l_{t+1}^p, the maximum loss is $-bdl_t$. This in turn implies that k is always greater than $-b$.

Then we have:

PROPOSITION 4.1   Suppose that θ_{t+1} is such that $l_{t+1}^p < l_t^p$; then $l_{t+1}^s = 0$.

Proof   Assume that $l_{t+1}^s > 0$. The FOC can be written

$$\theta_{t+1}f'(l_{t+1}^p + l_{t+1}^s) + \delta k(l_{t+1}^p) = a,$$

$$\theta_{t+1}f'(l_{t+1}^p + l_{t+1}^s) = s$$

$$\Rightarrow \delta k(l_{t+1}^p) = a - s \Rightarrow a - s > -\delta b > -b \Rightarrow s < a + b,$$

which is contrary to my hypothesis.   ∎

Hence, if the firm fires some primary workers, it will first fire all secondary workers.

PROPOSITION 4.2   Suppose that θ_{t+1} is such that $l_{t+1}^p > l_t^p$ and $l_{t+1}^s > 0$. Then there exists $\tilde{l}$ independent of l_t^p such that $l_{t+1}^p = \tilde{l}$.

Proof   Under the assumptions of the proposition, the FOC are

$$\theta_{t+1}f'(l_{t+1}^p + l_{t+1}^s) + \delta k(l_{t+1}^p) = a + b,$$

$$\theta_{t+1}f'(l_{t+1}^p + l_{t+1}^s) = s$$

$$\Rightarrow \delta k(l_{t+1}^p) = a + b - s,$$

which defines l_{t+1}^p in a unique way (since k is decreasing) and independently of l_t^p. Let $\tilde{l}$ be the solution to this equation:

$$\delta k(\tilde{l}) = a + b - s.$$

PROPOSITION 4.3   If θ_{t+1} is such that $l_{t+1}^p > l_t^p$ and $l_{t+1}^s = 0$, then $l_{t+1}^p \leq \tilde{l}$.

Proof   In this case we must have

$$\theta_{t+1}f'(l_{t+1}^p) + \delta k(l_{t+1}^p) = a + b,$$

$$\theta_{t+1}f'(l_{t+1}^p) < s.$$

The second condition states that it is not profitable to hire a secondary worker. Those two conditions imply that

$$\delta k(l^p_{t+1}) = a + b - \theta_{t+1} f'(l^p_{t+1}) > a + b - s = \delta k(\tilde{l}) \Rightarrow l^p_{t+1} < \tilde{l},$$

since k is decreasing.

Therefore, if l^p_t is once lower than $\tilde{l}$, it will always remain below it. If we assume that there is some initial date at which the firm enters the market with no labor force, then we have

THEOREM 4.1   For all t, $l^p_t \leq \tilde{l}$.

PROPOSITION 4.4   If $l^p_{t+1} < \tilde{l}$, then $l^s_{t+1} = 0$.

Proof If $l^p_{t+1} < l^p_t$, then we apply proposition 4.1; if $l^p_{t+1} > l^p_t$, proposition 4.2 implies that $l^s_{t+1} = 0$. Otherwise, l^p_{t+1} would be equal to $\tilde{l}$. Consider the case $l^p_{t+1} = l^p_t$. Assume that $l^s_{t+1} > 0$. Then the FOC are

$$a \leq \theta_{t+1} f'(l^p_{t+1} + l^s_{t+1}) + \delta k(l^p_{t+1}) \leq a + b,$$

$$\theta_{t+1} f'(l^p_{t+1} + l^s_{t+1}) = s$$

$$\Rightarrow \delta k(l^p_{t+1}) \leq a + b - s \Rightarrow l^p_{t+1} \geq \tilde{l}, \text{ which is false. Hence } l^s_{t+1} = 0. \qquad \blacksquare$$

COROLLARY   If $l^s_{t+1} > 0$, then $l^p_{t+1} = \tilde{l}$.

PROPOSITION 4.5 $l^s_{t+1} > 0$, if and only if $\theta_{t+1} > s/f'(\tilde{l}) = \underline{\theta}$.

Proof If $l^s_{t+1} > 0$, then $l^p_{t+1} = \tilde{l}$ and l^s_{t+1} is determined by $\theta_{t+1} f'(\tilde{l} + l^s_{t+1}) = s$.
   This will have a positive solution if and only if $\theta_{t+1} > \underline{\theta}$. $\blacksquare$

All the previous propositions imply the following theorem:

THEOREM 4.2   The solution of the firm's maximization problem is the following:

i. If $\theta_{t+1} > \underline{\theta}$, then $l^p_{t+1} = \tilde{l}$ and l^s_{t+1} is determined by the equation $\theta_{t+1} f'(\tilde{l} + l^s_{t+1}) = s$. In this case

$$\frac{\partial V}{\partial l^p_t} = \theta_{t+1} f'(l^p_{t+1} + l^s_{t+1}) + \delta k(l^p_{t+1}) - (a + b) = 0.$$

ii. If $\theta_{t+1} \leq \underline{\theta}$, then $l^s_{t+1} = 0$. In this case the solution in l^s_t is the primary's firm solution described in the previous appendix, provided that k is replaced by h. In particular, the values of the partial derivatives of V with respect to l^p_t are the same.

Theorem 4.2 allows us to derive an equation for $\tilde{l}$. Applying the formulas to the case where $l_t^p = \tilde{l}$, we get

$$k(\tilde{l}) = \frac{E\partial V}{\partial l(\tilde{l})} = -bG\left(\frac{s-b}{G'(\tilde{l})}\right) + \int_{(s-b)/f'(\tilde{l})}^{s/f'(\tilde{l})} (f'(\tilde{l}) - s)g(\theta)\,d\theta.$$

Given that $s = a + b - \delta k(\tilde{l})$, this equation in $k(\tilde{l})$ is exactly the same as equation (A3.5) in $h(\tilde{l})$. Therefore, using (A3.6),

$$k(\tilde{l}) = h(\tilde{l}) = -f'(\tilde{l})\int_{\theta_m(\tilde{l})}^{\theta_M(\tilde{l})} G(\theta)\,d\theta = -f'(\tilde{l})\int_{(s-b)/f'(\tilde{l})}^{s/f'(\tilde{l})} G(\theta)\,d\theta \qquad \text{(A4.1)}$$

$$\Rightarrow a + b - s = -\delta f'(\tilde{l})\int_{(s-b)/f'(\tilde{l})}^{s/f'(\tilde{l})} G(\theta)\,d\theta. \qquad \text{(A4.2)}$$

It is worth noting that the right-hand side of (A4.2) is monotonous in $x = f'(\tilde{l})$, so there exists at most one solution to (A4.2). Examination of (A4.2) reveals that there will be a solution if and only if $s - (a + b) < \delta b$. If this inequality does not hold, the solution is in fact $\tilde{l} = +\infty$ (or any value such that $(s - b)/x$ is beyond the support of θ), meaning that the firm will always be in the primary zone and never use secondary workers (because they are too expensive). Also, if θ is deterministic, its value must be smaller than $s/f'(\tilde{l})$ for (A4.2) to hold, meaning that the firm will not hire secondary workers.

Effect of a Median-Preserving Spread of θ on $\tilde{l}$

Let σ be an index of dispersion: When σ increases, the distribution of θ spreads in the way described in figure 4.2: The median $\hat{\theta}$ is unchanged and $(\hat{\theta} - \theta)\partial G/\partial\sigma(\theta, \sigma) \geq 0$. To compute the effect of an increase in σ on $\tilde{l}$, differentiate equation (A4.2) to get

$$\frac{f''(\tilde{l})}{f'(\tilde{l})}[a + b - s(1 - \delta(G(\theta_M(\tilde{l})) - G(\theta_m(\tilde{l})))) + \delta b G(\theta_M(\tilde{l}))]\frac{d\tilde{l}}{d\sigma}$$

$$= f'(\tilde{l})\int_{(s-b)/f'(\tilde{l})}^{s/f'(\tilde{l})} \frac{\partial G}{\partial\sigma}(\theta, \sigma)\,d\theta.$$

Suppose that $s/f'(\tilde{l}) = \theta = \theta_M(\tilde{l}) < \hat{\theta}$. This means that the firm operates in the dual zone more than half of the time. Then

$$\int_{(s-b)/f'(\tilde{l})}^{s/f'(\tilde{l})} \frac{\partial}{\partial\sigma} G(\theta)\,d\theta > 0.$$

Hence the right-hand side is positive. Now notice that $f''/f' < 0$ and that the term in brackets is positive. To see this, consider that

$$a + b - s = \delta h(\tilde{l}) > -\delta b G\left(\frac{s}{f'(\tilde{l})}\right),$$

since $s/f'(\tilde{l}) = \theta_M(\tilde{l})$, and it was shown in the appendix to chapter 1 that $h(l) > -bG(\theta_M(l))$. Thus the term in brackets must be greater than $\delta(s - b)(G(\theta_M) - G(\theta_m))$, which is positive. Hence $d\tilde{l}/d\sigma < 0$; a median-preserving spread in the distribution of θ lowers $\tilde{l}$.

5

Efficiency Wages and Segmented Labor Markets: The Empirical Debate

Theoretical developments in the field of efficiency wages have given rise to a large empirical literature trying to address hotly debated issues. These notably include testing the extent to which the existence of industry rents is due to competitive failures in the labor market and discriminating between the competing mechanisms that may generate such failures.

5.1 Competitive versus Noncompetitive Models of the Labor Market

There are many models that have similar predictions as the shirking model, including "insider models" where turnover costs and/or the existence of unions give bargaining power to the workers, and models of efficiency wages where firms pay above market-clearing wages to reduce costly turnover, or for fairness reasons. At the onset I should say that the link I have established (in chapter 3) between labor market failure and the existence of adjustment costs is quite robust to a variety of models. The only thing that is really needed is that employed workers expect to earn a rent over the unemployed, and that this rent be specified as *intertemporal*. That is, the rent is specified not as the difference between current wages and some alternative wage but as the difference between the present discounted value of being employed and that of being unemployed. Thus, when workers expect to lose their jobs with a higher probability, they must earn higher wages in order to earn the same expected discounted rent.

In discussing the empirical literature, I will not emphasize the differences across various versions of the efficiency wage model, nor the differences between efficiency wages and insider/outsider models. These models are so close to each other that it is difficult to discriminate. Many efficiency wage models as well as the insider models have very similar implications;

they all capture plausible, nonmutually exclusive phenomena that may be more or less important depending on which industry and time period one is looking at. I will therefore focus the discussion on the distinction between competitive and noncompetitive interpretations of observed regularities in the labor market.

5.2   The Debate on Interindustry Wage Differentials

One important piece of evidence which favors non-market-clearing models of wage determination is the existence of interindustry wage differences.

Krueger and Summers (1988) have documented the existence of large and persistent interindustry wage differentials and have argued that they hardly can be explained by market-clearing models of the labor market. The key finding is that by estimating an earnings function controlling for all worker characteristics available in the data, one finds significant coefficients on industry dummies that account for a substantial fraction of the variance in (log) wages.[1] Moreover these differentials are both persistent over time and correlated across countries.[2] This persistence rules out any neoclassical "frictional" interpretation of such differences. That is to say, they could arise in response to sectorial shocks as a response to imperfect labor mobility across sectors. But such differentials would surely go away quickly, whereas those that we observe have been there for decades. Another neoclassical interpretation is that the differentials are due to amenities and fringe benefits associated with job characteristics that are not controlled for (the so-called theory of compensating differentials; see Rosen 1986). Krueger and Summers control for these factors and find that taking fringe benefits into account *exacerbates*, rather than reduces, interindustry wage differentials. Such interpretation is further inconsistent with the fact that wage differentials are very correlated across occupations: High-wage sectors have both better-paid secretaries and better-paid production workers.

A more serious issue is whether interindustry wage differentials are explained by unobserved worker ability. By that interpretation, some industries would have a higher concentration of good workers than others, thus paying higher wages on average. The typical way to control for that problem is to look at the wage experience of workers who move from one

---

1. Dickens and Katz (1987a) and Katz and Summers (1989) report similar findings. See Dickens and Lang (1992a) for a survey of the evidence.
2. Dickens and Katz (1987b) and Helwege (1987).

industry to another. The typical pattern is that movers from one industry to another experience a change in wages roughly equal to the estimated wage differential between the two industries. Under the worker-specific unobserved ability interpretation, no such capital gain should exist. This therefore seems to rule out this interpretation. However, some problems remain. For one thing, not all studies reach the same result. Murphy and Topel (1987), for example, find that the change in wages experienced by movers is only 30% of the interindustry wage differential.[3] Also movers may have different characteristics from stayers. Blackburn and Neumark (1992) try to control for unobserved ability by using test scores. They find that unobserved ability at best accounts for a small share of the variance of wages across industries. Gibbons and Katz (1992) develop a model where skills are not equally valued across industries and where mobility occurs as a result of learning about one's ability. Clearly in such a model workers who improve their prior belief on their ability would move from industries with a low return to skill to industries with a high return to skill, and experience a wage change of the same sign and possibly same order of magnitude as the differential between the two industries. They then try to empirically correct for this possible source of bias by looking at a sample where job changes are due to plant closing—an event exogenous to learning about ability. They find that these exogenously displaced workers experience wage differentials that are very similar to the ones observed in a cross section or in a fixed-effect panel estimation. It is therefore unlikely that the bias generated by self-selection of movers is responsible for the observed magnitude of interindustry wage differentials.

The debate on interindustry wage differentials as evidence for market failures is therefore not totally settled. It is fair to say, however, that competitive models have a very hard time explaining wage differentials and that only part of the differential may be due to unobserved ability.

The next, much more difficult question is: Which noncompetitive models account for the pattern of interindustry wage differentials? As we have seen, many of these models are compatible with the pseudoadjustment cost derived in chapter 3. Let us, however, consider some of the findings and their implications for how various models fare. The evidence, not

---

3. Another dissenter is Keane (1993), who finds only small industry effects, using the NLS (National Longitudinal Survey) rather than the CPS (current population survey) used by Krueger and Summers. See also McNabb (1987). Edin and Zetterberg (1992) fail to find significant industry dummies in Sweden in a panel estimation of earnings function using individual fixed effects, but Arai (1994) does find significant and persistent industry effects in Sweden.

surprisingly, is far more inconclusive than when testing noncompetitive models as a whole against the competitive model.

Dickens and Katz (1987), who also survey the previous literature, have looked at the correlates of industry wage premia and find the following robust pattern: First, wage premia are higher in industries with a more educated labor force (remember that education was already controlled for when computing these premia), second, they are higher in more capitalistic and large firms, and third, they are higher in more profitable industries.

It is likely that detecting shirking is more difficult in large firms and that the cost of it to the employer is larger when the worker is more productive (meaning a higher education or a higher capital/labor ratio). Therefore the first two findings are quite compatible with the shirking model. On the other hand, the positive correlation with profits is more supportive of "rent sharing" or "insider-outsider" models of wage determination.

Arai (1994), using Swedish data, is able to correlate industry premia with a proxy for the "autonomy" enjoyed by workers, since it is more difficult to detect shirking if the worker enjoys greater autonomy. He finds a strong positive correlation between the wage premium and the degree of autonomy, thus supporting the shirking model.

5.3 Direct Evidence

Several pieces of literature have tried to test some implications of the efficiency wage models by directly looking at micro-data sets or surveys.[4]

One of the implications of the model is that jobs are rationed, especially when they pay more. Holzer, Katz, and Krueger (1991) have directly looked at the number of applicants to job openings and found that firms in high-wage industries tend to receive more applicants for their job openings. While this finding is hardly surprising, it is inconsistent with the market-clearing interpretations of interindustry wage differentials.[5]

Cappelli and Chauvin (1991) provide one of the most direct tests of the Shapiro and Stiglitz shirking model. They look at the discipline effects of wage premia in a cross section of plants of an automobile producer. While wages (determined by collective bargaining), work practices, and the moni-

---

4. Dickens et al. (1989) try to test one of the assumptions, rather than implications, of the shirking model, namely that there is a limit on the penalty that can be imposed for shirking. They argue that the fact that firms spend large resources preventing employee crime is evidence that penalties are limited; otherwise, firms would impose infinite penalty and an infinitesimal amount of monitoring would be enough to detect shirking.
5. Krueger (1988) presents similar findings.

toring technology are homogeneous across plants, the actual wage premium differs because these plants hire from different local labor markets associated with different outside options for the workers. Obviously in such a market above-market-clearing wages are mostly the product of union bargaining power. But for the purpose of directly testing the effect of wages on productivity, it is an appropriate experiment because variations in wage premia are clearly exogenous with respect to plant-level productivity. Cappelli and Chauvin have a direct measure of the extent of shirking, namely the rate at which workers are dismissed for disciplinary reasons. Their key finding is then that a higher-wage premium has a significant negative impact on the shirking rate. Similar evidence is provided in Drago and Heywood (1992). They use surveys of working conditions that include questions on both the extent of effort and the extent of monitoring. They find a positive impact on effort of both earnings and supervision intensity. They also find a negative (in accordance with the model) but insignificant effect on effort of the layoff probability. This is less good news for the model, although part of the effect of increased layoff probability will be picked up by higher wages.

A dual approach to testing the Shapiro-Stiglitz model consists in looking at the effects of changes in the efficiency of monitoring on equilibrium wages. This has been done by Krueger (1991). The natural experiment used is the coexistence of franchised and company-owned fast-food restaurants. In a franchised restaurant the owner is a residual claimant and has therefore a high incentive to monitor the employees. By contrast in a company-owned restaurant, the owner is paid a fixed wage by the company and has little incentives to monitor workers. The efficiency wage model therefore predicts that if the monitoring technology is the same, wages (and effort) should be higher in the franchised outlets. This is indeed what Krueger finds, although the gap is not very large: from 2 to 9%. Krueger also finds steeper wage-experience profile in the franchised restaurants, suggesting that both wage premia and deferred payments are used by these restaurants as effort-inducing devices.

Another piece of evidence related to the debate on efficiency wages is the recent finding that increases in the minimum wage in low-paying industries tend to raise employment. For example, Card and Krueger (1993) have looked at the fast-food industry in New Jersey and Pennsylvania and found that after the minimum wage was increased, those stores which were paying minimum wages prior to the reform increased employment by more than other stores. Katz and Krueger (1992) have similar results. These findings may simply be explained by a monopsonistic model of the labor market where firms artificially depress their demand for labor to get lower wages, thus exploiting a local, upward-sloping supply curve for labor. A rise in the minimum wage would then simply curtail the firm's markup of marginal product over wage, while at the same time raising employment and labor supply.[6] However, this finding may also be consistent with the fact that higher wages have increased labor productivity, for example, by raising the average quality of workers in the fast-food industry (for the adverse selection version of the efficiency wage model, see Drazen 1986 or Lang 1987). Rebitzer and Taylor (1991b) argue that in the shirking model an increase in the minimum wage may also have a positive impact on employment. The idea runs as follows: Rebitzer and Taylor assume that under the no-shirking condition wages must increase with the firm's current employment level. That may be due to a fixed supply of monitoring resources (the probability of being caught shirking falls with the size of the firm's labor force) or to an increased probability of losing one's job in the future (as in chapter 3). This puts the marginal cost of labor above the no-shirking wage, since firms realize that wages have to go up in order to expand employment—an effect very similar to monopsony but one that is entirely derived from the shirking model. From there it is not very difficult to realize that a binding minimum wage can increase employment: The minimum wage enforces the no-shirking condition with strict inequality, so there is no need to increase it further to elicit incentives when employment expands. The marginal cost of labor is now equal to the minimum wage. If the minimum wage is between the previous wage and the previous marginal cost of labor, employment will increase. What makes the efficiency wage theory intuitively appealing is that low-wage industries are likely to be pretty competitive, so the monopsony hypothesis is not very plausible.

Besides fast foods, another popular piece of evidence in favor of efficiency wages was the introduction of the $5-a-day minimum wage by Henry Ford in 1914. Raff and Summers (1987) studied this natural experiment, and they concluded that not only did the outcome support the efficiency wage model, but the idea was explicitly motivated by such consideration. The $5-a-day program generated large increases in productivity (between 40 and 70%), a fall in turnover and absenteeism, and an increase in the length of job queues. They, however, expressed caution at a strict shirking interpretation of the results and favored explanations based on fairness and insider mechanisms.

---

6. One may, however, find it difficult to believe in monopsony in such a competitive market as the fast-food retail trade in so densely populated areas in New Jersey.

Yet there is no scarcity of studies that find no support for efficiency wages: Leonard (1987) used a survey of supervision practices at 200 plants. He was thus able to run a regression of wages on supervisory intensity (measured by number of supervisors divided by number of employees).[7] One would believe that if the shirking model is correct, plants with higher supervisory intensity pay lower wages. None of that is apparent in Leonard's data. Neither has Neal (1993), using NLS data for 1977, found a negative correlation between supervision intensity and wages across industries. There is unfortunately a glaring endogeneity bias in these results: While truly exogenous changes in supervisory intensity would be negatively correlated with wages, plants where supervision is more of a problem can have *both* higher wages and higher supervisory intensity. Groshen and Krueger (1990), who looked at hospitals, in fact found a negative correlation between supervisory effort and wages.

More conventional econometric approaches have also been undertaken, and the results often support the efficiency wage model: Campbell (1993), for example, has found that higher unemployment for the industry or region tends to push wages down, while higher wages reduce the quit rate.[8] Wadhwani and Wall (1991), looking at a panel of U.K. firms, found a positive impact on productivity of both relative wages and outside unemployment. Rebitzer (1987) found positive productivity effects of unemployment.

5.4   Evidence on Dualism

The model developed in chapters 3 and 4 accounts for several realistic characteristics of dualism. The model predicts that workers in the primary sector (those who are paid efficiency wages) are typically paid higher and enjoy higher job security than those in the secondary sector. The secondary labor force is constantly queuing for jobs in the primary sector. The model also captures the intuition of Piore (1972) and Doeringer and Piore (1970) that dualism arises as a response to uncertainty and volatility (for both aggregate and idiosyncratic shocks). The model also predicts that such a dual structure will occur *within* firms, although this has to be qualified: The solution derived in chapter 4 may equally be achieved by using *subcontractors*. If treating identical workers differently affects work

---

7. For a formal model, see Calvo and Wellisz (1979).

8. Campbell is more interested in the turnover than the shirking version of the efficiency wage model. In a related work (Campbell 1991), he finds strong support for the turnover model by looking at the cyclical elasticity of real wages across sectors and finds that sectors with higher wage rigidity also have higher turnover costs.

morale, then it is a better option to use subcontractors than internal dualism.

Various authors have provided evidence of such internal dualism arising as a response to uncertainty. Abraham (1988), in an important empirical paper, has studied flexible staffing arrangements in the United States; included were agency temporaries, short-term hires (seasonal workers, student summer work, etc.), and on-call workers (laborers supplied by a union hiring hall and retirees who work a few days a month). Abraham found that 93% of the 450 firms surveyed in 1986 used flexible arrangements. This result suggests that internal dualism is a prevalent feature of the U.S. economy. However, secondary workers, on average, account for about 1.5% of the total labor input. This proportion rises to 8% for the 10% firms that use flexible arrangements most intensively. But these figures are likely to understate the true extent of dualism on the demand side of the U.S. labor market: First, no account is made of subcontractors; second, since regular labor contracts have low firing costs in the United States, some of the so-called regular employees (presumably the less senior) may in fact be "contingent" in the sense that they will disproportionately bear the burden of a slump. The survey used by Abraham also directly asks the reasons for flexible staffing. One of the reasons reported by 22% of respondents was to provide a buffer for regular staff against downturns in demand. Interestingly this proportion rises to 42% for the top 10% users. Abraham also studied the characteristics of heavy users versus low users of flexible staffing arrangements. She found that 12% of the top 10% users report having a highly variable demand, while the proportion is only 5% for the bottom 50% users. She also found that heavy users are likely to be smaller firms and to have experienced larger employment fluctuations in the five years preceding the survey.[9]

Rebitzer and Taylor (1991c) argue that part-time workers are used by firms as a contingent labor force. The theoretical appeal of that argument is that shirking models typically imply that unit labor costs are lower for full-time than part-time workers. This is because the rent that must be paid per worker is unchanged if the probability of being caught and the effort level are both proportional to the fraction of time worked, so wages per efficiency unit of labor have to rise. Rebitzer and Taylor find that average tenure is much shorter for part-time workers than for full-time ones. They then go on and test the model's prediction that the presence of secondary workers, by increasing job security for primary workers, reduces their wages. They indeed find a significant negative correlation between wages

---

9. See also Mangum et al. (1985) for similar evidence on the temporary help industry.

of full-time workers and the proportion of part-time workers in the firm. While this is supportive of the model presented in chapter 4, they interpret it as a sign that when there are more part-time workers around, full-time workers are also more likely to be "contingent." I find my interpretation of their results more rigorous and attractive from the point of view of testing the efficiency wage approach to dual labor markets.[10]

One aspect of dual labor market theory not captured in the model, and this ommission reflects the macroeconomic emphasis of the book, is the linkage between worker's characteristics and job type. Workers are identical and the model tells nothing about who will end up in the primary sector or about the extent of mobility across the two sectors. In the context of the efficiency wage model, there are two arguments that may lead to a correlation between worker characteristics and the likelihood of holding secondary jobs. First, because primary jobs are rationed, nothing prevents employers from allocating primary and secondary jobs on the basis of arbitrary criteria such as race or sex. In other words, the Beckerian claim that competition would eliminate discrimination is no longer valid in the imperfect world of dual labor markets. Second, it is more costly for the firm to assign some workers to primary jobs relative to others. All else equal, workers with a lower attachment to the work force will have a higher propensity to quit and therefore lower motivation. These workers will therefore end up in the secondary sector more often, since their efficiency wage is typically higher. This is likely to be true of part-time workers, youth, women, and possibly workers from disadvantaged neighborhoods.

A related argument that was central to the original theory of dual labor markets, and developed in the late 1960s in the debate over the advancement of minorities in the United States, is the idea that the returns to education are much lower in the secondary sector, implying that training programs may be a failure as a tool to tackle poverty. In this book I do *not* deal with that issue and the model I have developed does *not* necessarily have that implication. While there are good reasons to think that uneducated workers are more likely to end up in the secondary sector (see chapter 9), I do not rule out mobility between the two sectors and therefore do not accept the prediction that secondary workers have lower returns to education. Acquiring education may indeed be a valuable way of moving from the secondary to the primary sector (again see chapter 9).

Thus we leave aside that aspect of the theory. Let us, however, briefly discuss the related evidence. Dickens and Lang (1985) have tested such

---

10. Tilly (1992) argues that even within part-time workers, some are primary and others secondary.

aspects of dualism by estimating "dual earnings functions." That is, they assume that instead of a single relationship between earnings and worker's characteristics, there are two, and that which of them is relevant depends on worker's characteristics. Each of these earnings function represents one labor market, and the sorting of workers across these two markets is derived endogenously (in some sense, this amounts to introducing strong nonlinearities in earnings functions). Clearly such an exercise rests on the premise that there is no mobility across the two markets. Dickens and Lang find that the dual representation fits the data much better than the single one, that the returns to education are lower in the secondary market, and that blacks are more likely to be in the secondary market. Rebitzer and Robinson (1991) extend their framework and find that the impact of employer size on earnings is much higher in the primary sector than in the secondary sector. If we assume monitoring problems to be more important in large firms, this is supportive of the view that primary workers are paid efficiency wages to a greater extent than secondary ones. These papers build on an earlier, rather inconclusive literature where the assignment to primary and secondary sectors was arbitrary rather than endogenously generated by the data.[11] The problem with that literature, as well as the more recent evidence in Dickens and Lang and Rebitzer and Robinson, is that most of the distinction between primary and secondary workers boils down to a white/black distinction. Thus the evidence might simply be capturing "ghetto effects" that have little to do with efficiency wages or labor demand variability.

5.5   Conclusion

The efficiency wage hypothesis has been widely discussed and tested. While the evidence remains inconclusive as to which model best explains the data, the empirical literature has made, in my view, a strong case against a perfectly competitive view of the labor market. Much more empirical work remains to be done, on the other hand, about the implications of efficiency wages for the structure of labor market segmentation and labor market response to macroeconomic shocks. There is no abundance of studies that allows us to test some of the implications of chapter 4, for example.

---

11. See Cain (1976) for a survey Neumann and Zideman (1986) find support for the theory, McNabb and Psacharopoulos (1981) reject it, and Leigh (1976) and Rosenberg (1980) are quite inconclusive.

6 Dualism, Labor Market Reform, and Macroeconomic Performance

The preceding chapters have analyzed how dual labor markets naturally arise as a result of imperfect monitoring and demand fluctuations. In Europe, however, it is often argued that labor market regulation is responsible for dualism in the labor market: Regulation creates rents and job protection for "good jobs," while forcing those who cannot get them into the secondary sector.[1] Furthermore liberalization of European labor markets in the 1980s has taken place "at the margin" by allowing firms to use more flexible arrangements, such as temporary contracts, subject to restrictions that leave existing contracts unaffected.

In this chapter I consider a slightly different model from the one in chapter 4. I consider a continuous-time two-state Markov model where there are idiosyncratic shocks as well as aggregate shocks. The continuous-time structure allows us to introduce voluntary quits in a tractable form, and to analyze the equilibrium level of employment and its dynamic response to aggregate shocks. As in chapter 4, firms will use "flexible workers" at the margin to deal with fluctuations in demand, and "rigid workers" inframarginally as their "core labor force." Because of the two-state structure, they will only hire flexible workers in the "high state."

The real world policy experiment that motivates this study is the introduction of determined duration contracts (DDCs) in most countries of continental Europe as a device to reduce firing costs. To simplify the analysis, I will abstract from efficiency wage considerations and work under the assumption of exogenous real wages. The two contracts differ because they are associated with different firing costs; dualism arises because of this difference. Adjustment costs therefore come from the exogenous regulatory environment rather than incentive problems at the firm

---

This chapter builds on Bentolila and Saint-Paul (1992).
1. A theoretical analysis can be found in Lazear (1988).

levels. However, the logic of the efficiency wage model that has been discussed in the previous two chapters still holds in this chapter: First, I assume that workers who hold a permanent contract are better off than those with a temporary contract, who are unable to underbid primary workers. Hence there is no arbitrage condition that must hold between holding a permanent contract and holding a temporary contract. Second, as in chapter 4, unlike permanent workers, temporary workers have to be monitored, so their cost is assumed to be greater than the wage paid to permanent workers. This structure is exogenously imposed here, but it is shown in chapter 7 that under some conditions it will endogenously arise as an equilibrium outcome.

I therefore analyze three situations:

A. A world where only one type of contract (with a high firing cost) exists.

B. A world where two types of contracts, one with a firing cost and the other without a firing cost, coexist. This structure is similar to the one analyzed in chapter 4. The difference in cost structures is now simply interpreted as the result of labor market regulations rather than differences in monitoring technologies.

C. The transition path of an economy which is initially in world A and where flexible contracts are introduced.

6.1   The Model

The model is based on Bentolila and Saint-Paul (1992), who use a two-state Markov process that has been analyzed by Bertola (1990). There are two types of workers, who differ in their labor costs and firing costs. Type 1 workers, hereafter "rigid labor," enjoy a permanent contract, are paid w_1 per unit of time and cause the employer a firing cost F if fired. Type 2 workers, hereafter "flexible labor," are under a temporary contract and are more costly than primary workers because they have to be monitored. Their total unit cost is therefore $w_2 > w_1$.

There is a continuum of firms with a total mass of 1, and each firm can be in one of two states, represented by a demand (or productivity) parameter θ. In the high state (or "expansion") $\theta = \theta_H$ and in the low state ("recession") $\theta = \theta_L < \theta_H$.

Firms maximize the present discounted (at rate r) value of current and future profits. Current profits are given by

$$P = (\theta l - \tfrac{1}{2}bl^2) - w_1 l_1 - w_2 l_2 - \text{Adjustment costs,}$$

where the firm's real revenue is given by the term in parenthesis, l_1 is rigid employment, l_2 flexible employment, and $l = l_1 + l_2$ is total employment.

The state of an individual firm is governed by a Markov process, with ε being the flow probability of a firm switching from the bad to the good state and γ that of the reverse switch. Each firm's state is completely uncorrelated with other firms' states, implying that in steady state there is a constant proportion $\varepsilon/(\gamma + \varepsilon)$ of firms in expansion and $\gamma/(\gamma + \varepsilon)$ firms in recession. This assumption is relaxed in section 6.6 where I introduce aggregate fluctuations. In addition I assume that the rigid labor force can be reduced either by firing a number of workers and paying the firing cost, or by reducing it progressively and incurring a quadratic cost per unit of time of $\frac{1}{2}c_0(dl/dt)^2$ whenever $dl/dt < 0$. This alternative can be thought of as "(costly) quits induced by the employer." It is merely a way of modeling quits while preserving analytical tractability. Hence a change in c_0 can be thought of as a change in the quit rate.

These assumptions about adjustment costs can be summarized by a unique, convex adjustment cost function that is asymmetric (no hiring cost) and such that the marginal adjustment cost is bounded when the derivative of l_1 goes to infinity, thus allowing for discrete jumps in employment (figure 6.1). This adjustment cost function is simply the convex envelope of the two labor reduction technologies that I have just defined. As shown in figure 6.1, quadratic costs will be used to reduce the labor force up to $dl_1 = -F/c_0 dt$; further units of adjustment will be dealt with using firing costs (at $dl_1 = -F/c_0 dt$ the marginal quadratic adjustment cost is precisely equal to the firing cost F). Let $\Gamma(\Delta l_1)$ be this adjustment cost function; one clearly has $\Gamma(\Delta l_1) = 0$ if $\Delta l_1 = 0$, $\Gamma(\Delta l_1) = c_0(\Delta l_1)^2/(2dt)$ if $0 > \Delta l_1 > -F/c_0 dt$, and $\Gamma(\Delta l_1) = -F\Delta l_1 - F^2 dt/(2c_0)$ for $\Delta l_1 < -F/c_0 dt$. In practice, rather than using these formulas, one simply has to consider that if the marginal benefit of reducing the labor force by one unit is greater than F, the firm fires a mass of workers and uses firing costs, while if it is greater than zero but less than F, it gradually reduces its work force using quadratic costs.[2]

I first characterize the solution of the model in the case where flexible contracts are not available and then study the case where this type of contract is available.

---

2. Note that if there is a discrete jump in employment, the quadratic technology yields an infinite cost. Therefore only an infinitesimal level of adjustment may be achieved through that technology. For that reason the first $-F/c_0 dt$ units that are changed using the quadratic technology can be ignored whenever there is a discrete change in the labor force.

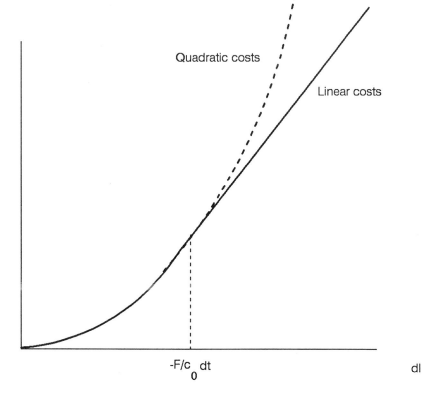

Figure 6.1
Labor adjustment costs

6.2   The Rigid World (Regime A)

I now characterize the solution to an individual firm's optimization problem, leaving the complete derivation to the appendix. To solve the problem, one has first to write down the firm's value function in both states of
nature H and L. This can be done recursively, using dynamic programming
(chapter 2), between date t and date $t + dt$. Hence the value function of the
firm in a recession is given by

$$V_L(l) = \max_{l'} [(\theta_L l' - \tfrac{1}{2} b l'^2) - w_1 l'] dt - \Gamma(l' - l)$$

$$+ (1 - rdt)[V_L(l')(1 - \varepsilon dt) + \varepsilon dt V_H(l')]. \tag{6.1}$$

Given its inherited labor force l, the firm sets its new labor force l' so
as to maximize its value function, given by the right-hand side of (6.1);

the maximum value it gets in turn defines its value function at l, hence the left-hand side of (6.1). The first term at the right-hand of (6.1) is the (infinitesimal) profits generated between t and $t + dt$ if the firm employs l' workers. The second term is the adjustment cost paid by the firm if it changes its work force from l to l'. This term is infinitesimal if the change in employment is differential, and finite if it is discrete. The last term is the contribution of the future to the firm's expected present discounted value. At $t + dt$ the firm will remain in the low state with probability $(1 - \varepsilon dt)$; in that case the present discounted value of its profits is by definition $V_L(l')$. With probability εdt it has shifted to the high state, which yields a value of $V_H(l')$. The sum of these two components is discounted at a factor $1 - rdt \approx e^{-rdt}$, the discount factor between t and $t + dt$.

The same equation can be written, mutatis mutandis, for firms in expansion:

$$V_H(l) = \max_{l'} [(\theta_H l' - \tfrac{1}{2}bl'^2) - w_1 l']dt - \Gamma(l' - l)$$

$$+ (1 - rdt)[V_H(l')(1 - \gamma dt) + \gamma dt V_L(l')]. \tag{6.2}$$

To determine the solution, we have to solve for (6.1) and (6.2). The first thing to be noted is that because there are no hiring costs, employment in expansions can jump to its optimal level regardless of its initial level. Therefore, over the relevant range, $V_H(l)$ does not depend on l, and employment in expansions is equal to a constant l_0^A, which satisfies the first-order condition:

$$\theta_H - bl_0^A - w_1 + \gamma V_L'(l_0^A) = 0. \tag{6.3}$$

Once it is known that V_H does not depend on l, it is easy to solve for the first-order condition in recessions:

$$(\theta_L - bl' - w_1)dt - \Gamma'(l' - l) + (1 - rdt)V_L'(l')(1 - \varepsilon dt) = 0. \tag{6.4}$$

In (6.4) two cases have to be distinguished. If $V_L'(l) < -F$, then the firm will fire a mass of people; in this case one may neglect terms in dt in (6.4). It then tells us that employment will drop to the level l_1^A such that

$$V_L'(l_1^A) = -F. \tag{6.5}$$

If $V_L'(l) > -F$, then adjustment is infinitesimal, and the firm uses quadratic costs. Equation (6.4) then becomes

$$V_L'(l) = c_0 \frac{dl}{dt}. \tag{6.6}$$

In this case employment dynamics can be fully recovered by rewriting (6.1) as

$$0 = \theta_L l - \frac{1}{2} b l^2 - w_1 l - \frac{c_0 (dl/dt)^2}{2} - (r + \varepsilon) V_L(l) + V'_L(l) \frac{dl}{dt}. \tag{6.7}$$

Differentiating (6.7) with respect to l and using (6.6) then allows us to derive a second-order differential equation in l (see the appendix) that yields simple partial adjustment dynamics for employment in recessions. Due to the absence of hiring costs, adjustment dynamics in recessions are similar to a deterministic model with quadratic adjustment costs (Sargent 1978; Nickell 1986).

The above discussion suggests that there are two regimes to be considered: If firing costs are large ($V'_L(l_0^A) > -F$), firms will not fire when falling into a recession. If they are not too large, they will fire. I concentrate on the latter case.

Optimal behavior is then as follows: The firm employs a constant number of employees l_0^A in the good state. When it suffers a bad shock (θ drops to θ_L), employment falls instantaneously to l_1^A; then it declines at rate $dl/dt = -\lambda(l - \bar{l})$ Until it reaches the static optimum in recessions, $\bar{l}$, or until the firm shifts back to an expansion. These employment levels are given by the following formulas:

$$\theta_H - b l_0^A = w_1 + \gamma F, \tag{6.8}$$

$$\theta_L - b \bar{l} = w_1, \tag{6.9}$$

$$\lambda c_0 (l_1^A - \bar{l}) = F, \tag{6.10}$$

where λ is the positive solution to the equation

$$c_0 \lambda^2 + (r + \varepsilon) c_0 \lambda - b = 0.$$

The solution is illustrated in figure 6.2 and is easy to interpret. Starting from expansion, the marginal worker is fired if a bad state occurs, implying that his shadow cost is equal to the sum of the wage and the firing cost times the probability of a recession. Equation (6.8) states that employment in expansions is determined by the equalization of the marginal product of labor and such shadow cost. In recessions the firm would like employment to drop to $\bar{l}$, the level where the marginal product of labor is equal to the wage (equation 6.9). It is not profitable, however, to do so instantaneously because of firing costs. Instead, the firm fires a mass of workers and then uses quadratic adjustment costs to reduce progressively its labor force down to $\bar{l}$. The marginal value of a worker when the firm uses quadratic

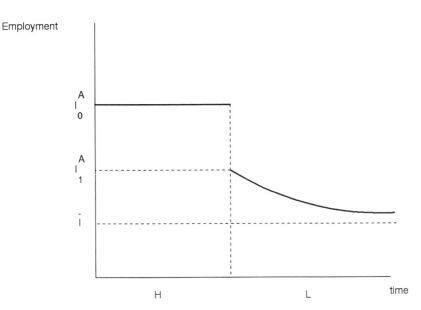

Figure 6.2
Employment response to a recession in world A

costs is equal to $-c_0\lambda(l - \bar{l})$, where λ is just the characteristic root of the first-order condition. Equation (6.10) states that at the start of a recession, employment drops to the point where the firm is indifferent between firing an additional worker or using quadratic costs.

Next I use these formulas to compute an explicit solution for *aggregate* employment in steady state. For this I compute the time path of employment in recessions, the stationary distribution of firms according to their state (H, L), and the time elapsed since they last changed state. To do this, simply remember that in steady state there is a proportion $\gamma/(\gamma + \varepsilon)$ of firms in recessions. These firms exit that state with flow probability ε, implying that the density of firms that have been in recession for a length of time between t and $t + dt$ is $\varepsilon\gamma/(\gamma + \varepsilon) \cdot e^{-\varepsilon t}dt$. These firms have an employment level that is between $\bar{l} + (l_1^A - \bar{l})e^{-\lambda t + dt}$ and $\bar{l} + (l_1^A - \bar{l})e^{-\lambda t}$. Aggregating these two exponential expressions for t between 0 and infinity allows us to compute the contribution of firms in recessions to aggregate employment. Similarly there is a proportion $\varepsilon/(\gamma + \varepsilon)$ of firms in expansion that employ a constant number of workers l_1^A. Adding these two contributions, we get the following result for aggregate employment (see the appendix for proof):

$$L_{\text{agg}}^A = \bar{l} + \varepsilon(\gamma + \varepsilon)^{-1}(l_0^A - \bar{l}) + \gamma\varepsilon[(\gamma + \varepsilon)(\lambda + \varepsilon)]^{-1}(l_1^A - \bar{l}). \tag{6.11}$$

Using (6.8)–(6.10), we can rewrite (6.11) as

$$L_{agg}^A = \frac{\theta_L - w_1}{b} + \frac{\varepsilon}{\gamma + \varepsilon}\left(\frac{\theta_H - \theta_L - \gamma F}{b}\right) + \frac{\gamma \varepsilon F}{(\gamma + \varepsilon)(\lambda + \varepsilon)\lambda c_0}. \tag{6.12}$$

Equation (6.12) allows us to do some simple comparative statics experiments: Increases in any of the θ raise aggregate employment, and increases in the wage reduce it. An increase in γ reduces employment for two reasons. There is a direct effect on the proportion of firms in recession, which increases, and an indirect effect on employment in firms in expansions, which goes down because the shadow cost of labor $w_1 + \gamma F$ has increased. Firms are more reluctant to hire because it is more likely that the marginal worker will be fired in the future. An increase in ε increases employment for two reasons. There is a direct positive effect on the number of firms in expansions, while firms fire less when falling in recessions and reduce their labor force at a slower pace thereafter (λ falls). Because firms expect to get out of the bad state sooner, they discount future losses from improductively keeping the marginal worker at a higher rate, which reduces these losses in present discounted terms relative to adjustment costs. Last, firing costs have an a priori ambiguous effect on aggregate labor demand. While employment in the good state falls (because the shadow cost of labor has increased), it raises in recessions because firms fire less. These two effects are captured by the second and third terms of (6.11), respectively. In fact it can be shown that with my specification a reduction in firing costs always *reduces* aggregate employment (see the appendix). As discussed in chapter 1, this result is very specific to the model. Bentolila and Bertola (1990) find a similar result, but it is numerical rather than analytical. Bentolila and Saint-Paul (1994), in the context of a model similar to the one in chapter 3, show that lower firing costs can have significant positive effects over some range.

6.3   Flexible Contracts Available (Regime B)

Let us now consider a world where in addition to the "rigid" contract with firing cost F studied above, there exist "flexible" contracts that have no firing cost. Workers hired under this type of contract will be referred to using subscript 2, and their unit cost is equal to w_2. Assume that $w_1 < w_2 < w_1 + \gamma F$, which means that rigid workers are preferred to flexible ones if the firm does not have to pay the firing cost (hence, in recession) but flexible workers are marginally preferred to rigid workers in expansion. Clearly, if $w_1 > w_2$, only flexible contracts are used, while only rigid ones are used if $w_2 > w_1 + \gamma F$. Therefore, for the two types of contract to coexist, it must be the case that the cost of the flexible contract is larger than the rigid wage but lower than the shadow cost of labor for a rigid worker who is fired when the firm falls into recession. The best interpretation of the assumption that $w_2 > w_1$ is not that they are paid more than rigid workers, which seems implausible from an empirical point of view but that, as in chapter 4, given their low employment security it is profitable to monitor them. Therefore w_2 is the sum of the flexible workers' wage and their monitoring cost.[3]

The solution can be derived using similar steps as for the rigid regime (see the appendix for details). The solution is as follows: The firm employs a constant number of flexible workers l_2^B in expansions as well as a constant number l_1^B of rigid workers. When it shifts to the bad state, it fires all its flexible workers but none of its rigid workers; it proceeds to reduce its rigid labor force progressively at a rate $dl_1/dt = -\lambda(l_1 - \bar{l})$ until it is back to the H state. The values of l_1^B and l_2^B are determined by the following equations:

$$\theta_H - b(l_1^B + l_2^B) - w_2 = 0, \tag{6.13}$$

$$w_2 - w_1 = \gamma c_0 \lambda (l_1^B - \bar{l}). \tag{6.14}$$

In this case firms use flexible workers on the margin in expansions because their marginal cost w_2 is less than $w_1 + \gamma F$, the marginal cost of a rigid worker fired in recession. For the same reason any rigid worker hired in expansion will not be fired in recession; otherwise, it would have paid to hire a flexible one instead. The solution is similar to the pattern derived in chapter 4: There is a dual regime where both types of workers are used and the marginal worker is flexible, and a rigid regime where only rigid workers are used. In a two-state model the dual regime is identical to the high state, and the rigid regime is identical to the low state. Equation (6.13) states that the marginal value product of a worker in expansion must be equal to his cost, taking into account that the marginal worker must be flexible. Conversely, in recessions all flexible workers in excess of $\bar{l}$ must have been fired, since their marginal cost w_2 is then greater than the marginal product of labor at $\bar{l}$, w_1. But since all inframarginal workers up to $\bar{l}$ must be rigid because these are cheaper than the flexible ones when not fired, no flexible worker is used in recession. Equation (6.14) states that the marginal product of a rigid worker hired in expansion is equal to w_2, since

---

3. Alternatively, we could assume that they are less productive, for example, because they provide lower effort. Such an assumption is made in Bentolila and Saint-Paul (1992).

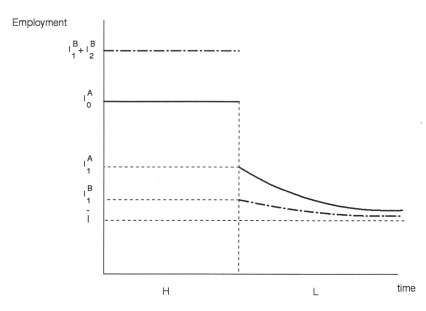

Figure 6.3
Employment response to a recession in world B

the marginal worker is flexible, and that this must be equal to the shadow marginal cost of a rigid worker, which is the sum of his wage and the opposite of his marginal value $(c_0 \lambda (l_1^B - \bar{l}))$ at the beginning of a recession, times the probability of a recession γ.

Using formulas (6.13) and (6.14), I can show that $l_1^B + l_2^B \geq l_0^A$ and that $l_1^B < l_1^A$. This inequality is illustrated in figure 6.3, where employment policies with and without flexible contracts are compared. The introduction of flexible contracts is therefore similar, as far as total employment is concerned, to a reduction in firing costs: Firms employ more people in expansions but fire more when falling into a recession.

The analogy with a reduction in firing costs, in this two-state model, can be pushed even further: Note that replacing l_0^A and l_1^A in (6.8) and (6.10) with $l_1^B + l_2^B$ and l_1^B, respectively, and replacing F with $(w_2 - w_1)/\gamma$, yields (6.13) and (6.14). As far as total employment is concerned, the flexible world is therefore identical to the rigid world, with a firing cost equal to $(w_2 - w_1)/\gamma$ instead of F. This "shadow firing cost" is the one that would make the firm in expansion indifferent between hiring a flexible worker or a rigid worker at the margin, since both alternatives would yield the same shadow cost of labor w_2. Interestingly this analogy tells us that introducing flexible contracts amounts to reducing the firing cost and at the same time indexing it on parameters such as w_1, w_2, and γ. The implicit indexation on γ, the probability of falling in recession, amounts to a fall in the "shadow firing cost" when γ rises which prevents the shadow marginal cost of labor in expansions from rising (it stays equal to w_2). In the flexible world firms in expansion are therefore less vulnerable to shifts in idiosyncratic volatility γ than in the rigid one. Equation (6.14) tells us that these changes are met through a substitution of flexible workers for rigid workers but that total employment in expansions is unaffected. The counterpart of this is that employment will drop to lower levels when the firm falls into recession, which was not the case in the rigid world, since l_1^A did not depend on γ.

Let us now aggregate and study the effect of flexible contracts on aggregate employment. In particular, aggregate flexible employment is equal to flexible employment in any firm in expansion times the proportion of firms in expansion:

$$L_{2\mathrm{agg}}^B = \frac{\varepsilon l_2^B}{\gamma + \varepsilon} = \frac{\varepsilon}{\gamma + \varepsilon}\left[\frac{\theta_H - \theta_L - (w_2 - w_1)}{b} - \frac{(w_2 - w_1)}{\gamma c_0 \lambda}\right], \qquad (6.15)$$

and aggregate rigid employment is

$$L_{1\mathrm{agg}}^B = \bar{l} + [\varepsilon\gamma + \varepsilon(\lambda + \varepsilon)][(\gamma + \varepsilon)]^{-1}(l_1^B - \bar{l})$$

$$= \frac{\theta_L - w_1}{b} + \frac{\varepsilon\gamma + \varepsilon(\lambda + \varepsilon)}{(\gamma + \varepsilon)(\lambda + \varepsilon)}\left(\frac{w_2 - w_1}{\gamma c_0 \lambda}\right). \qquad (6.16)$$

Total aggregate employment is then obtained by summing the two components, which yields an equation similar to (6.12), with F now replaced with the "shadow firing cost" $(w_2 - w_1)/\gamma$:

$$L_{\mathrm{agg}}^B = \frac{\theta_L - w_1}{b} + \frac{\varepsilon}{\gamma + \varepsilon}\left(\frac{\theta_H - \theta_L - (w_2 - w_1)}{b}\right) + \frac{\varepsilon(w_2 - w_1)}{(\gamma + \varepsilon)(\lambda + \varepsilon)\lambda c_0}. \qquad (6.17)$$

Equations (6.15)–(6.17) can be used for comparative statics purposes. An increase in γ, for example, has an ambiguous impact on flexible employment: There are less firms in expansion, but they are more flexible. The effect on rigid employment is unambiguous, it drops as all firms in expansion hire less primary workers. The net effect on aggregate employment is also unambiguous from (6.17): It drops. Therefore an increase in γ reduces employment in both the rigid world and the flexible world. The difference is that in the rigid world, a higher share of employment reductions takes place in firms in expansions than in the flexible world.

Is aggregate employment higher in world B than in world A? Given that I have shown that world B was identical to world A with a reduction in the firing cost from F to $(w_2 - w_1)/\gamma$, we know that the answer is in principle ambiguous, and that in my particular case employment will in fact be *lower* in world B. Another interesting, paradoxical, corollary is that a reduction in *the wage* of flexible workers may well *reduce* aggregate employment. This is because the wage of flexible workers only intervenes through the shadow firing cost. Firms hire more in expansions but also replace rigid workers with flexible ones, so in recessions they are left with less labor. In the aggregate, employment may well fall, and since lowering firing costs reduces employment in that particular model, it will.

6.4   The Transition between the Two Regimes

Let us now turn to study how an economy that does not have flexible contracts behaves when such flexibility is introduced. The main feature of the transition is that firms suddenly find that they have too many rigid workers and want to replace some of them with flexible ones. Because the rigid labor force entails adjustment costs, this process will be sluggish.

The adjustment path for individual firms can be computed using the same dynamic programming technique used above. Firms in expansion enter the transition with l_0^A rigid workers, while their long-run desired level is $l_1^A < l_0^A$. Their optimal transition path is the one that solves the Bellman problem:

$$V_H(l_1) = \max_{l_1', l_2} [(\theta_H(l_1' + l_2) - \tfrac{1}{2}b(l_1' + l_2)^2) - w_1(l_1' + l_2)]dt$$

$$- \Gamma(l_1' - l_1) + (1 - rdt)[V_H(l_1')(1 - \gamma dt) + \gamma dt V_L(l_1')], \qquad (6.18)$$

and a similar problem must be simultaneously solved for V_L.

The solution is computed in the appendix and has the following properties. At the microeconomic level, when flexible contracts are introduced, firms in the good state hire a mass of flexible workers up to the point where the marginal product of labor is equal to w_2. Because total employment must increase in firms in expansion and because rigid workers are inframarginal, the fact that they are too numerous does not affect the firm's optimal policy for total employment, which is determined by the identity between the marginal product of labor and the marginal cost of a flexible worker. Then they progressively replace rigid workers with flexible ones, using quadratic adjustment costs until rigid employment reaches its long-run level l_1^B. Also the point above which firms in recession fire a mass of rigid workers drops from l_1^A to $\hat{l}$, where $l_1^A > \hat{l} > l_1^B$ (see the appendix). This latter result comes from the fact that the firm now wants to get rid of rigid workers in excess of l_1^B in expansions, which creates an additional value to firing them when falling in recession.

As a consequence firms that enter the transition in the midst of a recent recession (where their employment level is still above $\hat{l}$) will fire an additional mass of rigid workers so that their employment drops to $\hat{l}$.

At the macroeconomic level, when flexible contracts are introduced, total employment will overshoot its long-run level (see the appendix). To understand the intuition behind this result, we need to distinguish between firms in expansion and in recession when the change occurs. When flexible contracts are introduced, firms in expansion hire flexible workers to equate their marginal product to their wage w_2. Thus total employment in these firms instantaneously reaches its long-run level (it immediately satisfies equation 6.13). Furthermore, since the total number of firms in expansion is constant, their contribution to total employment will not rise in the future. On the other hand, if flexible contracts had always existed, firms in recession would reduce employment starting from l_1^B, whereas now they do it starting from $\hat{l}$. Hence the contribution of firms in recession to total employment is higher in the short run than in the long run. Thus aggregate employment overshoots its long-run level.

This last result implies that one should not draw overoptimistic conclusions from the observation that aggregate employment substantially rises after the introduction of flexible contracts.

6.5   Introducing Business Cycles

I now show how business cycles can be introduced into the model without altering an individual firm's optimal policy. I thus define an aggregate recession as a situation in which a proportion $1 - \phi$ of firms in the H state simultaneously drop into the low state. The arrival of aggregate recessions is governed by a Poisson process independent of the process for idiosyncratic recessions. Therefore each firm now faces a probability of falling into recession of $\gamma = \hat{\gamma} + \pi(1 - \phi)$, where π is the flow probability of an aggregate recession and $\hat{\gamma}$ the flow probability of an idiosyncratic recession. Here the hat stands for intrinsic of any one firm: $\hat{\gamma}$ is the same for all firms but refers to shocks uncorrelated across firms, while γ is the overall probability for a firm of falling into recession, which includes the arrival

rate of aggregate recessions $\pi(1 - \phi)$.[4] Given the partial equilibrium nature of the model, these aggregate recessions are identical, from the point
of view of the firm, to idiosyncratic ones (in both cases it falls into the bad
state θ_L), so the only thing the firm cares about is the sum of the two
arrival rates γ. That is to say, the firm's optimal policies are the same as
above, but the way these optimal policies are aggregated is different. I
now define a *pseudosteady state* (PSS) as the steady state to which the
economy converges if no aggregate recession has ever happened. To
compute the pseudosteady state, we have to replace γ with $\hat{\gamma}$ *whenever* γ
enters in the steady-state distribution of employment and leave γ unchanged
whenever it is part of the firm's optimal policy. Thus aggregate employment in world A's PSS can be computed applying this transformation
to (6.12):

$$L_{\text{agg}}^A(\text{PSS}) = \frac{\theta_L - w_1}{b} + \frac{\varepsilon}{\hat{\gamma} + \varepsilon}\left(\frac{\theta_H - \theta_L - \gamma F}{b}\right) + \frac{\hat{\gamma}\varepsilon F}{(\hat{\gamma} + \varepsilon)(\lambda + \varepsilon)\lambda c_0}.$$

$$(6.19)$$

Let us first compute the impact on total employment of an *aggregate*
recession in world A. Suppose that the economy, starting from a PSS, is hit
by an aggregate recession at $t = 0$. There is a proportion $1 - \phi$ of firms
in expansion who fall in recession, so aggregate employment drops by
$\varepsilon/(\hat{\gamma} + \varepsilon)(1 - \phi)(l_0^A - l_1^A)$. Aggregate employment subsequently evolves
according to (see the appendix)

$$L_{\text{agg}}^A(t) = L_{\text{agg}}^A(\text{PSS})$$

$$- \frac{(1 - \phi)\varepsilon}{\hat{\gamma} + \varepsilon}e^{-\varepsilon t}\left[\frac{\lambda(l_1^A - \bar{l})e^{-\lambda t} + [\hat{\gamma}(l_0^A - l_1^A) - \lambda(l_0^A - \bar{l})]e^{-\hat{\gamma}t}}{\hat{\gamma} - \lambda}\right].$$

$$(6.20)$$

Studying this formula, we find two cases:

1. If $\lambda(l_0^A - \bar{l}) < (\varepsilon + \lambda + \gamma_i)(l_0^A - l_1^A)$, the pattern of employment is as in
figure 6.4: Employment reaches its minimum at the start of the recession,
increasing steadily thereafter.

2. If $\lambda(l_0^A - \bar{l}) > (\varepsilon + \lambda + \gamma_i)(l_0^A - l_1^A)$, employment is as in figure 6.5: It
goes on diminishing after the start of the recession until it reaches a trough
and then goes up again.

---

4. This modeling allows us to refer to aggregate recessions, whose probability is known by
firms but does not alter their optimal policy.

Employment

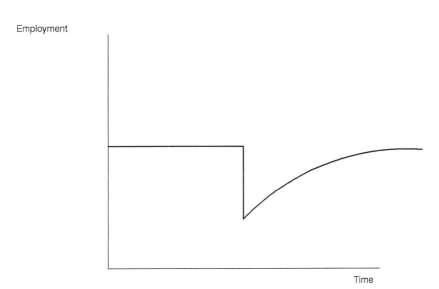

Figure 6.4
Employment response to an aggregate recession in world A: Case 1

Employment

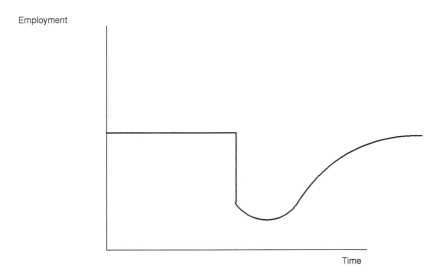

Figure 6.5
Employment response to an aggregate recession in world A: Case 2

Intuitively there must be an initial drop in employment, since a mass of firms fall into recession. Thereafter, because the proportion of firms in recession is higher than in steady state, the flow from recession to expansion is greater than the opposite flow, implying a positive effect on employment, while firms that stay in recession go on reducing their labor force, implying a negative effect on employment. When the first effect dominates, figure 6.4 applies; when the second effect dominates, figure 6.5 is the relevant one.

Let us further compute the effect of an aggregate recession on each type of labor and on aggregate employment in world B and then compare the effect on the latter with that in regime A. First note that employment levels in PSS are now given by

$$L^B_{2\text{agg}}(\text{PSS}) = \frac{\varepsilon l^B_2}{\hat{\gamma} + \varepsilon} = \frac{\varepsilon}{\hat{\gamma} + \varepsilon}\left[\frac{\theta_H - \theta_L - (w_2 - w_1)}{b} - \frac{w_2 - w_1}{\gamma c_0 \lambda}\right] \quad (6.21)$$

and that aggregate rigid employment is

$$L^B_{1\text{agg}}(\text{PSS}) = \bar{l} + [\varepsilon\hat{\gamma} + \varepsilon(\lambda + \varepsilon)][(\hat{\gamma} + \varepsilon)(\lambda + \varepsilon)]^{-1}(l^B_1 - \bar{l})$$

$$= \frac{\theta_L - w_1}{b} + \frac{\varepsilon\hat{\gamma} + \varepsilon(\lambda + \varepsilon)}{(\hat{\gamma} + \varepsilon)(\lambda + \varepsilon)}\left(\frac{w_2 - w_1}{\gamma c_0 \lambda}\right). \quad (6.22)$$

Adding the two, we find aggregate employment in world B's PSS, which can also be obtained by replacing F with the shadow firing cost $(w_2 - w_1)/\gamma$ in (6.19):

$$L^B_{\text{agg}}(\text{PSS}) = \frac{\theta_L - w_1}{b} + \frac{\varepsilon\hat{\gamma}}{(\hat{\gamma} + \varepsilon)(\lambda + \varepsilon)}\left(\frac{w_2 - w_1}{\gamma c_0 \lambda}\right)$$

$$+ \frac{\varepsilon}{\hat{\gamma} + \varepsilon}\left[\frac{\theta_H - \theta_L - (w_2 - w_1)}{b}\right]. \quad (6.23)$$

Suppose that, starting from PSS, the economy is hit by an aggregate recession at $t = 0$. Then aggregate employment at date t is equal to (see the appendix)

$$L^B_{2\text{agg}}(t) = L^B_{2\text{agg}}(\text{PSS})(1 + (\phi - 1)e^{-(\varepsilon + \hat{\gamma})t}) \quad (6.24)$$

for flexible workers and

$$L^B_{1\text{agg}}(t) = L^B_{1\text{agg}}(\text{PSS}) - \frac{(1 - \phi)(l_1 - \bar{l})\varepsilon}{\hat{\gamma} + \varepsilon}\frac{e^{-\varepsilon t}\lambda(e^{-\lambda t} - e^{-\hat{\gamma} t})}{\hat{\gamma} - \lambda} \quad (6.25)$$

for rigid workers. Adding these two numbers, we find the evolution of aggregate employment. Figures 6.6 and 6.7 illustrate the response of each

Primary
Employment

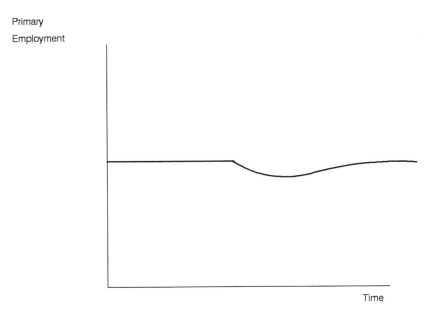

Time

Figure 6.6
Employment response to an aggregate recession in world *B*: Primary employment

Secondary
Employment

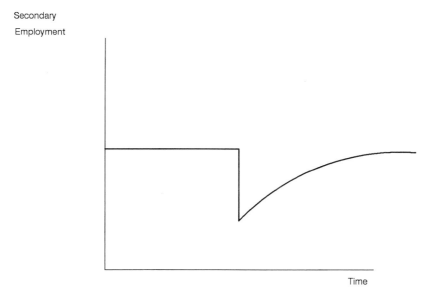

Time

Figure 6.7
Employment response to an aggregate recession in world *B*: Secondary employment

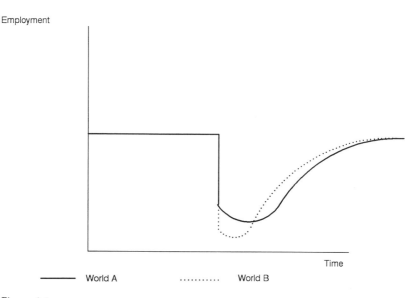

Employment

Time

——————— World A   ··········· World B

Figure 6.8
Employment response to an aggregate recession

labor type. The response of rigid employment is smooth, while the burden
of the recession is borne by flexible workers.

Finally, comparing the response of total aggregate employment in regime B to that in regime A, we observe (see the appendix) that recessions
are more violent, in the sense that the relative fall in total employment at
the start of a recession is larger. This again is not surprising given the
equivalence between the two-tier system and a general fall in firing costs.

Recessions are also less persistent in two senses. Consider first the
following index of persistence:

$$t_\alpha = t | \{ L_{agg}(t) = (1 - \alpha)L_{agg} + \alpha L_{agg}(0) \},$$

where L_{agg} is aggregate employment, and choose the largest value of t_α
satisfying this equation. Then t_α is lower, when flexible contracts are available, for any α. Furthermore the trough of total employment comes earlier
when flexible contracts are available. Both results are illustrated in figure
6.8.

6.6   Empirical Evidence on the Effect of Two-Tier Systems on Labor Demand

In the 1980s many European countries increased labor market flexibility
"at the margin" by introducing various forms of flexible contracts, mostly

Table 6.1
Share of temporary jobs in total employment (1989, %)

Country	Temporary jobs
Belgium	5.1
Denmark	9.9
France	8.5
Germany	11.0
Italy	6.3
Netherlands	3.4
Portugal	18.7
Spain	26.6
United Kingdom	5.4

Source: *OECD Employment Outlook*, 1991.

determined duration contracts. Table 6.1 reports the proportion of such contracts in some European countries. We see that they typically account for 10% of the work force, with the notable exceptions of Spain and Portugal. So the use of these contracts has been relatively limited, although not negligible.

The Spanish experience is of particular relevance, since flexible contracts have been much more widespread. In particular, given that flexibility is still on the agenda for many European countries and that it is likely to come in a two-tier fashion, there are lessons to be drawn from the Spanish experience. Bentolila and Saint-Paul (1992) have analyzed the impact of the liberalization of these contracts, which took place in 1984, on aggregate and firm-level labor demand in Spain.

In the wake of the first oil shock in 1973 and the political shock caused by Franco's death in 1975, Spain found itself with a quite rigid labor market. On the one hand, the wage flexibility prevalent in the earlier period was lost due to, among other factors, jockeying for position between the labor unions and strong pressures for lower wage dispersion (see Bentolila and Blanchard 1990). On the other hand, the employment relation was supposed to be long term (indefinite) and firing costs were relatively high. This rigidity was most likely a cause for the initially slow response of employment to the shocks, although it eventually contributed to the bankruptcy of firms with excessive labor hoarding, causing a larger employment drop afterward.

As in most European countries the Spanish government was in the early 1980s under strong pressure to increase labor market flexibility. It was in fact one of the first to react, by opening in 1980 the possibility of flexible, or fixed-term, labor contracts (*contratos temporales*). These are of two types: with cause and without cause. The former applies to work that is temporary in nature (like building jobs, tourism services, or harvest activities) and has always existed. The latter applies to any type of work and includes several types, like youth training and practice contracts, contracts for new workers substituting old ones and, most important, the so-called employment promotion fixed-term contracts (*contratos temporales de fomento del empleo*), which have no specificity other than the firm wanting to hire a worker on a fixed-term contract.

The most important characteristics of without-cause flexible contracts are (1) they can be signed for very short periods (three to six months) but renewed only up to three years in total, (2) at termination there are no firing costs (for some types) or low firing costs (for other types), and (3) their extinction cannot be appealed to the labor courts.[5] These conditions are not necessarily less restrictive than in other European countries (see table 6.2), but given that temporary contracts were much more widely used in Spain, labor market flexibility actually increased more than in other countries following the introduction of these contracts. It should also be noted that in 1994, the government has, under the pressure from unions, reduced the scope for using these contracts.

These contracts were not much used in the first half of the 1980s given the very low job creation. While some restrictions on the type of firms or workers who could sign these contracts existed in the 1980 law, they were lifted in 1984 in order to promote employment growth. Also incentives for the use of these contracts, like reductions in social security contributions, were instituted. Starting in 1986, when the economy picked up, almost all (98%) of the contracts registered in employment offices have been flexible. This flow has changed the stock quite fast: In the second quarter of 1987 (first available figure) 15.6% of all employees had this type of contract; in the fourth quarter of 1990 31.6% did. In the early 1990s this share stabilized at this level, in part because of the constraints put on the renewal of flexible contracts. The impact of this type of contract has been quite different by sector and type of worker (see Segura et al. 1991 or Jimeno and Toharia 1991), but it has been significant everywhere.

Bentolila and Saint-Paul then note that the introduction of flexible contracts has been followed by a boost in aggregate employment. In particular, employment growth has been quite high from 1986 to 1990, both by

---

5. See Segura et al. (1991) for a description of all types of flexible labor contracts.

Table 6.2
Regulation of fixed-term contracts in Europe

	Requisities of job	Maximum length	Renewals	Conversion to perma-nent job
Belgium	None	2 years	None	Automatic if exceeds length
Denmark	None	No limit	No restriction	
France	Temporary jobs only	2 years	2 renewals	Automatic if exceeds length
Germany	Temporary jobs only	1.5 years	No restriction	
Greece	Specific conditions	No limit	2 renewals	Automatic if exceeds length
Ireland	None	No limit	No restriction	
Italy	Specific conditions	3 months to 2 years	1 renewal (exceptional)	Automatic if exceeds length
Luxemburg	Specific conditions	No limit		Implies automatic renewal
Netherlands	None	No limit	1 renewal (by permission)	Implies automatic renewal
Portugal	Temporary jobs only	Maximum for renewals	No restriction within length	Automatic if exceeds length
Spain	None	3 years	No restriction within length	Automatic if exceeds length
United Kingdom	None	No limit	No restriction	

Source: Segura et al. (1991).

Table 6.3
Product and employment growth rates

	1964–74	1975–85	1986–90
Real GDP	6.3	1.5	4.8
Total employment	1.0	−1.7	3.0
Labor productivity	5.3	3.2	1.8
Employees	2.2	−1.5	4.8

international and Spanish standards. For example, over this period aggregate employment has grown by 1.5% in the European Community and by 1.9% in the United States. To illustrate previous Spanish experience, table 6.3 presents the growth rate of employment and related variables. It shows that the responsiveness of employment to output has been rising over time and has been specially high from 1986 to 1991, with the growth rate of dependent employment being truly remarkable (and even higher for private employees, of 5.1%). Another characteristic of this expansion is that while aggregate employment has increased, employment under rigid contracts has actually fallen.

All these features are consistent with the model outlined above. Although the effects of flexible contracts on aggregate employment in the long run are ambiguous, we know that they imply a higher cyclical elasticity of employment and that aggregate employment overshoots its long-run level at the time these contracts are introduced. Given that 1986 to 1990 was an expansion period, these two factors explain why the introduction of flexible contracts was followed by an employment boost in Spain. The model also predicts that the stock of rigid contracts should be gradually reduced in response to the introduction of flexible contracts, which is what happened in Spain.

During the 1991–94 recession, employment fell very sharply in Spain. This is again consistent with the prediction that aggregate employment is much more reactive to the business cycle due to the introduction of flexible contracts. The disappointing performance of the Spanish economy during that period suggests that one should not be overoptimistic about the impact of flexible contracts on total employment and that much of the initial increase may be due to overshooting.

Bentolila and Saint-Paul then estimate labor demand functions with firm level data to test for the implications of the model. They find that following the introduction of flexible contracts labor demand became more responsive to product demand shocks. However, they fail to find a drop in persistence, as measured by the coefficient of employment on lagged employment.

6.7   Conclusion

In summary, in this chapter we have studied the impact on the level and dynamics of employment of the introduction of a flexible tier into the labor market, under the assumption that both the primary sector and the secondary sector coexist and that firms use the flexible tier, as in chapter 4, to deal with fluctuations in their product demand.

We first saw that the introduction of flexible contracts is equivalent to a reduction in the firing cost and that therefore its effect on aggregate employment is ambiguous. Firms in expansions hire more because their marginal worker is flexible and has a lower shadow marginal cost than a rigid worker who would be expected to be fired in recessions. However, all flexible workers will be fired when the firm falls into a recession, and firms hire fewer rigid workers than the number of workers they keep when falling into the bad state in world A. Therefore employment in firms in recessions falls relative to world A, so the net effect on aggregate employment is a priori ambiguous. In fact the specification is such that aggregate employment is *lower* in world B than in world A.

Second, the shift to the two-tier system is equivalent to an indexation of the firing cost on labor costs for each type of worker and on the probability of falling into a recession γ. When this probability increases, firms in expansion do not reduce their work force because the shadow cost of labor has not changed. On the other hand, firms remain with fewer workers when falling in recession because they have hired fewer rigid workers (i.e., the shadow firing cost has fallen). The contrary happens in world A: Firms employ fewer workers in expansion because the shadow cost of labor has increased, while their firing point in recession is unaffected because the firing cost is unchanged.

Third, an increase in the cost of employing secondary workers increases the shadow firing cost and for that reason may have counterintuitive effects on aggregate employment. Firms in expansion substitute rigid workers for flexible ones, so firms in recessions employ more workers, even though firms in expansion employ fewer workers. Again, within the model's specification, aggregate employment increases.

Fourth, macroeconomic fluctuations are less persistent and sharper in world B than in world A, as would be the case with any form of reduction of labor adjustment cost in any model.

Fifth, *there is overshooting*. The *impact* effect of introducing flexible contracts on aggregate employment is larger than its long-run effect. This is because firms can lower their primary labor force only progressively, while they can adjust their total labor force upward instantaneously by hiring secondary workers.

Sixth, while introducing flexible contracts is equivalent to a reduction in firing costs, it has different distributional properties. Workers lucky enough to keep permanent contracts enjoy more employment security than before, even though the labor market is more flexible from an aggregate point of view. Conversely, workers with flexible contracts bear the burden of adjustment and have less employment security than if firing costs had been reduced uniformly.

6.8 Appendix: Derivation of Theoretical Results

The Model without Flexible Contracts (World A) Individual Firm's Demand Policies

First, notice that employment necessarily increases when there is a switch from L to H. Because there are no hiring costs, the level of employment before an expansion has no impact on the present discounted value of a given employment level provided that it increases. Hence there is no state variable, so a shift to an expansion yields a constant value V_H independent of the level of employment prior to the expansion.

Therefore a firm in recession maximizes

$$V_L(l) = \max\left(\theta_L l' - \frac{bl'^2}{2} - w_1 l'\right) dt - \Gamma(l' - l)$$

$$+ (1 - rdt)(1 - \varepsilon dt) V_L(l') + (1 - rdt)\varepsilon dt V_H, \tag{6.1}$$

where l is the initial employment level, l' the level to which it drops instantaneously, and dt a small time interval; Γ is the adjustment cost function defined in the text. Maximization takes place with respect to l'. The solution to (6.1) can be in one of two regimes:

1. If $V'_L(l) < -F$, the firm fires a mass of workers. Clearly employment drops to the point where $V'_L(l') = -F$.[6] Therefore, if the firm fires, it will fire a mass of people at one point in time (when it falls into the L state) and use quadratic costs thereafter. Let l_1^A be the resulting employment level:

$$V'_L(l_1^A) = -F. \tag{A6.1}$$

2. If $V'_L(l) \geq -F$, the firm uses quadratic costs and gradually adjusts its work force. l' differs from l infinitesimally: $l' = l + \dot{l}dt$. Maximization of (6.1) is equivalent to

$$\max V_L(l) = \left(\theta_L l - \frac{b\dot{l}^2}{2} - w_1 l\right) dt - \frac{c_0(\dot{l})^2}{2} dt$$

$$+ (1 - rdt)(1 - \varepsilon dt) V_L(l + \dot{l}dt) + (1 - rdt)\varepsilon dt V_H, \tag{A6.2}$$

---

6. Note that the problem is concave, so V' is decreasing.

where I have neglected second-order terms. The solution to this problem is

$$V'_L(l) = c_0 \dot{l}. \tag{A6.3}$$

The more negative $V'_L(l)$ is, the more remote the firm is from its optimum, and the faster it wants to reduce its labor force. Eliminating $V_L(l)$ from both sides of (A6.2) allows us to write an equation for V_L:

$$0 = \left(\theta_L l - \frac{bl^2}{2} - w_1 l\right) - \frac{c_0(\dot{l})^2}{2} - (r + \varepsilon)V_L(l) + \dot{l}V'_L(l) + \varepsilon V_H. \tag{A6.4}$$

It is convenient to differentiate (A6.4) with respect to l, which yields, using the envelope theorem,

$$0 = \theta_L - bl - w_1 - (r + \varepsilon)V'_L(l) + \dot{l}V''_L(l). \tag{A6.5}$$

Plugging (A6.3) into (A6.5) and noting that $d(V'_L(l))/dt = \dot{l}V''_L(l)$ yields a differential equation for the dynamics of l:

$$0 = \theta_L - bl - w_1 - (r + \varepsilon)c_0\dot{l} + c_0\ddot{l}. \tag{A6.6}$$

Equation (A6.6) defines a standard linear differential equation for l. The solution to this equation is

$$l(t) = \bar{l} + (l(0) - \bar{l})e^{-\lambda t}. \tag{A6.7}$$

In (A6.7), $-\lambda$ is the only negative characteristic root of (A6.6), meaning that λ satisfies $c_0\lambda^2 + c_0(r + \varepsilon)\lambda - b = 0$. Combining (A6.3) and (A6.7), we have the derivative of V_L which is equal to

$$V'_L(l) = -\lambda c_0(l - \bar{l}). \tag{A6.8}$$

We assume that parameters are such that firms fire at the beginning of a recession. The level at which employment drops is then determined by

$$l_1^A = \bar{l} + \frac{F}{\lambda c_0}. \tag{A6.9}$$

Equation (A6.9) is obtained by eliminating V'_L between (A6.8) and (A6.1).

Let us now turn to the optimal policy of firms in expansions. Given that firms fire in recessions, the marginal cost of a worker at the beginning of a recession is F. Hence firms in expansions maximize

$$V_H(l) = \left(\theta_H l - \frac{bl^2}{2} - w_1 l\right)dt$$

$$+ (1 - \gamma dt)(1 - r dt)V_H(l) + \gamma dt(-F(l - l_1^A) + V_L(l_1^A)).$$

The optimum is defined by $V_H'(l) = 0$:

$$\theta_H - bl - w_1 - \gamma F = 0, \tag{A6.10}$$

implying that

$$l = l_0^A = \frac{\theta_H - w_1 - \gamma F}{b}. \tag{A6.11}$$

The θs must be far enough apart from each other for $l_0^A > l_1^A$.

Aggregation of Individual Firms' Demand Policies

In steady state the outflow of firms in expansions must be equal to the inflow. If x denotes the proportion of firms in expansion, this implies that $\gamma x = \varepsilon(1 - x)$; that is, $x = \varepsilon/(\varepsilon + \gamma)$. All firms in expansion have an employment level equal to l_0^A. Firms in recession have an employment level equal to

$$l(t) = \bar{l} + (l_1^A - \bar{l})e^{-\lambda t},$$

where t is time spent in the L state. Firms exit the L state with flow probability ε, implying that the proportion of firms having been in recession for a duration between t and $t + dt$ is $\gamma\varepsilon/(\gamma + \varepsilon)e^{-\varepsilon t}dt$. Aggregate employment is thus equal to

$$\frac{\varepsilon l_0^A}{\gamma + \varepsilon} + \frac{\gamma\varepsilon}{\gamma + \varepsilon}\int_0^{+\infty} (\bar{l} + (l_1^A - \bar{l})e^{-\lambda t})e^{-\varepsilon t}dt. \tag{A6.12}$$

Solving (A6.12) yields (6.11).

The Model with Flexible Contracts

First, notice that in recessions $(\theta_L - bl)$ will not exceed w_1; otherwise, the firm would hire a mass of rigid workers. Hence $\theta_L - bl < w_2$, implying that $l_2 = 0$, which proves that all flexible workers are fired at the beginning of the recession. Second, no rigid worker will be fired at the beginning of a recession because such worker would cost $w_1 + \gamma F > w_2$ and the firm would hire a flexible worker instead.

Hence firms in recessions solve the same optimization problem as in (6.1), implying that the (rigid) labor force diminishes at a rate

$$\frac{dl_1}{dt} = -\lambda(l_1 - \bar{l})$$

and that the marginal value of a rigid worker in a recession is

$$V_L'(l_1) = -c_0\lambda(l_1 - \bar{l}).$$

In an expansion the firm chooses l_1 and l_2 to maximize

$$V_H(l_1, l_2) = \left(\theta_H(l_1 + l_2) - b\frac{(l_1 + l_2)^2}{2} - w_1 l_1 - w_2 l_2\right)dt$$

$$+ (1 - rdt)(1 - \gamma dt)V_H(l_1, l_2) + \gamma dt V_L(l_1).$$

The first-order conditions are

$$\theta_H - b(l_1 + l_2) - w_2 = 0, \tag{6.13}$$

$$w_2 - w_1 = -\gamma V_L'(l_1) = \gamma c_0 \lambda(l_1 - \bar{l}),$$

which completes the derivation of equations (6.13) and (6.14).

Using these formulas, we can easily prove that $l^B = l_1^B + l_2^B$ and l_1^B are, respectively, identical to l_0^A and l_1^A for firing costs equal to $(w_2 - w_1)/\gamma < F$. Equations (6.15), (6.16), and (6.17) can then be derived using the distribution of firms in recessions and their employment levels as we have done above.

The Transition from World A to World B

When flexible contracts are introduced, firms in expansion, and some firms in recession, start with a rigid labor force higher than the one they desire in the presence of flexible contracts. Hence firms in expansion reduce their rigid labor force until they reach l_1^B. Therefore, rigid employment is now a state variable for firms in both states. To characterize the path of flexible and rigid employment following the introduction of flexible contracts, it is necessary to solve for the two value functions:

$$V_H(l_1) = \max\left(\theta_H(l_1' + l_2) - b\frac{(l_1' + l_2)^2}{2} - w_1 l_1' - w_2 l_2\right)dt$$

$$+ (1 - rdt)(1 - \gamma dt)V_H(l_1') + \gamma dt(1 - rdt)V_L(l_1') - \Gamma(l_1' - l_1), \tag{A6.13}$$

$$V_L(l_1) = \max\left(\theta_L l_1' - b\frac{l_1'^2}{2} - w_1 l_1'\right)dt + (1 - rdt)(1 - \varepsilon dt)V_L(l_1')$$

$$+ \varepsilon dt(1 - rdt)V_H(l_1') - \Gamma(l_1' - l_1), \tag{A6.14}$$

where maximization takes place with respect to l_2 and l_1'. Notice that whenever $l_1 \leq l_1^B$, the previous analysis prevails, yielding $V_L'(l_1) = -c_0\lambda(l_1 - \bar{l})$ and $V_H(l_1) = $ constant; that is, $V_H'(l_1) = 0$.

Let us first consider the first-order conditions associated with (A6.13). Maximization with respect to l_2 implies that

$$\theta_H - b(l_1' + l_2) = w_2. \tag{A6.15}$$

The marginal product of labor is therefore pinned down by w_2. Consider now maximization with respect to l_1'. The logic is the same as above:

1. If $V_H'(l_1) < -F$, then l_1 drops to l_1' such that $V_H'(l_1') = -F$.
2. If not, then the firm uses quadratic costs to reduce l_1 down to l_1^B.

We have

$$c_0 \dot{l}_1 = V_H'(l_1), \tag{A6.16}$$

$$0 = w_2 - w_1 - (r + \gamma)V_H'(l_1) + \gamma V_L'(l_1) + \dot{l}_1 V_H''(l_1). \tag{A6.17}$$

Equations (A6.16) and (A6.17) are equivalent to (A6.3) and (A6.5), respectively.

Similar equations can be derived for recessions. If $V_L'(l_1) \geq -F$, we have

$$c_0 \dot{l}_1 = V_L'(l_1), \tag{A6.18}$$

$$0 = \theta_L - bl_1 - w_1 - (r + \varepsilon)V_L'(l_1) + \varepsilon V_H'(l_1) + \dot{l}_1 V_L''(l_1). \tag{A6.19}$$

The above equations extend the model's solution to the zone where $l_1 > l_1^B$. In the zone where $l_1 \leq l_1^B$, V_L and V_H are the same as derived above, in particular V_H no longer depends on l_1. These equations can be solved numerically. Two properties, however, can be formally established. First, firms in expansions do not fire but reduce their primary labor force progressively; second, the firing point for firms in recessions will drop from l_1^A to $\hat{l}_1$, with $l_1^A > \hat{l}_1 > l_1^B$.

To prove the first point, notice that equations (A6.16), (A6.17), and the concavity of V imply that $V_H'(l_1) \geq (w_2 - w_1)/(r + \gamma) - \gamma F/(r + \gamma) > -F$, since $w_2 > w_1$. This implies that $l_1' = l_1$. Hence firms in expansions do not fire anybody when the system is introduced.

To see that the firing point of firms in recessions goes down, let us suppose that it does not. Then all firms in recessions when the system is introduced will continue reducing progressively their labor force, with $l_1' = l_1$ (and $V_L'(l_1) = -c_0\lambda(l_1 - \bar{l})$). Notice that (A6.19) implies that

$$0 \leq \theta_L - bl_1 - w_1 - (r + \varepsilon)V_L'(l_1) + \dot{l}_1 V_L''(l_1)$$

or

$$0 \leq \theta_L - bl_1 - w_1 - (r + \varepsilon)c_0 \dot{l}_1 + c_0 \ddot{l}_1, \qquad (A6.20)$$

with equality for $l_1 \leq l_1^B$ and strict inequality for $l_1^A > l_1 > l_1^B$. At $l_1 = l_1^B$, we have $\dot{l}_1 = -\lambda(l_1^B - \bar{l})$. Let $x = (l_1 - \bar{l})e^{\lambda t}$. Note that at $l_1 = l_1^B$, we have $dx/dt = 0$. Now (A6.20) can be rewritten as

$$\dot{x}((r + \varepsilon)c_0 + 2\lambda) < c_0 \ddot{x}$$

where the second-degree equation defining λ has been used. This inequality implies that if $\dot{x}$ is positive at some point, it increases forever. But in this case $\dot{x}$ cannot reach 0, which is impossible since it is equal to 0 at l_1^B. Hence $\dot{x} < 0$, implying that $dl_1/dt < -\lambda(l_1 - \bar{l})$, or equivalently that $V_L'(l_1) < -c_0\lambda(l_1 - \bar{l})$. This inequality must be true for $l_1 = l_1^A$, where it implies that $V_L'(l_1^A) < -F$. This is clearly in contradiction with the assumption that the firing point does not drop below l_1^A. Hence the firing point of firms in recessions must go down. Since $V_L'(l_1^B) = (w_1 - w_2)/\gamma > -F$, it remains higher than l_1^B.

Overshooting

At the time when flexible contracts are introduced there are:

1. A density $\varepsilon/(\gamma + \varepsilon)$ of firms with $l_1^B + l_2^B$, satisfying (A6.15), that is, (6.13); the contribution of these firms to total employment is thus the same as in the long run.

2. A density $\gamma\varepsilon/(\varepsilon + \dot{\gamma})e^{-\varepsilon u}$ of firms having been in recessions for a length of time u. These have employment $\min((l_1^A - \bar{l})e^{-\lambda u} + \bar{l}, \hat{l}_1)$.

These firms would employ $(l_1^B - \bar{l})e^{-\lambda u} + \bar{l}$ workers if the economy were in its long-run steady state, which is smaller than $\min((l_1^A - \bar{l})e^{-\lambda u} + \bar{l}, \hat{l}_1)$. Hence total employment is necessarily higher than in the long run. This proves the overshooting result.

Evolution of Aggregate Employment after a Recession

Suppose that at $t = 0$ the economy is in a pseudosteady state, as if no aggregate recession ever occurred. The distribution of firm's individual states and durations in the L state is the same as that used to derive (A6.12), with γ replaced by $\hat{\gamma}$. Assume that a recession occurs at $t = 0$. To compute the evolution of aggregate employment after the economy has fallen into a recession, we need to compute the distribution of firms according to their state and how long they have stayed in the L state for any date $t \geq 0$.

At $t = 0$ there is a proportion $1 - \phi$ of firms in the H state that falls into the L state. This creates a mass of $(1 - \phi)\varepsilon/(\hat{\gamma} + \varepsilon)$ firms in the L state. This mass subsequently erodes at rate ε. Therefore we know that at date t there is a mass of $N_t(t) = e^{-\varepsilon t}(1 - \phi)(\varepsilon/(\hat{\gamma} + \varepsilon))$ firms that have been in the L state since $t = 0$. Concerning firms that fell in recession at some date $t - u < 0$, their number is the same as for the stationary distribution, since the economy was in PSS when they fell into the L state, and the number of these firms goes on being eroded at rate ε after the aggregate recession. Therefore at date t there is a density of $n_u(t) = \hat{\gamma}\varepsilon/(\hat{\gamma} + \varepsilon)e^{-\varepsilon u}$ firms in recession for a time $u > t$. Consider now firms in expansions; their total number $N_e(t)$ evolves according to $dN_e/dt = -\gamma N_e + \varepsilon(1 - N_e)$. At $t = 0$ we know that $N_e = \varepsilon/(\hat{\gamma} + \varepsilon)\phi$. Solving for N_e, we find that $N_e(t) = \varepsilon/(\hat{\gamma} + \varepsilon) + (\phi - 1)\varepsilon/(\hat{\gamma} + \varepsilon)e^{-(\varepsilon + \hat{\gamma})t}$ firms in expansion. The flow of firms falling into the L state at some date $t - u > 0$ is therefore $\hat{\gamma}N_e(t - u)$. These firms subsequently shift back to the H state at rate ε, so at date t there is a density of $n_u(t) = \hat{\gamma}e^{-\varepsilon u}[\varepsilon/(\hat{\gamma} + \varepsilon) + (\phi - 1)\varepsilon/(\hat{\gamma} + \varepsilon)e^{-(\varepsilon + \hat{\gamma})(t - u)}]$ firms having been in recession for a length of time $u < t$.

Once this distribution is computed, it is easy to compute the path of aggregate employment. In world A aggregate employment is equal to, at date t,

$$L_{\text{agg}}^A(t) = N_t(t)(\bar{l} + (l_1^A - \bar{l})e^{-\lambda t})$$

$$+ \int_0^{+\infty} n_u(t)(\bar{l} + (l_1^A - \bar{l})e^{-\lambda u})du + N_e(t)l_0^A. \tag{A6.21}$$

Integrating (A6.21), we find (6.20). Similarly in world B aggregate employment of type 1 workers evolves according to

$$L_{1\text{agg}}^B(t) = N_t(t)(\bar{l} + (l_1^B - \bar{l})e^{-\lambda t})$$

$$+ \int_0^{+\infty} n_u(t)(\bar{l} + (l_1^B - \bar{l})e^{-\lambda u})du + N_e(t)l_1^B, \tag{A6.22}$$

which can be integrated into (6.25). Equation (6.24) is then obtained by simply noting that $L_{2\text{agg}}^B(t) = N_e(t)l_2^B$.

Comparison of Effects of Recession with and without Flexible Contracts

First, notice that equations (6.8), (6.10), (6.13), and (6.14) imply that $l_2^B > l_0^B - l_1^A$ and $l_1^B < l_1^A$. Second, notice that equations (6.19)–(6.25) imply that the relative drop in employment at the start of a recession is

$$\left(\frac{\Delta L}{L}\right)^B = \frac{(1 - \phi)\varepsilon l_2^B}{(\hat{\gamma} + \varepsilon)L_{\text{agg}}^B}$$

in the flexible case and

$$\left(\frac{\Delta L}{L}\right)^A = \frac{(1 - \phi)\varepsilon(l_0^A - l_1^A)}{(\hat{\gamma} + \varepsilon)L_{\text{agg}}^A}$$

in the rigid one.

Third, equations (6.19), (6.8), (6.9), and (6.10) imply that

$$\frac{L_{\text{agg}}^A}{l_0^A - l_1^A} = \frac{\varepsilon}{\hat{\gamma} + \varepsilon} + \frac{\bar{l}}{l_0^A - l_1^A} + \frac{l_1^A - \bar{l}}{l_0^A - l_1^A} \frac{\varepsilon(\hat{\gamma} + \lambda + \varepsilon)}{(\varepsilon + \lambda)(\hat{\gamma} + \varepsilon)}$$

and similarly that

$$\frac{L_{\text{agg}}^B}{l_2^B} = \frac{\varepsilon}{\hat{\gamma} + \varepsilon} + \frac{\bar{l}}{l_2^B} + \frac{l_1^B - \bar{l}}{l_2^B} \frac{\varepsilon(\hat{\gamma} + \lambda + \varepsilon)}{(\varepsilon + \lambda)(\hat{\gamma} + \varepsilon)}.$$

The second expression is smaller than the first, implying that $(\Delta L/L)^B > (\Delta L/L)^A$. This proves that recessions are sharper in world B. Now using equations (6.20), (6.24), and (6.25) (or equation 6.20 with F replaced with $(w_2 - w_1)/\gamma$), notice that t_α is defined by

$$e^{-(\varepsilon + \hat{\gamma})t} + (\text{Ratio})e^{-\varepsilon t}\lambda\frac{e^{-\lambda t} - e^{-\hat{\gamma}t}}{\hat{\gamma} - \lambda} = \alpha,$$

where Ratio $= (l_1^B - \bar{l})/l_2^B$ in the flexible case and Ratio $= (l_1^A - \bar{l})/(l_0^A - l_1^A)$ in the rigid case, and where the largest solution for t_α is selected, implying that the left-hand side is locally decreasing in t around the solution. Then Ratio is smaller in the flexible case, implying that t_α is smaller.

To prove that the trough comes earlier in world B, differentiate aggregate employment with respect to time in both cases, and check that the date at which the minimum is reached comes earlier when F goes down. Then apply the analogy between world B and world A with a lower firing cost.

7   Impact of Dualism on Wage Formation

Up to now, we have focused on the effects of a two-tier labor market on aggregate labor demand and shown that the secondary sector tends to make the labor market more flexible *at the* margin. In those exercises we have held the wage for a given type of contract fixed, both across idiosyncratic and aggregate states of nature. We have also assumed, when dealing with the effects of introducing temporary contracts, that the wage paid to workers with permanent contracts is unaffected.

An important question is, however, whether the introduction of the secondary labor market will have any impact on wage formation in the primary sector. Will flexible contracts moderate or stimulate wage increases for workers with permanent contracts? This chapter addresses these issues by closing the model developed in chapter 6 with endogenizing wage formation.[1]

In this chapter we will confine ourselves to a steady state with no "quits," $c_0 = +\infty$. We will assume that wage formation is competitive in the secondary sector,[2] while in the primary sector workers require that

---

1. Throughout the book I stick with models of the labor market, meaning employment and wage determination rather than models of the economy as a whole. It would be easy to spell out the models in a general equilibrium fashion by making enough linearity assumptions about tastes and technology in the rest of the economy: for example, constant marginal utility of consumption, a single homogeneous good, etc. But this would be more for the sake of "political correctness" (internal to the economics profession) than anything else. Taking general equilibrium seriously in a world of imperfect markets is associated with a range of problems (existence, uniqueness, continuity, comparative statics) which are far different from the ones I deal with here, and far from settled. The general philosophy of modeling in this book is to make assumptions stick to the intuition being conveyed, eliminating effects that may introduce complications and are irrelevant to the argument.

2. Secondary workers are often thought to receive efficiency wages, as is the case in the work of Krueger (see chapter 5) on fast foods. The assumption I make is an approximation of the idea that monitoring problems are less important in the secondary sector than in the primary one (indeed the rents estimated by Krueger in the secondary sector are small).

their present discounted income exceed that of an unemployed (or equivalently a worker with a flexible contract) by a constant markup. This is what is typically the case in a continuous time efficiency wage model (e.g., see Shapiro and Stiglitz 1984), but it can also be taken as a good approximation of the outcome of bargaining between firms and insiders.

7.1 Flexible Contracts and Wage Formation

The main conclusions of the analysis is that introducing flexible contracts has several effects on wage formation in the primary tier of the labor market:

First, as we have seen in chapters 4 and 6, primary workers will have a greater employment security than in a world without flexible contracts. This is because temporary workers are used to adjusting to fluctuations in product demand and are fired before the primary workers are fired. Since primary workers have more employment security, they in fact require *lower* wages than in the world with only permanent contracts available. Recall the analysis in chapter 3: An increase in job security increases the employed's intertemporal utility holding everything else equal. This allows firms to match the no-shirking condition with lower wages.

Second, firms that shift from the low to the high state will hire fewer rigid workers than if flexible contracts were not available (see chapter 6). Therefore it will be more difficult for an unemployed individual to find such a job. This tends to push down the value of being unemployed, which in turn lowers wages in the primary sector. Under the efficiency wage interpretation of the model, becoming unemployed is a tougher punishment because the likelihood of finding a "good job" has fallen. A lower wage is therefore required to enforce effort. Under the bargaining interpretation, the threat point of the insiders has deteriorated, so the negotiated wage is lower.

Third, the possibility of getting a flexible contract may in fact increase the utility of being unemployed. As we will see, this will occur in the model provided that the introduction of flexible contracts lifts the economy to a full-employment equilibrium. By the same argument as in the previous paragraph, this effect will tend to push wages up the primary sector.

These three arguments rest on the assumption that the markup of the primary workers' discounted utility over the unemployed is unaffected by the introduction of flexible contracts. This may, however, not be the case.

For one thing, greater job security will increase the bargaining power of insiders, which will tend to push up wages. For another, the firm now has the option of replacing a primary worker with a secondary one, which will tend to reduce its bargaining power. This will lower wages in the primary sector.

We can conclude that the net effect of introducing flexible contracts on wages in the primary sector is ambiguous. But my personal feeling is that the first two arguments above are likely to be more relevant; that is, flexible labor contracts will have a moderating impact on wage formation in the primary sector.

The model in this chapter also provides a foundation for the assumption that was made in the previous chapter that workers holding flexible contracts queue for rigid jobs. It shows that under some plausible conditions the firm will want to offer rigid contracts to those workers that are paid efficiency wages and flexible contracts to those who are monitored. This builds a bridge between the institutional dualism of chapter 6 and the efficiency dualism of chapter 4.[3]

7.2   A Model of Wage Formation

Let us first analyze wage formation in a world A where only rigid contracts prevail. This is the same model as in chapter 6, but here we simplify the analysis by ruling out the option of reducing the labor force by means of quadratic adjustment costs. This is equivalent to letting c_0, the parameter describing the level of these costs, go to infinity.

How is labor demand affected by this assumption? Let us start with firms in the low L state. Let $V_L(l)$ be the present discounted value of employing l workers when the firm is in the low state. Let F be the firing cost. One clearly has to cases. If $V_L'(l) < -F$, then the firm fires its workers up to the point where $l = l_L$, where l_L is determined by $V_L'(l_L) = -F$.[4] If $0 > V_L'(l) > -F$, then the firm keeps its workers until it is brought back to the expansionary state (because the firm is in the low state one can rule out the case where $V_L'(l_L) \geq 0$, in which case it would hire). Now the firm's present discounted flow of profits is given by

---

3. The impact of two-tier systems on wage formation has also been analyzed in Bentolila and Dolado (1992) who construct a rather different bargaining model, focusing on sometimes related, sometimes different effects. Their conclusion is similar to the present one in that some effects tend to push wages up, others down. I return to their empirical findings in section 5.8.

4. To simplify the analysis, we will assume that the firing cost F is paid to a third party rather than directly to the worker as a severance payment.

$$V_L(l) = \frac{\theta_L l - b l^2/2 - w_{1L} l + \varepsilon V_H}{r + \varepsilon}. \tag{7.1}$$

As in chapter 6 we have assumed that firms do change their labor force when shifting from one state to another. Because of linear adjustment costs, the firm's employment in the high state is independent of l and so is its value V_H. In (7.1), w_{1L} is the wage paid to workers when the firm is in the low state. Contrary to what was assumed in chapter 6, it here differs from the wage paid in the high state.

Equation (7.1) implies that in recessions employment will drop to l_L, defined by

$$l_L = \frac{\theta_L - w_{1L} + (r + \varepsilon)F}{b}. \tag{7.2}$$

For firms in the high state, we let $V_H(l)$ be the value of employing l workers. As in chapter 6 firms will hire workers up to the point where $V_H'(l_L) = 0$. This is equivalent to stating that the marginal revenue of labor is equal to its shadow marginal cost. Because the marginal worker is expected to be fired when the firm drops to the low state, the latter is simply equal to $w_{1H} + \gamma F$, where w_{1H} is the wage paid in the high state. Employment in the high state is therefore simply determined by

$$\theta_H - b l_H - w_{1H} - \gamma F = 0 \tag{7.3}$$

or

$$l_H = \frac{\theta_H - w_{1H} - \gamma F}{b} \tag{7.4}$$

Firing and hiring will occur if the solutions to (7.2) and (7.4) satisfy $l_L < l_H$:

$$\theta_H - \theta_L - (w_{1H} - w_{1L}) > (r + \varepsilon + \gamma)F. \tag{7.5}$$

If (7.5) fails to hold, then the economy is in a regime such that $l_H = l_L$, which will not be analyzed here.

Let us now turn to wage determination. We will assume that workers are only prepared to work if being employed yields them an expected present discounted income that exceeds that of the unemployed by a fixed markup Q:

$$V_e = V_u + Q, \tag{7.6}$$

where V_e is the present discounted value of being employed and V_u the present discounted value of being unemployed. This type of relationship is exactly the one that would be obtained in the efficiency wage model of Shapiro and Stiglitz (1984). In their model, Q is simply equal to e/q, where e is the required effort level and q the flow probability of being caught shirking. The no-shirking condition then simply reads as $q(V_e - V_u) = e$, which means that effort (the benefit of shirking) must be equal to the flow probability of being caught time the present discounted loss from being dismissed (the annuity cost of shirking). In the model of chapter 3 the discrete time equivalent to (7.6) is (3.3).

In a bargaining framework there would be an intertemporal surplus-sharing rule which would typically yield an equation of the following form:[5]

$$V_e = V_u + Q + \delta W. \tag{7.7}$$

Here W is the firm's expected present discounted marginal profit. That is, the employed not only require a markup over the unemployed's welfare but extract some of the surplus of the match. In this model we simply have $W = 0$ in the H state and $W = -F$ in the L state. The bargaining outcome would therefore be very similar to the efficiency wage outcome, except that the markup would be smaller in recessions. In the remainder we will stick to the simpler formulation given by (7.6).

What does (7.6) imply for wages? Let $V_e(H)$ (resp. $V_e(L)$) be the present discounted value of being employed in a firm in the high (resp. low) state. Assume that workers have perfect access to financial markets (or equivalently are risk neutral with a discount rate equal to the interest rate). Then these value functions can be written recursively as

$$V_e(H) = w_{1H}dt + (1 - rdt)\left[(1 - \gamma dt)V_e(H) + \gamma dt(V_e(L)\frac{l_L}{l_H} \right.$$

$$\left. + \left(1 - \frac{l_L}{l_H}\right)\right] \tag{7.8}$$

$$V_e(L) = w_{1L}dt + (1 - rdt)[(1 - \varepsilon dt)V_e(L) + \varepsilon dt V_e(H)]. \tag{7.9}$$

Equations (7.8) and (7.9) are continuous time counterparts of (3.1). The value of being employed today (at time t) is equal to the flow of income (the wage rate times the small time interval dt) plus tomorrow's expected present discounted value. In the right-hand side of (7.8), tomorrow's expected PDV is equal to $V_e(H)$ if the firm is still in the high state (probability $1 - \gamma dt$)), $V_e(L)$ if the firm falls into the low state but the worker retains

---

5. An example is Pissarides (1990).

his job (probability $\gamma dt(l_L/l_H)$, and V_u (the value of being unemployed) if the firm falls into the low state and the worker loses his job (probability $\gamma dt(1 - l_L/l_H)$). A similar interpretation applies to (7.9).

As in chapter 3 the firm's employment policy (here determined by l_H and l_L) enters wage formation through the probability of being dismissed. Contrary to chapter 3, we now assume that firms do not take into account the impact of their employment policy on wage formation when optimizing. This is witnessed by the fact that wages were held exogenous when the first-order conditions (7.2) and (7.3) were derived. If, as in chapter 3, firms were taking into account the effect of their future employment policies on current incentives, they would set a lower l_H and a higher l_L (see Strand 1992). Furthermore the ability to make commitments over one's future employment policy would eliminate any reason to go on using rigid contracts. One therefore has to keep in mind that in this chapter, rigid contracts go on being used despite the firing cost because they provide firms with a commitment device to reduce the worker's probability of being fired. In chapter 3 it was assumed that they could make such a commitment at no cost.

Plugging (7.6) into (7.8) and (7.9) and simplifying, it is now easy to compute wages in both states as a function of V_u:

$$w_{1H} = r(V_u + Q) + \gamma\left(1 - \frac{l_L}{l_H}\right)Q, \tag{7.10}$$

$$w_{1L} = r(V_u + Q). \tag{7.11}$$

Firms in the good state pay higher wages than firms in the bad state because workers must be compensated for the higher probability of being fired if the firm falls into the bad state. This effect is embodied in the last term of (7.10), which is equal to the flow probability of losing one's job, $\pi = \gamma(1 - l_L/l_H)$, times the rent lost when such event occurs, Q. In addition to the interest on the rent, rQ, the firm must pay an annuity value πQ to the worker; this may be interpreted as an insurance premium for the risk of being fired. The wage differential will be higher the lower l_L/l_H (i.e., when firing costs are lower and idiosyncratic volatility $\theta_H - \theta_L$ is higher) and the higher γ (higher industry turnover).

Closing the Model

The model is closed by computing V_u. Let a be the flow probability of an unemployed worker's finding a job. Then we can write a recursive equation for V_u that is similar to (7.8) and (7.9):

$$V_u = \bar{w}dt + (1 - rdt)[(1 - adt)V_u + adt(V_u + Q)], \tag{7.12}$$

where $\bar{w}$ is the level of unemployment benefits and (7.6) has been used. Equation (7.12) is clearly equivalent to $V_u = (\bar{w} + aQ)/r$. Plugging this into (7.10) and (7.11), we get an expression of wages as a function of a:

$$w_{1H} = \bar{w} + (r + a)Q + \gamma\left(1 - \frac{l_L}{l_H}\right)Q, \tag{7.13}$$

$$w_{1L} = \bar{w} + (r + a)Q. \tag{7.14}$$

A tighter labor market, meaning a higher value of a, is associated with higher wages.

Let u be the level of unemployment. In steady states, au workers leave unemployment per unit of time. This must be equal to the number of workers hired by firms shifting from the low state to the high state. Let us normalize the total number of firms to 1. In steady state there are $\gamma/(\gamma + \varepsilon)$ firms in the low state. A fraction ε of them per unit of time shift back to the high state, and each of them hires $l_H - l_L$ workers. Hirings per unit of time are therefore equal to

$$\varepsilon\gamma\frac{l_H - l_L}{\gamma + \varepsilon} = au. \tag{7.15}$$

Last, we normalize total labor force to be 1, which implies that

$$\frac{\varepsilon l_H}{\gamma + \varepsilon} + \frac{\gamma l_L}{\gamma + \varepsilon} + u = 1. \tag{7.16}$$

The first term is total employment in H firms, the second term total employment in L firms, and the last term unemployment. Equilibrium in l_H, l_L, w_{1H}, w_{1L}, a, and u is therefore computed as the solution to equations (7.2), (7.4), (7.13), (7.14), (7.15), and (7.16).

Equilibrium determination is graphically portrayed in figure 7.1. On the x-axis is $z = l_L/l_H$, the fraction of the labor force that is retained when a firm falls into the low state. On the y-axis is a, the index of labor market tightness. Equilibrium is determined by the intersection of the AA locus and the BB locus. The AA locus describes the effect of labor market tightness a on the cost of labor in one state relative to the other.[6] It is

---

6. The AA locus is obtained by plugging (7.13) and (7.14) into the right-hand side of (7.2) and (7.4) and dividing (7.4) by (7.2). The result is the following equation:

$$z = \frac{l_L}{l_H} = \frac{\theta_L - \bar{w} - (r + a)Q + (r + \varepsilon)F}{\theta_H - \bar{w} - (r + a)Q - \gamma(1 - z)Q - \gamma F}.$$

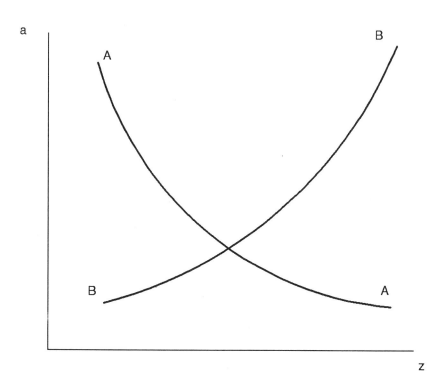

Figure 7.1
Equilibrium determination

downward sloping because an increase in labor market tightness a increases wages by the same amount in both states, which tends to increase the cost of workers in the low state relative to the high state, thus reducing l_L/l_H. The BB locus describes the effect of z on job creation, through wage formation and labor demand in both states.[7] It is upward sloping because an increase in z reduces wages in the high state, thus boosting labor demand and therefore labor market tightness.

Next we want to compute the model's solution when flexible contracts are available. We assume, as in chapter 6, that flexible contracts entail no firing cost. Furthermore we assume that wage formation in the flexible tier of the labor market is perfectly competitive. This assumption is a stylized representation of the casual observation that the secondary labor market is

---

7. BB is obtained by eliminating wages from (7.2) and (7.4) using (5.13) and (5.14), plugging the resulting expressions into (5.15) and (7.16), and eliminating u between the two resulting equations. The end result is

$$a = \frac{\varepsilon\gamma[(\theta_H - \theta_L) - \gamma(1 - z)Q - (r + \gamma + \varepsilon)F]}{\gamma + \varepsilon - \gamma(\theta_L - \overline{w} - (r + \varepsilon)F) - \varepsilon(\theta_H - \overline{w} - \gamma F - \gamma(1 - z)Q) + (\gamma + \varepsilon)(r + a)Q}.$$

more competitive than the primary one. It is possible, however, to give it a more rigorous content. This is what is done in the next section, which may be skipped without altering the understanding of the remainder of the chapter.

7.3   Flexible Contracts and Competitive Wage Setting

If we stick to the efficiency wage interpretation of (7.6), the assumption that flexible workers earn competitive wages while rigid ones are paid efficiency wages may be rationalized as an equilibrium outcome. Let us assume that firms can elect to pay workers either an efficiency wage that matches the no-shirking condition (7.6) or a competitive wage equal to w_c and to monitor them at a cost c per worker per unit of time. If the firm decides to pay efficiency wages, then it will have to pay a wage that matches conditions (7.13) and (7.14), or more generally

$$w = w_c + (r + a + \pi)Q, \tag{7.17}$$

where w_c is the competitive wage, π is the flow probability of a worker losing one's job, and a is now interpreted as the flow probability of finding a job in the *primary* sector. In the primary world considered in the previous section, the competitive wage w_c is simply equal to $\bar{w}$, since there is equilibrium involuntary unemployment; π is equal to 0 in the L state and $\gamma(1 - l_L/l_H)$ in the H state (hence equations 7.13–7.14).

Let us first consider what options the firm will choose in world A where there is a firing cost equal to F. In the high state, if the marginal worker is fired, then the shadow cost of labor is

$$w + \gamma F = w_c + (r + a + \pi)Q + \gamma F \qquad \text{if the firm pays efficiency wages,}$$

$$= w_c + c + \gamma F \qquad \text{if it does not.}$$

Firms will decide to pay efficiency wages if and only if

$$(r + a + \pi)Q < c. \tag{7.18}$$

This will be true if a and π are low. High firing costs will of course tend to lower π, the probability of being fired, and a, the probability of finding a job (since fewer firings also imply fewer hirings in equilibrium). *It is therefore more likely that firms will decide to pay efficiency wages if firing costs are high.* This is a crucial result. It tells us that workers who hold flexible contracts will earn less rents than those who own rigid contracts. A similar result would be obtained in an insider/outsider model of wage bargaining à la Lindbeck and Snower (1989), where precisely the existence of turnover costs creates a rent to be split between firms and incumbents. Here the mechanism is quite different: High firing costs force firms to lower the cyclical variability of their employment policy, which, by increasing job security, makes it cheaper to use efficiency wages rather than monitoring.

Let us turn to what happens in world B. The decision the firm has to make is twofold: It has to decide what type of contract to offer and whether to pay efficiency wages or to monitor. Consider, first, workers with a flexible contract. The cost of labor is

$$w = w_c + (r + a' + \pi')Q \qquad \text{if the firm pays efficiency wages,}$$

$$= w_c + c \qquad\qquad\qquad \text{if it monitors.}$$

Now π' is the worker's flow probability of being fired in world B, while a' is the flow probability of finding a *rigid* job. Since flexible contracts entail no firing costs, π' is likely to be higher than π. Therefore for some configurations it is indeed optimal for the firm to pay efficiency wages to workers with a rigid contract and to monitor workers with a flexible contracts. The corresponding condition is

$$(r + a' + \pi')Q > c. \qquad\qquad\qquad\qquad\qquad\qquad (7.19)$$

In chapter 4 dualism arose as an equilibrium outcome with a single type of contract. By employing workers who were monitored and preferentially fired, the firm was reducing the perceived probability of being fired for those workers who are paid efficiency wages. This requires that the firm actually make some commitment over *who* would be fired in case of a slump. As in chapter 3 this commitment was technically due to the fact that employment decisions had to be made one period in advance.

It is clear that if I were making this assumption here, rigid contracts would no longer be used in world B. Any worker with a rigid contract could be offered a flexible contract associated with the same wage and the same probability of being fired, and the firm would economize on firing costs.

However, I rule out such commitment. Let us assume that firings are random so that π' is the same for all workers with a flexible contract. The only way the firm can grant more employment security to some workers is to offer them a rigid contract. Formally, if π'' is the equilibrium probability of being fired when one holds a rigid contract in world B, rigid workers will coexist with flexible ones iff

$$(r + a' + \pi'')Q + \delta\gamma F \le c, \qquad\qquad\qquad\qquad\qquad (7.20)$$

where $\delta = 1$ if the marginal rigid worker is fired when the firm falls into a recession and 0 if not.[8] Note that $\pi''(1 - \delta) = 0$. If (7.20) holds, then $(r + a' + \pi'')Q \leq c$, implying that rigid workers will be paid efficiency wages. It is not profitable to give a rigid contract to a worker who is monitored, since exactly the same wage can be obtained by a flexible contract, allowing the firm to economize on firing costs. Therefore, in any configuration where both types of contracts coexist, it must be the case that rigid workers are paid efficiency wages and flexible workers are monitored. Also note that $(r + a' + \pi'')Q \leq c$ is more likely to hold than (7.18), since $\pi'' < \pi$; that is, rigid workers have a lower probability of being fired in world B than in world A. Therefore, there is a configuration of parameters where workers are monitored in world A, while rigid workers are paid efficiency wages in world B. In this case the introduction of flexible contracts triggers an increase in the rent paid to rigid workers (from zero to some positive number) and thus pushes their wages upward.

Last, flexible contracts will actually be used when introduced if

$$(r + a + \pi)Q + \gamma F > c. \tag{7.21}$$

If (7.21) holds, then the marginal cost of a flexible, monitored worker, starting from world A's equilibrium, is lower than the marginal cost of a rigid, efficiency-wage worker.

Let us proceed under the working assumption that (7.18)–(7.21) hold, implying that (1) flexible workers are paid competitive wages, (2) rigid workers are paid efficiency wages, (3) both types of contracts are used in equilibrium.

7.4   The Underemployment Case with Full Job Protection

Consider now what happens to wages in the rigid sector when flexible contracts are introduced. First, let us look at equilibrium determination when the economy stays at an underemployment equilibrium. This is the case when labor demand is not high enough to restore full employment. We thus consider equilibria where workers are indifferent between holding a flexible contract and being unemployed, while holders of rigid contracts are strictly better off. The competitive wage is then equal to the level of

---

8. As will be made clear below, equality must hold in (7.20) if $\delta = 1$. Otherwise, the marginal cost of a rigid worker would be lower than that of a flexible worker, and firms would substitute rigid workers for flexible workers up to the point where either equality in (7.20) is restored or no flexible worker is employed.

unemployment insurance $\bar{w}$. The cost of a secondary worker is $\bar{w} + c$. The value of being unemployed will be equal to the value of holding a flexible contract. Rigid workers will still earn a rent Q above this value. As a result the value of being unemployed is still given by equation (7.12), but a is now interpreted as the flow probability of getting a type 1 job. Type 1 wages w_{1H} and w_{1L} are still given by (7.13) and (7.14), but l_H and l_L should be replaced with l_{1H} and l_{1L}, the number of type 1 employees.

If $a(A)$ is the equilibrium value of labor market tightness a in the world with no flexible contracts, firms in the high state will hire a positive number of flexible workers when they become available if their marginal cost is lower than the shadow cost of a rigid worker;

$$\bar{w} + c < \bar{w} + (r + a(A))Q + \gamma F + \gamma(1 - z(A))Q, \tag{7.22}$$

where $z(A) = l_L/l_H$ is the ratio between low-state employment and high-state employment in world A. If (7.22) does not hold, then flexible contracts will not be used and the economy will remain at the same equilibrium.

We want to know what would happen if, as in chapter 6, the economy shifts to a regime where no rigid worker is fired when a firm drops into the low state. As will be clear in the next section, there may be cases where rigid workers are still fired, which was ruled out in chapter 6.

Given the absence of voluntary quits and/or quadratic adjustment costs, the number of rigid workers will be constant over the firm's product demand cycle, $l_{1L} = l_{1H} = l_1$. *There is no hiring of rigid workers in steady state.* Therefore a drops to 0.[9] Equations (7.13) and (7.14) then become

$$w_{1H} = w_{1L} = \bar{w} + rQ = w_1. \tag{7.23}$$

Wages will *fall* in the primary sector after the introduction of flexible contracts. This is due to two effects. First, rigid workers in booming firms have more employment security, so they require lower wages—the $\gamma(1 - l_L/l_H)Q$ term in (7.13) disappears. Second, there are many less primary jobs created because fluctuations in product demand are dealt with using flexible contracts. This lowers the unemployed's probability of earning rents in the future, and therefore the value of being unemployed and wages in the primary sector. We here have an example where the introduction of flexible contracts, by lowering both the stock and the flow of so-called good jobs available, depresses the welfare of both the employed and the unemployed (while increasing profits).

---

9. This can be seen by plugging $l_H = l_L$ into (7.15).

Another property of (7.23) is that wages in the rigid sector will be less reactive to demand conditions than in world A. Quantities are then determined in a way that is totally similar to chapter 6. Employment in the high state is $l_1 + l_2$ and is given by

$$l_1 + l_2 = \frac{\theta_H - (\overline{w} + c)}{b}, \tag{7.24}$$

where l_1 is determined by the condition

$$\overline{w} + c = w_1 - \gamma V_L'(l_1). \tag{7.25}$$

The left-hand side of equation (7.25) is the marginal product of labor. The right-hand side is the shadow cost of a rigid worker, which is equal to his wage plus the expected marginal losses from shifting to the low state. V_L is defined by (7.1), implying that $V_L'(l_1) = (\theta_L - bl_1 - w_1)/(r + \varepsilon)$.

Last, note that the economy will find itself in this regime if secondary workers are more costly than primary workers, but less than a primary worker who would be fired when the firm falls into the low state. This is equivalent to $\overline{w} + rQ < \overline{w} + c < \overline{w} + rQ + \gamma F$, or

$$rQ < c < rQ + \gamma F. \tag{7.26}$$

7.5   The Underemployment Case with Incomplete Job Protection

What happens if (7.22) but not (7.26) holds so that we have

$$rQ + \gamma F < c < (r + a(A)Q) + \gamma F + \gamma(1 - z(A))Q. \tag{7.27}$$

When flexible contracts are introduced, firms find that the marginal cost of a flexible worker is lower than that of a rigid worker. When shifting from recession to expansion, they will hire less rigid workers and more flexible workers. As they do so, the flow probability of finding a rigid job falls, and firms realize that they can pay rigid workers less. The process stops when the shadow cost of a rigid worker becomes equal to the cost of a flexible worker, that is, when a has dropped to a level such that

$$c = (r + a)Q + \gamma F + \gamma(1 - z)Q, \tag{7.28}$$

where $z = l_{1L}/l_{1H}$. In the new equilibrium firms in the high state are indifferent between hiring a flexible worker and hiring a rigid worker. Contrary to what happened in chapter 6 and in the previous section where the marginal worker was flexible and rigid workers were inframarginal, the marginal worker is now indifferently rigid or flexible. When falling into the low state, firms will fire all flexible workers and a mass of rigid workers up to the point where $V'_L(l_1) = -F$. In the high state firms are indifferent with respect to which type of contract they offer, but in general equilibrium this must be determined by the requirement that z must be such that (7.28) holds.

Note that this regime was ruled out in the model of chapter 6 where wages were exogenous. In that model rigid workers were more expensive than flexible ones if fired and cheaper if not fired. Since only the marginal worker mattered, reducing the probability of firing rigid workers could only reduce their marginal cost provided that the marginal rigid worker were not fired, which in the end meant that no rigid worker was fired. In the present model, reducing the probability of firing rigid workers reduces their wages through the last term in (7.13) and through the induced drop in a in general equilibrium. In the regime considered here rigid workers become less costly than flexible ones for a small enough, but strictly positive, value of this probability.

In this regime the model is closed in a way similar to world A. Equations (7.13) and (7.14) still hold, with l_H and l_L replaced by l_{1H} and l_{1L}. Rigid employment in the low state is still determined by (7.2). Eliminating u between (7.15) and (7.16) and writing $l_{1H} = l_{1L}/z$, we can get a relationship between z and l_{1L}:

$$z = \frac{l_{1L}(a)\varepsilon(a + \gamma)}{a(\gamma + \varepsilon) + \gamma(\varepsilon - a)l_{1L}(a)}. \tag{7.29}$$

In this expression l_{1L} as been written as a decreasing function of a as determined by (7.2).

Equilibrium is determined in figure 7.2. Equation (7.28) defines an upward-sloping relationship CC between a and z. It is the locus along which the cost of a rigid worker is exactly equal to the cost of a flexible worker. A higher rate of job finding in sector 1, a, pushes up wages in that sector. An increase in z (i.e., an increase in job security) is required to bring back wages to the level that matches the cost of rigid workers with that of flexible workers.

Equation (7.29) defines a downward-sloping relationship DD between a and z. It is a steady-state relationship that tells us that fewer primary jobs are destroyed and therefore created when z is larger, so a falls.

Interestingly, it is possible to "read" world A's equilibrium on figure 7.2. To see this, first note that (7.29) is still valid in world A. Second, note that (7.27) implies that world A's economy will lie *above* CC in the (z, a) plane. This simply says that the cost of labor is higher in world A than in world B. Therefore introducing flexible contracts shifts the economy from a point like E in figure 7.2 to a point like E'. In the new equilibrium a is

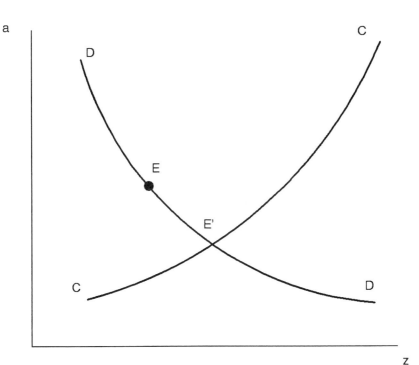

Figure 7.2
Equilibrium determination

lower and z higher: There are less rigid jobs created, and rigid workers have more employment security. For both reasons flexible contracts lower wages in the rigid tier of the labor market. The phenomenon is essentially the same as in the previous section but it does not go all the way through to no job creation and full-employment security.

To conclude this section, note that in the two regimes just studied both employed and unemployed workers would actually oppose flexible con-tracts (i.e., V_u falls). This is because the prospects for earning rents are less favorable due to a lower chance of getting a permanent job, while the economy is not productive enough to generate flexible jobs that pay more than unemployment insurance. I return to the issue of the political econ-omy of two-tier systems in chapter 11.

7.6   The Full-Employment Case

Let us characterize the economy's equilibrium in the case where introduc-ing flexible contracts restores full employment. The wage paid to flexible workers is now $w_c > \bar{w}$. w_c is endogenously determined as the marginal product of labor in firms in expansion minus the monitoring cost. Besides that, most of the analysis developed in the previous two sections carries through with $\bar{w}$ replaced with w_c. In particular, the conditions for full and incomplete job protection, (7.26) and (7.27), are unaffected (note that $\bar{w}$ had been eliminated from these conditions).

Let us limit ourselves to the case where (7.26) holds so that there is full job protection. Employment is then $l_1 + l_2$ in the high state and l_1 in the low state. Plugging $u = 0$ into (7.16), we get a relationship between l_1 and l_2:

$$l_2 = \frac{(\gamma + \varepsilon)(1 - l_1)}{\varepsilon}. \tag{7.30}$$

The marginal product of labor in the H state must be equal to the cost of a flexible worker, $w_c + c$. The competitive wage therefore satisfies

$$w_c = \theta_H - b(l_1 + l_2) - c = \theta_H - b + \frac{b\gamma l_1}{\varepsilon} - c \tag{7.31}$$

Employment of type 1 workers l_1 is still determined by (7.25). w_1, however, is now equal to $w_c + rQ$ rather than $\bar{w} + rQ$. Using (7.31), we can now compute l_1:

$$l_1 = \frac{(r + \varepsilon)(c - rQ) + \gamma(\theta_L - rQ + c - \theta_H + b)}{\gamma b(1 + \gamma/\varepsilon)}. \tag{7.32}$$

Equations (7.30)–(7.32) allow us to compute the competitive wage w_c, and then $w_1 = w_c + rQ$.

The two effects previously discussed, namely the reduction in wages that comes from a drop in the rigid worker's alternative option and their increase in job security are still present. However, we now have a countervailing effect that will push w_1 up, namely the increase in the competitive wage from $\bar{w}$ to w_c.

7.7   Impact of Flexible Contracts on the Markup

In the preceding sections we analyzed the impact of flexible contracts on wage formation *through the structure of labor demand*. By affecting the level and dynamics of the demand for both types of workers, flexible contracts change the level of wages that allows primary workers to earn a certain rent over their alternative value. In this section we see how this rent itself may be changed when flexible contracts are introduced.

First, the level of the rent Q may be affected by the fact that rigid workers typically stay longer within their firms since they are fired less often. If tenure is associated with more bargaining power (e.g., if compensation for dismissal is indexed on seniority), or if older workers can device more efficient ways of shirking, then this may increase Q. The use of flexible workers as a buffer to deal with demand fluctuations may thus prompt rigid workers to ask for higher wages. (This argument is developed by Bentolila and Dolado 1992 within a model that does not allow for the intertemporal effects studied in the preceding sections of this chapter) Such a hike in the equilibrium rent Q may occur if after flexible contracts are introduced, firms find profitable to pay higher wages to rigid workers and to monitor them less. Going back to the discussion of section 7.3, we have seen that under certain parameter values, firms will monitor in world A but pay efficiency wages to rigid workers in world B. In that case the rent for rigid labor contracts will jump from 0 to Q when flexible contracts are introduced. Note that the move is associated with some efficiency gain since the economy spends less resources on monitoring.

Second, Q will also be affected by the presence within the firm of flexible workers.[10] Suppose, for example, that the worker's bargaining power comes from the fact that it is costly for the firm to screen workers and that firing costs make it costly to recruit the wrong person. In the absence of flexible contracts, the firm knows that the job will be kept idle for some time if the match breaks down. This allows the incumbent worker to earn some rent. When flexible contracts are introduced, the firm can instantaneously fill the position with a flexible contract until an appropriate worker is found (Ortega 1994 has developed an argument along these lines). This will increase its threat point and therefore reduce the rent paid to the incumbent worker.

The bottom line is that while one expects flexible contracts to affect Q, the net effect is not obvious. There are reasons to believe that both firms and primary workers will become "tougher."

7.8   Empirical Evidence on the Effect of Two-Tier Labor Markets on Wage Formation

Bentolila and Dolado (1992) have studied the impact on wages of the introduction of temporary contracts in Spain (discussed in the preceding chapter). Bentolila and Dolado use data on bargained wages and wage

---

10. Lindbeck and Snower (1988) have analyzed the impact of "outsiders" and "entrants" on wage formation.

drift, that is, the deviation of actual wages from bargained wages. They then make the following key identifying assumption: Bargained wages are a proxy for the wages paid to permanent workers, while wage drift is a proxy for wages paid to temporary workers (more precisely the difference between their wage and the rigid wage). Bentolila and Dolado then study how wage drift and bargained wage growth have evolved in the second half of the 1980s and the early 1990s, following the introduction of flexible labor contracts. They observe that while wage drift has dropped and even become negative, there has been more upward pressure in the bargained wage. They conclude that this is suggestive that temporary workers earn less than permanent ones and that the introduction of flexible labor contracts has tended to reinforce the bargaining power of rigid workers. In other words, there has been an increase in Q high enough to offset the drop in rigid wages associated with more employment security.

Bentolila and Dolado then go on and use data from a panel of Spanish firms to study whether workers on temporary contracts participate in wage negotiations, namely whether they are members of the team of so-called insiders who set wages. If this were true, an additional temporary worker would reduce bargained wages because insiders are more numerous and thus need to ask for lower wages to preserve their probability of being employed. They conclude that they cannot reject the hypothesis that temporary workers are not part of the team of insiders.

In a related study Jimeno and Toharia (1991) estimate, in accordance with the above model, that workers under temporary contracts are paid 11 percent less, on average, than workers under permanent contracts. They conclude that overall the reform has tended to push wages downward, which is somewhat at variance with Bentolila and Dolado.

7.9   Conclusion and Summary

This chapter has asked the following question: When there is a move to greater labor market flexibility through the introduction of a two-tier system, what happens to wages? We have worked under the stylized hypothesis that the flexible tier will be paid competitive wages and have reached the following conclusions:

1. If there is a "reserve army" of labor, then the competitive wage will not rise above the level of unemployment insurance. There will remain a group of unemployed workers that is indifferent between holding a flexible contract and being unemployed. Wages in the primary sector fall relative to

the world without flexible contracts both because the value of being unemployed falls due to lower opportunities to find permanent jobs and because primary workers enjoy greater employment security. The welfare of both employed and unemployed workers falls because the flow of primary jobs created falls, thus lowering the probability of finding one and consequently the value of being unemployed. This in turn lowers equilibrium wages in the primary sector.

2. If the economy moves to a full-employment equilibrium with a competitive wage above the level of unemployment insurance, then the value of being unemployed may rise. In this case wages in the primary sector may also rise.

3. Third, there are reasons to believe that the rent earned by primary workers over their alternative values will change when flexible contracts are introduced. General considerations suggest that it can either rise or fall, although the model provides a rationale for them to rise: The trade-off between paying efficiency wages to primary workers and monitoring them is altered in favor of the first alternative when flexible contracts are available.

8   Dualism and Labor Market Flows

Traditional macroeconomic thinking has long been dominated by the representative agent framework. Growth and business fluctuations were thus implicitly thought of as affecting all firms and sectors identically. This view has recently been challenged by the literature on gross labor market flows. If it were true that business cycles affected all firms identically, then one would observe that employment reductions in recessions would be met by a large drop in job creation and a large increase in job destruction. Similarly one would observe a large increase in the employment-to-unemployment flow and a large decline in the unemployment-to-employment flow. The literature on gross flows has pointed out that this is not what is observed in practice. In the United States, recessions are met by large increases in job destruction but job creation falls only moderately. Furthermore gross worker flows move together in Europe: The number of unemployed people who find jobs actually increases in expansions. This chapter will analyze how the dual approach may help to explain these findings.

8.1   Facts about Flows

Gross labor market flows have been studied, among others, by Davis and Haltiwanger (1990, 1992), Blanchard and Diamond (1990), and Burda and Wyplosz (1994).

Davis and Haltiwanger, using a large panel of U.S. manufacturing firms, have studied gross *job flows*, namely how many jobs are created and destroyed in an economy. Two of their findings are of interest to us. First, they find that job destruction and job creation are quite large: 5 percent of jobs are, on average, destroyed (or created) every quarter. Second,

---

This chapter elaborates on Saint-Paul (1992a).

employment reductions in recessions are chiefly met by increases in job destruction rather than reductions in job creation. In other words, there is still a large amount of job creation going on during recession. Davis and Haltiwanger then define the gross job reallocation flow as the sum of job creation and job destruction and argue that there is more reallocation going on during recessions (since job destruction is more procyclical than job creation is countercyclical, the sum of the two is bound to be counter-cyclical).

Burda and Wyplosz (1994) have focused on worker flows in Europe rather than job flows. They again find that despite all the complaints about Eurosclerosis, worker flows in Europe, as in the United States, are large. The order of magnitude is a yearly flow between unemployment and employment of around 10 percent of the total labor force. These flows are therefore as large as the unemployment rate itself. Second, and in accordance with the results of Davis and Haltiwanger, they find that the gross flow from unemployment to employment is countercyclical, as is the flow from employment to unemployment. That is, the *number* of unemployed workers who find jobs is higher in recessions than in expansions. However, total *hirings* drop in recessions. For this procyclical behavior of hirings to be compatible with the countercyclicality of the unemployment-to-employment flow, it must be the case that (1) hirings are only *moderately* procyclical (as is job creation in Davis and Haltiwanger), while (2) quits and the flow from nonparticipation to employment are strongly pro-cyclical.

Let us see how the dual model can shed light on these stylized facts about labor market flows.

8.2   Job Creation and Job Destruction in the Dual Model

As I have pointed out above, the flow literature insists on the fact that there is continuing large labor reallocation going on in the economy. This view stands in sharp contrast with the conventional view that European economies are plagued by sclerosis and lack of labor mobility. A recent OECD study (OECD 1995, table 1.8) found that in France job turnover (as measured by the sum of job creation and job destruction) amounted to 27.6 percent of total employment in 1989–92, more than the equivalent figure of 23.7 percent for the United States. If, as this result suggests, so many jobs are created and destroyed every year, it must be the case that oft-emphasized issues such as firing costs and low mobility are irrelevant.

The dual model studied in this book shows that these two views are not necessarily incompatible. It is possible that high turnover is concentrated in the "flexible" tier of the labor market, without affecting most of the workers in the rigid sector. For example, 20 percent of the work force could have a 100 percent turnover rate (meaning changing jobs on average once a year) and the remainder a 0 percent turnover rate. The aggregate turnover would then be 20 percent, a very high number, yet 80 percent of jobs would last forever.

Let us go back to the model developed in chapter 6 and analyze its implications for the behavior of labor market flows. First, let us study the determinants of job creation and job destruction in steady state in both the rigid and flexible worlds. Clearly job destruction and job creation would be equal in steady state; hence they must move together at low frequencies.

Starting with the rigid world (world A), we begin by noting that the number of jobs destroyed using firings is equal to the product of three terms:

1. The flow probability of falling into a recession γ.

2. The number of firms in expansion $\varepsilon/(\varepsilon + \gamma)$.

3. The number of workers being fired at the start of an individual recession $l_0^A - l_1^A$. Total firings are therefore equal to

$$\Phi = \frac{\gamma\varepsilon(l_0^A - l_1^A)}{\gamma + \varepsilon}. \tag{8.1}$$

In declining firms, jobs continue to be destroyed, as firms use the quadratic component of adjustment costs: voluntary quits. These jobs disappear at rate $\lambda(l_t - \bar{l})$. As shown in chapter 6, there is a density $\varepsilon\gamma \exp(-\varepsilon t)/(\gamma + \varepsilon)$ of firms being in recession for a length of time between t and $t + dt$. These firms employ $\bar{l} + (l_1^A - \bar{l})e^{-\lambda t}$ workers. Therefore total job destruction using quits is equal to

$$\Sigma = \int_0^{+\infty} \lambda(l_1^A - \bar{l})\exp(-(\varepsilon + \lambda)t)\frac{\varepsilon\gamma}{\gamma + \varepsilon}dt$$

$$= \frac{\varepsilon\gamma\lambda(l_1^A - \bar{l})}{(\gamma + \varepsilon)(\lambda + \varepsilon)}.$$

Gross job flows are equal to

Job creation = Job destruction

$$= \Phi + \Sigma = \frac{\gamma\varepsilon}{\gamma + \varepsilon}\left[l_0^A - l_1^A + \frac{\lambda(l_1^A - \bar{l})}{\lambda + \varepsilon}\right] \tag{8.2}$$

Plugging into (8.2) the first-order conditions (6.8)–(6.10) for employment at the firm level, we get

$$\Phi + \Sigma = \frac{\gamma \varepsilon}{\gamma + \varepsilon} \left[\frac{-F\varepsilon}{c_0 \lambda (\lambda + \varepsilon)} - \frac{\gamma F}{b} + \frac{(\theta_H - \theta_L)}{b} \right] \tag{8.3}$$

Equation (8.3) has a number of interesting features. The first factor $\varepsilon\gamma/(\gamma + \varepsilon)$ can be interpreted as *firm turnover*: It is the number of firms that change state per unit of time. The term in brackets is *job turnover at the firm level*. It tells us how many jobs are destroyed, on average, by a firm that falls into a recession (or equivalently how many jobs are created by a firm that shifts to the expansionary state).

We can see that (8.3) has the following properties:

1. There is less turnover when firing costs are higher. Firing costs lower hirings in good times and firings in bad times. In the model they lower l_0^A but increase l_1^A.

2. There is more turnover when $\theta_H - \theta_L$ is higher, which means that product demand shocks are larger; firms hire more in expansions and fire more in recessions.

3. An increase in γ, i.e a higher probability of bad times, has conflicting effects on job flows. It tends to increase firm turnover, since firms fall more often into the bad state. (This concomitantly increases the number of firms who shift from the bad state to the good state since the stock of firms in the bad state is higher.) Second, it tends to reduce job turnover; because the shadow cost of labor has increased, firms in the good state employ less people. However, because the firing cost is linear, their firing point at the start of a recession l_1^A is left unchanged. Consequently there is a reduction in the number of people fired by firms at the beginning of recessions.

4. An increase in ε, the probability of switching to the expansionary state, affects flows through two channels. On the one hand, firm turnover increases. Firms in recessions switch back more often to expansions, while firms in expansions are more numerous, so more of them fall into recession. On the other hand, the losses from having to keep unprofitable workers in the bad state of nature are discounted more heavily, so firms fire less when falling into a recession. This tends to reduce turnover at the firm level. Algebraically λ falls as ε rises, which lowers the first negative term in the brackets of (8.3). The net effect of ε on turnover is therefore a priori ambiguous.

These properties suggest that in world A an increase in product demand volatility through γ may have only a moderate impact on job flows: While firm turnover increases, job turnover per firm falls. In principle, the net effect may even be to reduce total job creation and destruction. This is in sharp contrast to what happens in the dual world.

Let us now turn to the analysis of job flows in the flexible world (world B). Computations are the same as in world A except that l_0^A and l_1^A must be replaced with $l_1^B + l_2^B$ and l_1^B, respectively. Therefore we have

$$\Phi = \frac{\gamma \varepsilon l_2^B}{\gamma + \varepsilon} \tag{8.4}$$

and

$$\Sigma = \frac{\varepsilon \gamma \lambda (l_1^B - \bar{l})}{(\gamma + \varepsilon)(\lambda + \varepsilon)} \tag{8.5}$$

Note that in steady state Φ and Σ are equal to H_2, the hiring flow in the secondary sector, and to H_1, the hiring flow in the primary sector, respectively. Plugging the first-order conditions (6.13)–(6.14) and (6.9) into (8.4) and (8.5), we can again compute total turnover:

$$\Phi + \Sigma = \frac{\gamma \varepsilon}{\gamma + \varepsilon} \left[\frac{-(w_2 - w_1)\varepsilon}{c_0 \lambda (\lambda + \varepsilon)\gamma} - \frac{w_2 - w_1}{b} + \frac{\theta_H - \theta_L}{b} \right]. \tag{8.6}$$

As argued in chapter 6, the dual regime's aggregate behavior is the same as that of the rigid regime, with γF replaced with $(w_2 - w_1)$. Equation (8.6) is therefore identical to (8.3) once this transformation has been done.

The properties of (8.6) are as follows:

1. An increase in $\theta_H - \theta_L$ increases flows, as in the rigid regime.

2. An increase in the relative cost of flexible workers $w_2 - w_1$ reduces flows: Firms hire fewer flexible workers and more rigid workers in expansions, so they fire less in recessions. Since w_2 is the sum of the flexible worker's wage, which tends to be lower than the rigid worker's wage, and of the monitoring cost, the model predicts lower flows when the monitoring cost is higher and when wage inequality is lower.

3. An increase in volatility due to γ now has unambiguous effects on job flows: Both firm turnover and job turnover at the firm level increase. A higher value of γ increases the shadow cost of labor for rigid workers, but it has no effect on the marginal cost of labor for firms in expansions, since

the marginal worker in those firms is flexible. Therefore firms hire more flexible workers and fewer rigid workers, implying that they can fire more when falling into recessions, thus getting closer to their long-term optimum.

4. An increase in ε has an effect similar to that in world A. While firm turnover increases, it is less costly for firms to hire primary workers because they expect bad times to be short. This reduces the expected marginal cost from having to keep them.

5. There is more turnover in world B than in world A. This observation is straightforward. For world B to be relevant, we must have $w_2 < w_1 + \gamma F$, implying that the "apparent" firing cost in world B, $(w_2 - w_1)/\gamma$, is lower than F. Given that a reduction in F increases turnover in (8.3), flows are larger, given F, in world B than in world A.

Note that the comparative statics with respect to γ are changed compared to world A, while those with respect to ε are unchanged. This is because the shadow firing cost depends on γ but not on ε.

Let us summarize our findings and relate them to the empirical literature discussed above: First, we have seen that more flexible economies have larger turnover. This is true in various senses: World A has higher turnover when F falls, world B has higher turnover when flexible workers become cheaper relative to rigid workers, world B has higher turnover than world A. This characteristic may explain why flows have increased in some European countries. The increase in labor flows may be due to increases in labor market flexibility such as the introduction of temporary contracts. For example, Jaslin et al. (1988), looking at the French labor market, found that in 1987, 25 percent of the unemployed fell into that state due to termination of a temporary contract. The same figure was 5.6 percent in 1976.

Second, the uncertainty parameter γ may or may not increase flows in the rigid world, but it will increase flows in the flexible world. The difference is that while the shadow marginal cost of labor increases in good times in the rigid world, it is unaffected in the flexible world because the marginal worker is on a temporary contract. By contrast, the cost of rigid workers increases, so at the margin firms substitute temporary workers for permanent workers. This may explain why there is still large job creation going on in recessions: If a recession means an increase in γ, then it will be associated with job destruction in the rigid sector but job creation in the flexible one. In steady state, firms hire more because they are left with fewer rigid workers in the bad state of demand and have to hire more flexible workers when shifting to the good state of demand. Higher job creation therefore comes from two sources: higher firm turnover and a substitution of bad (precarious) jobs for permanent jobs.

Note, however, that the *anatomy* of a recession is crucial in assessing its impact on job flows. The type of aggregate recession we have studied in chapter 6, whereby most firms fall into the bad state with no changes in underlying parameters, would be associated with large job destruction in the flexible sector, contrary to the increase in γ. Alternatively, if we think of a recession as a reduction in ε rather than an increase in γ, then its effects on job flows in world B are ambiguous.

Therefore we have to keep in mind that recessions will be associated with creation of flexible jobs only to the extent that firms perceive them as an increased probability of bad news.

8.3   From Job Flows to Worker Flows

In the previous section the discussion focused on the implications of the dual model for job creation and job destruction. How can these results be translated into flows between states in the labor force, such as employment-to-employment flow or the unemployment-to-employment flow studied by Blanchard and Diamond (1990) and Burda and Wyplosz (1994)? The simple model constructed in this section allows us to compute labor flows from the job flows computed in the previous section. The model can generate a countercyclical unemployment-to-employment flow along with a procyclical employment-to-employment flow, as given by Burda and Wyplosz, and is suggestive of a dual labor markets explanation for the observed pattern.

The model is illustrated in figure 8.1. The assumption is that most quits (arrow c) are from the secondary sector to the primary sector. This is consistent with the view that primary jobs are rationed, so flexible workers will constantly seek a primary job and accept it as soon as they find one. By contrast, in the model, there is no reason for a worker to leave his job for a similar job. Therefore employment flows within each sector are neglected. This is clearly an approximation of reality, but it is a reasonable assumption, since the primary sector is characterized by internal promotions and low turnover, while the precarity of secondary jobs implies that secondary workers are likely to experience unemployment spells between two jobs in the secondary sector. Last, there is no flow from the primary sector to the secondary sector: Primary workers would leave their jobs for worse jobs only if they are fired, in which case it is reasonable to assume that they first experience a spell of unemployment.

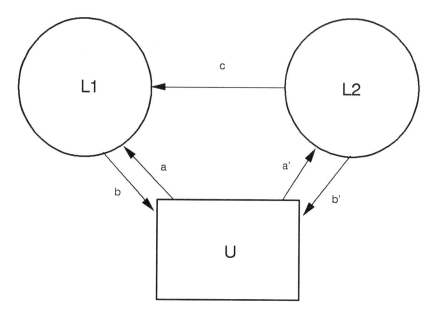

Figure 8.1
Structure of labor market flows

In the previous section we were able to compute H_1 and H_2, the flow of hires per unit of time in each sector. How can we recover worker flows from H_1 and H_2? In this model hirings under rigid contracts are simply equal to the sum of quits c and the flow a from unemployment to work in the primary sector:

$$H_1 = a + c. \tag{8.7}$$

Furthermore, since only the unemployed are assumed to be willing to work under a flexible contract, secondary hirings are equal to the flow a' from unemployment to the secondary sector:

$$H_2 = a'. \tag{8.8}$$

To close the analysis, we need to specify how primary hirings are allocated between the unemployed and secondary workers. We assume that this occurs on a proportional basis; that is, that the share of unemployed workers in total hirings is simply equal to their share in total primary job seekers. The probability of finding a job is then the same for all job seekers and equal to $H_1/(U + L_2)$. This assumption is not straightforward for two reasons. First, we could believe that employers rank applicants according to unemployment duration, as in Blanchard and Diamond

(1994). Second, since the unemployed search for jobs in the whole labor market and secondary workers look only for primary jobs, we could believe that they would have more chances of getting one. However, this assumption is chiefly motivated by simplicity, and the results do not crucially hinge on a proportional allocation of hirings. Therefore we will write the flows from unemployment and secondary employment to primary employment as

$$a = \frac{H_1 U}{U + L_2} \tag{8.9}$$

and

$$c = \frac{H_1 L_2}{U + L_2}. \tag{8.10}$$

Total employment inflows are

$$a' + a + c = H_1 + H_2, \tag{8.11}$$

while total unemployment outflows are

$$a' + a = H_2 + \frac{H_1 U}{U + L_2}. \tag{8.12}$$

In world B the steady-state values of H_1 and H_2 are given by the right-hand sides of (8.5) and (8.4), respectively (since separations and hirings coincide in steady state). Equations (8.11) and (8.12) therefore allow us to compute how labor market flows react to changes in the parameter values of the model.

We are now in a position to investigate how business cycles affect flows in the dual model. To do this, consider the effects of a "recession," that is, a drop in ε (the transition probability from recession to expansion) along with an increase in γ (the transition probability from expansion to recession).

First, note that the effect of such a change on firm turnover will clearly depend on how big is the drop in ε relative to the hike in γ. If the drop in ε dominates, firm turnover will fall, while if the rise in γ dominates, firm turnover will increase. This suggests, as mentioned above, that the correlation between aggregate fluctuations and job flows crucially depends on the anatomy of these fluctuations.

To isolate the effects of labor market dualism on the cyclical behavior of labor market flows, let us simply assume that firm turnover is unaffected by a recession. Therefore ε drops and γ increases in such a way that

$\varepsilon\gamma/(\varepsilon + \gamma)$ remains constant. We then know, from chapter 6 and the previous section's analysis, that both the drop in ε and the rise in γ reduce l_1^B. Primary workers are more costly for two reasons. (1) The marginal loss these workers inflict on the firm during the recession is larger in present discounted value because the recession, on average, lasts longer. (2) This recession is more likely to occur. Since the marginal worker is flexible, total employment in the good state is unaffected, implying that H_1 must fall while H_2 must rise. This is apparent from looking at the right-hand sides of (8.4) and (8.5). Total hirings in (8.6) unambiguously increase, since total employment in expansions has not changed, and firings increase as well. Therefore, in the dual world, *controlling for firm turnover, hirings are countercyclical*. By contrast, in world A the effect would be ambiguous because firms employ fewer people in both states, so the effect on total firings is ambiguous.

Second, *the unemployment-to-employment inflow is more countercyclical than hirings*. The key reason for this is that H_2 accounts for a larger share of the former than of the latter. This is because all hires in the secondary sector are from unemployment, while hires in the primary sector are both from unemployment and the secondary sector. In a recession there are more bad jobs available for the unemployed, and fewer good jobs for those who hold bad jobs. Hence quits fall, and more unemployed workers find jobs.

This property that $a' + a$ is more countercyclical than $H_1 + H_2$ holds regardless of firm turnover, since firm turnover affects H_1 and H_2 by the same multiplicative factor. It is therefore possible to reproduce the pattern evidenced in Burda and Wyplosz (1994) simply by calibrating γ and ε so that recessions reduce firm turnover enough to induce a fall in hirings but not enough to prevent $a' + a$ to increase.

8.4 Dynamic Simulations

An obvious problem with the approach of the previous section is that we deduce the cyclical behavior of employment flows from comparative statics exercises. It would be interesting to know whether these properties are also true on the adjustment path toward the steady state. For this, we have performed a numerical simulation of an economy subject to a shock, such that γ rises permanently and ε drops permanently. The simulation can be performed using the solution technique of section 6.5, which was used to analyze the transition toward the new regime.

A simulation is presented in figure 8.2. From the figure we can conclude the following: At the start of the recession, H_2 drops, then it increases progressively, asymptotically reaching its long-run level, which is higher

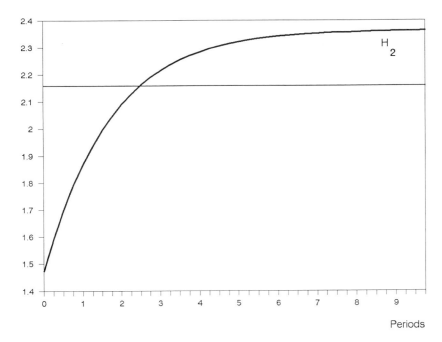

Figure 8.2
Dynamic response of secondary hirings

for the simulation parameters than the initial level. Hence we see that secondary hirings fall and then rise in response to a recession. This happens despite the presence of an additional effect not included in the steady-state analysis of the previous section: Firms want to use more flexible workers and fewer rigid workers, so they progressively replace the latter with the former, thus implying an additional inflow of secondary workers at the start of the recession.

This "undershooting" result is due to the fact that at the start of a recession, the stock of firms in the bad state is below its long-run level, while ε drops. Hence the flow of firms from the bad to the good state is much lower than its long-run level, implying a drop in secondary hirings. Figure 8.3 presents a simulation where γ increases, but ε is unchanged. In this case, secondary hirings jump at the start of the recession, although by less than in the long run.

8.5 Do Dual Labor Markets Lead to a Dual Society?

An important issue related to the discussion of labor market flows is whether or not always the same people end up in the bad jobs. If so, then

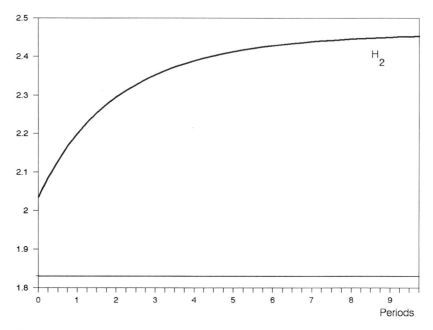

Figure 8.3
Dynamic response of secondary hirings

the dual labor market would lead to a segregated society. If, on the contrary, there is a lot of mobility between the two tiers, the dual nature of the labor market has less dramatic social consequences.

Fougère and Kamionka (1992) have estimated transition probabilities in the French labor market between permanent jobs, precarious jobs, and unemployment. Their estimated probabilities point to the optimistic conclusion that the transition probability from temporary to permanent jobs is quite high: roughly 75 percent a year for people between 36 and 50, and 56 percent for the 21-to-25 age group. However, when assuming heterogeneity in the transition probabilities within each age group, Fougère and Kamionka identify a core of "stayers" within each age group who never find permanent employment. The estimated percentages of stayers are 5, 25, and 13 percent for the age groups 21–25, 26–35, and 36–50 respectively. The particularly high figure for the 26–35-age group casts doubts on the impression of high mobility one gets from looking at average transition probabilities.

8.6   Conclusion and Summary

As this chapter has shown, a two-tier vision of the labor market may explain why rigidity is still a serious issue, even though high turnover rates are observed at the aggregate level. These high turnover rates are concentrated in the flexible sector, but the majority of the workers belong to the rigid sector.

Dual labor markets help explain why hirings and job creations are still large in recession: To the extent that recessions are associated with an increased probability of "bad times" at the firm level (i.e., an increase in γ), firms begin to replace primary workers with secondary workers. This creates more jobs in the secondary sector.

For this reason the flow from unemployment to employment may be countercyclical, while total hirings may be procyclical. Some unemployed persons will take secondary jobs, which are relatively abundant during recessions. But the employment-to-employment flow falls because it is chiefly made of secondary workers who find a primary jobs, of which much fewer are available during recessions.

9   Skilled versus Unskilled Workers

Until now we have considered the case of workers who are homogeneous in their skills. If they differed in pay, firing costs, and employment security, it was essentially because imperfections in wage formation prevented those worse off from underbidding those better off. Heterogeneity was thus sustained in equilibrium, and good jobs were rationed and randomly allocated across identical workers.

This chapter looks at another dimension of the dual labor market by introducing differences in skill levels among the working population. So we get close to one of the most debated economic phenomena: the deterioration in the unskilled's relative position in the labor market, in terms of unemployment rates and/or earnings. This trend has been observed since the early 1980s in all major industrial countries. The most widespread explanation is that technical progress has biased labor demand against the unskilled and in favor of the skilled.

This chapter takes a rather different perspective. We want to study how labor market institutions, in particular, firing costs, affect the relative demand for skilled and unskilled labor. We are also interested in how labor market institutions affect the link between technical change and the structure of unemployment.

The model developed here has two types of workers, skilled and unskilled, who compete for jobs in a world where firing is costly. The model is a search model, so vacancies are not filled instantaneously. This is summarized by the use of a matching function (see chapter 2) that relates hirings to the stock of vacancies (v) and unemployment (u). Despite the fact that there are no shocks to product demand, firing costs depress the demand for unskilled labor because they prevent firms from replacing unskilled workers with skilled workers. This creates an *option value* of

---

This chapter is based on Saint-Paul (1992b).

maintaining a vacancy until a skilled worker is found rather than immediately filling it with an unskilled worker. This option value further increases the value of posting a vacancy in the skilled rather than the unskilled labor market. When firing costs are high enough, firms will exercise that option, and both skilled and unskilled workers will end up in permanent jobs (the rigid regime). When they are lower, firms will be willing to pay the firing cost and hire unskilled workers to eventually replace them with skilled ones. Unskilled workers will thus have lower job security and higher turnover than skilled ones (the flexible regime). This is in accordance with the empirical regularity that unskilled workers have shorter job durations and more precarious jobs.[1]

The two main messages of the chapter are the following: First, there exist supply effects that are likely to reinforce demand effects: The less educated are likely to suffer more from unemployment when there are more educated people in the work force. Second, if labor market institutions are more rigid (in the sense of high firing costs), the less educated are also likely to suffer more from unemployment.

In the model it is shown that the economy must satisfy an arbitrage condition in terms of the *relative* unemployment rate of the unskilled: The unskilled must be relatively more abundant than the skilled for firms to want to hire them. The main results are the following:

1. When the relative productivity of the skilled increases, the unskilled unemployment rate increases, the skilled unemployment rate decreases, and aggregate unemployment *unambiguously increases* in the rigid regime.

2. When the proportion of skilled workers in the labor force rises, the unemployment rate for *both* the skilled and the unskilled increases. As a result aggregate unemployment may increase or decrease, but simulations suggest that it will only decrease if the initial proportion of skilled workers is quite high.

3. There effects are weaker when firing costs go down because the option value of filling a vacancy with a skilled worker is reduced, which increases the value of hiring an unskilled worker and reduces its responsiveness to the supply and productivity of skilled workers.

The model implies that technological advances may generate unemployment directly by increasing the productivity of the skilled relative to

---

1. See Mincer (1991). Alba-Ramirez and Freeman (1990) find that in Spain unskilled workers are more likely to end up in temporary jobs. Similarly Fougèbre (1989) has shown that in France less educated workers are more likely to exit from unemployment with a determined duration contract.

the unskilled and indirectly by increasing the supply of skilled workers in the economy. The unemployability of the unskilled is reinforced by the above-mentioned option value of letting a job position idle until a skilled worker is found. This option value is higher when firing costs are higher and when the probability of finding a skilled worker is higher. Hiring an unskilled worker therefore entails a capital loss that is greater when their relative productivity is lower and when the skilled are found more easily.

While relative demand effects have often been emphasized as a key factor behind the rise in the unemployment rate of the less educated, the present model shows that relative supply effects may also have an impact. Testing whether these effects are empirically important is quite difficult, for the mechanism emphasized here also works its way through labor demand. However, these supply effects are consistent with the observation that there has been no marked increase in measured "mismatch," contrary to what would have been predicted if relative demand effects had prevailed.[2] In most countries the skilled and unskilled unemployment rates have moved together at both high and low frequencies, so it is difficult to see an exogenous relative demand shock.[3]

The chapter is organized as follows: The basic model, where firms cannot fire workers, is set up in section 9.1. Section 9.2 studies the impact of relative productivity levels and of the skill composition of the labor force. Section 9.3 considers what happens if firms can fire workers at a cost, thus being able to replace unskilled workers with skilled workers. Section 9.4 derives the main conclusions.

9.1   The Basic Model

The model is a continuous-time matching model in the fashion of Pissarides (1990, 1992) with two types of workers: high-skilled workers (type 1) and low-skilled workers (type 2). Each type of worker has a separate labor market, and on any market i ($i = 1$, 2) the number of matches per unit of time is determined by a matching function $m(V_i, U_i)$, where U_i is the number of type i unemployed workers and V_i is the number of vacancies in this market. In other words, we assume that vacancies are directed at a specific type of skill ex ante and that firms cannot post a general vacancy and decide which type of worker to hire in the course of the application process. This is a realistic feature provided

---

2. Layard et al. (1991) review the mixed evidence on mismatch.
3. See Nickell and Bell (1994).

that the skills are differentiated enough: Skill requirements are often associated with jobs, and jobs announcements always specify what type of worker is needed, including degrees and work experience.

The total number of jobs is held fixed and equal to K. K may alternatively be thought of as the capital stock, overhead labor, or an index of aggregate activity. Each job may be held by either type of worker. Low-skilled workers are less productive in any given job than high-skilled workers. A high-skilled worker generates 2 units of output per unit of time, and a low-skilled worker 2ρ units of output, with $\rho < 1$.

The assumption that K is fixed is an extreme form of decreasing returns. Decreasing returns are important for my results because they generate a linkage between the two labor markets. In the case of a fixed number of jobs, it implies that each job held by a low-skilled worker decreases the number of jobs available for high-skilled workers by exactly one unit. With weaker forms of decreasing returns, it will decrease the productivity of high-skilled workers.

Because K is fixed, firms have to decide for each vacant job whether they should hire a low-skilled worker or a high-skilled worker. This will generate an arbitrage condition between the value of a vacancy in market 1 and the value of a vacancy in market 2.

We also assume that firms cannot post more than one vacancy per job. That is to say, the matching process is really defined in terms of jobs rather than vacancies. In Pissarides (1990), what prevents the number of vacancies from becoming infinite is the fact that vacancies are costly, implying that their net value becomes negative as the labor market becomes tighter. Here vacancies are costless but they cannot exceed K. As a result the total number of vacancies is simply equal to the number of vacant jobs.[4]

Last, we assume a simple form of wage bargaining: The output of any worker is equally split between the firm and the worker. As a result firms make a profit per unit of time equal to 1 for each job held by a type 1 worker, and $\rho < 1$ for each job held by a type 2 worker. (This is the option taken in Pissarides 1992.)

Alternatively, we could assume Nash bargaining to allow for wages reacting to labor market conditions. Intuitively this would weaken the results (since part of higher unemployment is absorbed by lower wages) but not make them disappear. This is indeed what happens in our case: The

---

4. Implied is a positive relationship between vacancies and unemployment: Therefore, the shifts in u (unemployment) and v (vacancies) considered here correspond to shifts of the Beveridge curve, and not shifts along the Beveridge curve. Shifts along the Beveridge curve are generated by changes in the index of aggregate labor demand, K. For evidence and discussions about whether the Beveridge curve has shifted, see Bean (1994).

model's solution under continuous-time Nash bargaining with permanent renegotiation is derived in the appendix. It turns out that the results are not qualitatively affected.

Because of bargaining, firms get less surplus from unskilled than from skilled workers. Therefore it is profitable for them to post vacancies in the skilled labor market for jobs currently held by unskilled workers so that they can fire the unskilled worker and replace him with a skilled worker whenever one is found. In this section, we assume that firing costs are high enough to prevent that scenario, which will be studied in the next section.

The equations of the model are written in a dynamic form, but we will limit ourselves to a comparison of steady states, since the dynamical system has too high a dimension to be tractable.

The Arbitrage Condition for Vacancies

Since ρ is less than 1, firms will prefer that a job be held by a high-skilled rather than a low-skilled worker. Therefore, if their chances of hiring a type 1 worker are the same as those of hiring a type 2 worker, they will prefer to post vacancies in market 1. This of course tightens market 1 and slackens market 2. As a result type 2 vacancies are filled more quickly than type 1 vacancies. This raises the value of type 2 vacancies and decreases the value of type 1 vacancies. The process will continue until the relative tightness of the two markets is such that firms are indifferent between either type of vacancies. Hence, because of wage rigidity, the arbitrage between the two types of workers is realized through arrival rates instead of wages.

More formally, let λ_{1t} be the probability per unit of time of getting a type 1 applicant for a type 1 vacancy, and λ_{2t} the arrival rate of type 2 applicants. The value to the firm of a type 1 vacancy is therefore

$$\text{VAC}_{1t} = (1 - rdt)[\lambda_{1t}dtJ_{1t+dt} + (1 - \lambda_{1t}dt)\text{VAC}_{1t+dt}], \tag{9.1}$$

where dt is a small time interval, r is the discount rate, and J_{1t} is the PDV to the firm of a job held by a type 1 worker. This equation can be rewritten

$$0 = -(r + \lambda_{1t})\text{VAC}_{1t} + \lambda_{1t}J_{1t} + \frac{d\text{VAC}_{1t}}{dt}. \tag{9.2}$$

Similarly we have for market 2,

$$0 = -(r + \lambda_{2t})\text{VAC}_{2t} + \lambda_{2t}J_{2t} + \frac{d\text{VAC}_{2t}}{dt}. \tag{9.3}$$

Provided that type 2 workers are not all unemployed in equilibrium firms must in equilibrium be indifferent between either type of vacancy.[5] This implies that

$$\text{VAC}_{1t} = \text{VAC}_{2t} = \text{VAC}_t \tag{9.4}$$

for all t. Using (9.2) and (9.3), we can rewrite (9.4) as

$$\lambda_1[J_1 - \text{VAC}] = \lambda_2[J_2 - \text{VAC}]. \tag{9.5}$$

Equation (9. 5) states that the arrival rate of unskilled workers must exceed that of skilled workers by the ratio of the capital gain from hiring a skilled worker over the capital gain from hiring an unskilled worker.

Let us assume that there is an exogenous quit rate equal to s. The value to the firm of a job held by a skilled worker is defined by

$$0 = 1 - (r + s)J_1 + \frac{dJ_1}{dt} + s\text{VAC}. \tag{9.6}$$

The similar formula for type 2 workers is

$$0 = \rho - (r + s)J_2 + \frac{dJ_2}{dt} + s\text{VAC}. \tag{9.7}$$

In steady state $dJ_1/dt = dJ_2/dt = 0$. Eliminating J_1 between (9.6) and (9.2) then yields

$$\text{VAC} = \frac{\lambda_1}{r(r + \lambda_1 + s)} \tag{9.8}$$

for skilled workers and symmetrically

$$\text{VAC} = \frac{\lambda_2 \rho}{r(r + \lambda_2 + s)} \tag{9.9}$$

for unskilled workers. Equations (9.8) and (9.9) can be combined to yield the arbitrage condition in terms of the arrival rates:

$$\frac{\lambda_1}{r + \lambda_1 + s} = \frac{\lambda_2 \rho}{r + \lambda_2 + s}. \tag{9.10}$$

Equation (9.10) is the first fundamental equation of the model. It may be rewritten:

---

5. The corner case is examined later in this chapter.

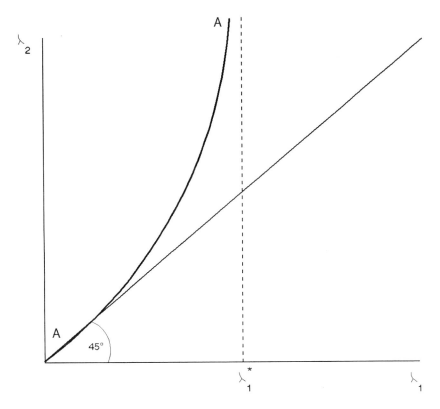

Figure 9.1
Arbitrage condition for vacancies

$$\lambda_2 = \frac{\lambda_1}{\rho - \lambda_1(1 - \rho)/(r + s)} \qquad (9.10')$$

This equation defines a curve AA in the (λ_1, λ_2) locus (figure 9.1). AA, which goes through the origin, is convex and upward sloping. It is always above the 45-degree line, and its slope is greater than 1. This reflects the fact that since firms make more money on skilled workers, they must lose less time in finding unskilled workers. Otherwise, they would strictly prefer to hire skilled workers.

AA has the following interpretation: The ratio of the two arrival rates must be equal to the ratio between 1 (the income from hiring a skilled worker) and ρ (the income from hiring an unskilled worker) *minus* the annuity equivalent of the loss made from losing the option of filling the vacancy with a skilled worker, $\lambda_1(1 - \rho)/(r + s)$.

AA has a vertical asymptote at

$$\lambda_1 = \lambda_1^* = \frac{\rho(r + s)}{1 - \rho}. \tag{9.11}$$

This means that if λ_1 is greater than λ_1^*, a type 1 vacancy has a greater value than a type 2 job. In this case no level of λ_2 can match VAC_1 and VAC_2, so the arbitrage condition (9.4) no longer holds and has to be replaced by an inequality: $VAC_1 \geq VAC_2$. In this zone all type 2 workers are unemployed.

The Flow Equilibrium Locus

We can now close the model and derive the second relation between λ_1 and λ_2. We will assume that the matching function $m(V_i, U_i)$ is concave with constant returns to scale. In market i the worker arrival rate λ_i is the number of matches divided by the stock of vacancies:

$$\lambda_i = \frac{m(V_i, U_i)}{V_i} = m\left(1, \frac{U_i}{V_i}\right), \tag{9.12}$$

where I have used the constant returns assumption. Note that the matching function is assumed to be the same in both markets: there is no a priori reason to believe that there is a systematic correlation between skill levels and the efficiency of the matching process.

Equation (9.12) may be inverted as

$$U_i = V_i h(\lambda_i), \tag{9.13}$$

where $h = m(1, \cdot)^{-1}$ is a convex, increasing function. For each type of worker, the change in employment is just hirings minus quits:

$$\frac{dL_i}{dt} = -sL_i + \lambda_i V_i = -sL_i + m(V_i, U_i). \tag{9.14}$$

The total number of vacancies must equal the number of available jobs:

$$V_1 + V_2 = K - L_1 - L_2, \tag{9.15}$$

where L_i is the number of type i workers who are employed.

Let us normalize the total labor force to 1, and let us assume that there is a proportion x of skilled workers. Hence

$$U_1 = x - L_1, \tag{9.16}$$

$$U_2 = 1 - x - L_2. \tag{9.17}$$

Using (9.13), (9.14), (9.16), and (9.17), we can solve for for U_i, V_i, and L_i in steady state. If u_i and v_i denote the unemployment and vacancy rates for type i (relative to labor supply), we get

$$u_i = \frac{h(\lambda_i)}{\lambda_i/s + h(\lambda_i)},$$
(9.18)

$$v_i = \frac{1}{\lambda_i/s + h(\lambda_i)}.$$
(9.19)

Together, (9.18) and (9.19) define a Beveridge curve for market i, which is parameterized by the index of labor market slack λ_i. Clearly u_i is increasing and v_i decreasing in λ_i; that is, a tighter labor market, with either more vacancies or less unemployment, must be associated with lower arrival rates of workers in equilibrium. Also an increase in s, given λ_i, increases both u_i and v_i (the Beveridge curve shifts up); that is, higher turnover increases both the unemployment rate and the proportion of vacant jobs. From this we can compute the aggregate unemployment and vacancy rates:

$$u = xu_1 + (1 - x)u_2$$
(9.20)

and

$$v = xv_1 + (1 - x)v_2.$$
(9.21)

It is then possible to express (9.15) in terms of λ_1 and λ_2:

$$x\frac{1 + \lambda_1/s}{\lambda_1/s + h(\lambda_1)} + (1 - x)\frac{1 + \lambda_2/s}{\lambda_2/s + h(\lambda_2)} = K.$$
(9.22)

This equation defines a locus BB which we will call the *flow equilibrium locus* (see figure 9.2). Equation (9.22) can be rewritten

$$xw(\lambda_1) + (1 - x)w(\lambda_2) = K,$$

where $w(\lambda_i) = (1 + \lambda_i/s)/(\lambda_i/s + h(\lambda_i)) = 1 - u_i + v_i = w_i$ is the steady state *job rate* for type i workers, that is, the total number of jobs available for this type, whether vacant or not, divided by the supply of workers of this type. Equation (9.22) obviously states that the total number of jobs must be equal to K.

BB is downward sloping in the (λ_1, λ_2) plane and has two asymptotes at $\lambda_1 = \bar{\lambda}_1$ and $\lambda_2 = \bar{\lambda}_2$, respectively. The $\bar{\lambda}_i$ are defined by

$$x\frac{1 + \bar{\lambda}_1/s}{\bar{\lambda}_1/s + h(\bar{\lambda}_1)} = K \quad \text{and} \quad (1 - x)\frac{1 + \bar{\lambda}_2/s}{\bar{\lambda}_2/s + h(\bar{\lambda}_2)} = K.$$

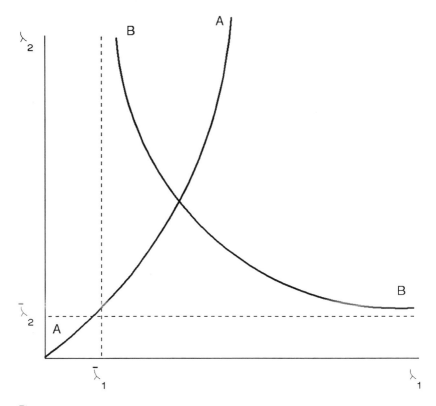

Figure 9.2
Equilibrium determination

In the case depicted figure 9.2, $\bar{\lambda}_1 < \lambda_1^*$, and there is a unique equilibrium determined by the intersection of AA and BB. Since AA is above the 45-degree line, the equilibrium satisfies $\lambda_1 < \lambda_2$. Hence the unemployment rate for the unskilled is higher than for the skilled. The converse is true for vacancy rates.

Whenever $\lambda_1^* < \bar{\lambda}_1$, AA and BB do not cross. The unemployment rate for type 2 is thus equal to 1, so $\lambda_2 = +\infty$ and $\lambda_1 = \bar{\lambda}_1$. In that case the unskilled are literally unemployable even though their relative wage is exactly equal to their relative productivity ρ.

9.2   Impact of the Productivity Differential and the Skill Composition of the Population

The two variables ρ and x capture the transmission of technical progress to unemployment via the heterogeneity of skills and the composition of the

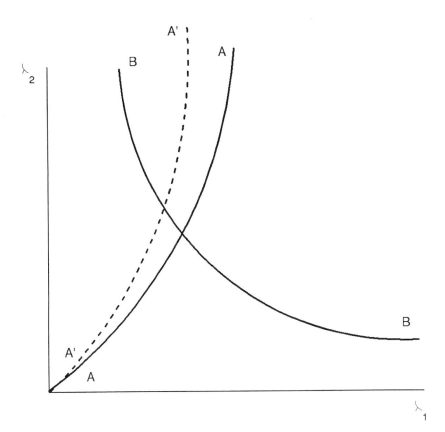

Figure 9.3
Impact of a reduction in ρ

work force. We will focus on a fall in ρ and a rise in x, since recent research emphasizes that both the supply of and demand for skilled workers has increased over the last twenty years (see Katz and Murphy 1992).

Impact of a Change in ρ

It should first be noted that ρ captures the *relative* productivity differential of unskilled labor. Multiplying the profits from both types of labor by the same constant a results in the right-hand side of (9.8) and (9.9) being multiplied by a, leaving (9.10) unaffected.[6] Therefore an increase in the productivity of skilled relative to unskilled labor implies a *decline* in ρ, even though the absolute productivity of type 2 workers may rise.

---

6. Equation (9.10) would also be unaffected if there was a vacancy cost proportional to productivity.

The impact of a decline in ρ is clear from equation (9.10) and figure 9.3: The AA locus shifts upward. Firms require a greater probability of finding an unskilled worker in order to compensate for the lower profits they make relative to type 1 workers. Consequently λ_1 declines and λ_2 rises. As a result the unskilled unemployment rate rises and the skilled unemployment rate goes down (equation 9.18). Interestingly the aggregate unemployment rate goes up unambiguously:

PROPOSITION 9.1 $\partial u / \partial \rho < 0$.

Proof   See the appendix for a proof.

Proposition 9.1 tells us that in some sense there should be a correlation between work force heterogeneity and unemployment: The more the unskilled are remote from the skilled in terms of productivity, the higher the unemployment rate. The intuition behind this result is as follows: Proposition 1 means that when one moves along the BB curve away from the 45-degree line, the aggregate unemployment rate increases. Suppose that we try to increase unskilled unemployment and reduce skilled unemployment while leaving aggregate unemployment unaffected. Say that there is one more unemployed unskilled and one less unemployed skilled worker. In order to sustain this change in steady state, there must be more vacancies for type 1 workers and fewer vacancies for type 2 workers. Since the skilled labor market is more congested than the unskilled one, and since there are decreasing marginal returns to posting a vacancy, the increase in the number of vacancies for market 1 must be larger than the decline in vacancies for market 2.

Since employment is held constant, the aggregate job rate must rise above K, thus creating disequilibrium. To restore equilibrium the aggregate unemployment rate must therefore rise. In other words, proposition 9.1 is essentially a mismatch result related to the convexity of the Beveridge curve and the concavity of the matching function. It tells us that a given increase in labor demand creates fewer new matches when the labor market is tight to begin with. Therefore a shift of labor demand from the slack to tight labor market creates fewer jobs in the latter than it destroys in the former.

Impact of a Change in x

The x variable allows us to analyze how the skill composition of the population affects unemployment, in particular, whether an increase in the number of people with higher education has a positive or adverse effect on

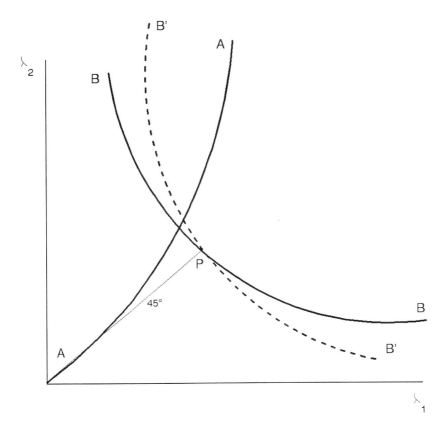

Figure 9.4
Impact of an increase in x

unemployment. A change in x affects unemployment through a shift in the flow equilibrium locus; more precisely:

PROPOSITION 9.2   When x increases, the BB locus rotates clockwise around its intersection with the 45-degree line. As a result both λ_1 and λ_2 increase (figure 9.4).

Proof   At $\lambda_1 = \lambda_2$ the left-hand side of (9.22) is independent of x. Therefore the new BB locus has the same intersection with the 45-degree line. Consider a point of BB above the 45-degree line such that $\lambda_2 > \lambda_1$. Since $(1 + \lambda/s)/(\lambda/s + h(\lambda))$ decreases with λ, it is lower for λ_2 than for λ_1. As a result an increase in x tends to increase the left-hand side of (9.22). To compensate and maintain it equal to K, λ_2 has to increase for the same value of λ_1. Therefore BB is above its previous location when x increases. The converse holds in the zone where $\lambda_2 < \lambda_1$.

Since unemployment rates are increasing functions of the λ's, proposition 9.2 tells us that the unemployment rate will increase for *both* types of workers. That it increases for skilled workers is not surprising, since they are relatively more abundant. But because of the arbitrage condition, it will also increase for unskilled workers: Since employers have more chances to hire a skilled worker, they will want to hire unskilled workers only if their market slackens enough. Therefore the unemployment rate of unskilled workers rises.

What does this imply for the aggregate unemployment rate? Since the unemployment rate for the skilled is lower than for the unskilled, the two negative effects on skill-specific unemployment rates are balanced by a positive composition effect: There are more people in the low-unemployment portion of the population. Therefore the aggregate unemployment rate may either rise or decline when x increases. It is possible to show that both things must happen for $x \in [0, 1]$:

PROPOSITION 9.3   The unemployment rate is the same for $x = 0$ and $x = 1$.

Proof Note that for $x = 1$, λ_2 becomes irrelevant and that λ_1 is determined by

$$\frac{1 + \lambda_1/s}{\lambda_1/s + h(\lambda_1)} = K$$

which is equation (9.22) with $x = 1$. But for $x = 0$, equation (9.22) is just

$$\frac{1 + \lambda_2/s}{\lambda_2/s + h(\lambda_2)} = K.$$

Therefore $\lambda_2(x = 0) = \lambda_1(x = 1)$, implying that $u(x = 0) = u_2(x = 0) = u_1(x = 1) = u(x = 1)$.

Proposition 9.3 is just an application of the remark that what matters is relative, not absolute productivity: The single-type cases $x = 0$ and $x = 1$ are in reality the same thing. Since unemployment is the same at both ends of the $[0, 1]$ interval, by continuity it must both increase and decrease when x goes from 0 to 1. Numerical simulations with a Cobb-Douglas matching function indicate that it first rises and then declines, and that it declines over a smaller range than it rises (an example is given in figure 9.5).

An element of intuition for this hump-shaped response is as follows: When x is small, a given increase in x has a large impact on the skilled's arrival rate λ_1 because it is large in relative terms. Since AA's slope is

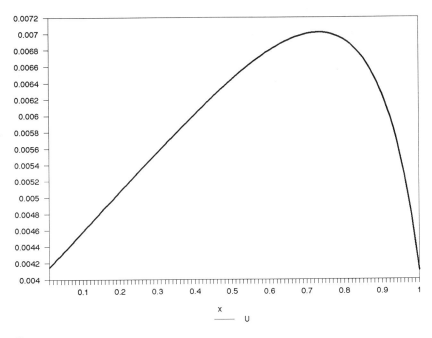

Figure 9.5
Effect of x on aggregate unemployment

greater than 1, this must be matched by a large effect on λ_2. The fact that most of the workers are unskilled generates a large effect on aggregate unemployment, which dominates the composition effect. In other words, even though the skilled are a small minority, the large relative increase in their number has strong effects on the option value of hiring a skilled worker, so employment prospects for the majority deteriorate. By contrast as x becomes large, BB and AA become steeper at the equilibrium point. At high values of x, firms will require only a small increase in the skilled's arrival rate in order to match an increase in the unskilled's arrival rate. This implies that a given increase in x will only have a small effect on λ_1. The effect on λ_2 will be quite large, but the arbitrage effect on employment will be small relative to the composition effect, since the majority of the workers are skilled.

This again suggests that unemployment is higher when there is more heterogeneity in the work force, that is, for intermediate rather than extreme values of x. Given that one would rather believe that x is relatively low, the case for a positive effect of the proportion of educated workers on unemployment has to be taken seriously.

Before concluding this section, we should note that the unemployability of the unskilled becomes a more severe problem as x increases, since λ_2/λ_1

increases along the AA locus. In fact an increase in x can lead the economy to the "corner solution" zone where $u_2 = 1$.

9.3   The Flexible Regime and the Role of Irreversibility

Until now we have assumed that it was not profitable for firms to post a type 1 vacancy for jobs held by type 2 workers and replace them when a suitably skilled applicant comes along. In this section we assume that it is possible to do so provided that the firm pays a firing cost F when it gets rid of the unskilled worker. If F is not too high, then it will indeed be optimal for firms to post vacancies for jobs held by type 2 workers and replace them with type 1 workers. This will be referred to as the "flexible regime." We want to characterize the range of parameters over which the economy will be in the flexible regime, perform the comparative statics exercises with respect to F, ρ and x, and analyze how irreversibility affects the unemployment effects of heterogeneity (analyze the crosseffects of F and x).

There are various motivations for this exercise. First, it gives the model a touch of realism, since, as stated in the introduction, less educated workers have more precarious jobs. Second, it allows us to analyze the effects of firing costs on the level and structure of unemployment, an important problem in the light of the debate on European unemployment. Up to this point we have followed the literature by focusing on the effect of firing costs on labor demand through the shadow cost of labor. Here we want to suggest that firing costs also have a negative impact on the *relative* demand for unskilled labor because of the already mentioned option value effect. Third, it allows us to show how the effects highlighted in the previous section depend on irreversibility, in that higher firing costs make unskilled labor demand more reactive to skilled labor supply.

If one assumes that firms have the option of replacing unskilled workers with skilled workers, the value of an unskilled job must now embody this possibility, so equation (9.7) is rewritten as

$$0 = \rho - (r + s)J_{2t} + s\mathrm{VAC}_t + \frac{dJ_{2t}}{dt} + \max[0, \lambda_{1t}(J_{1t} - F - J_{2t})]. \quad (9.23)$$

In the equation the second term in the brackets is the value of posting a type 1 vacancy for this job and replacing the type 2 worker when an applicant is found.

Equation (9.23) implies that the firm will replace workers if and only if

$$J_{1t} - F - J_{2t} \geq 0. \tag{9.24}$$

If (9.24) is satisfied, the economy is in the flexible regime. In steady state equations (9.2) and (9.6) determine J_1 and VAC as a function of λ_1, with no change with respect to section 9.2:

$$VAC = \frac{\lambda_1}{r(r + \lambda_1 + s)} \tag{9.8}$$

implying that

$$J_1 = \frac{r + \lambda_1}{r(r + \lambda_1 + s)} \tag{9.25}$$

Equations (9.3) and (9.23) now determine VAC and J_2 as a function of λ_2, λ_1, and J_1:

$$VAC = \frac{\lambda_2 \rho + \lambda_1 \lambda_2 (J_1 - F)}{(r + \lambda_2)(r + \lambda_1) + rs} \tag{9.26}$$

$$J_2 = \frac{\rho + sVAC + \lambda_1 (J_1 - F)}{r + s + \lambda_1}. \tag{9.27}$$

Eliminating (VAC) and (J_1) from (9.8), (9.25), and (9.26) yields the new arbitrage condition:

$$\lambda_2 = \frac{\lambda_1}{\rho - F\lambda_1}. \tag{9.28}$$

Solving for J_2, condition (9.24) may be rewritten

$$F < \frac{1 - \rho}{r + s}. \tag{9.29}$$

The interpretation of (9.29) is clear. Its right-hand side is what is lost, in present discounted terms, by a firm that can hire a skilled worker today and does not do so: it is the present discounted value of the profit differential between employing a skilled worker and an unskilled worker. Equation (9.29) states that the economy will be in the flexible regime if this loss is greater than the firing cost; in that case the firm will prefer to pay the firing cost rather than forgo the capital gain from replacing an unskilled worker with a skilled worker. Therefore the flexible regime is more likely whenever (1) firing costs are lower, (2) ρ is lower, (3) interest rates are lower, or (4), quits are lower.

Note that if we replace F by $(1 - \rho)/(r + s)$ in (9.28), we get exactly (9.10′): The discounted loss from not being able to replace a type 2 worker with a type 1 worker plays, in the rigid regime, the same role as the firing cost in the flexible regime. Since (9.29) has to hold, in the flexible regime the AA curve (defined by equation 9.28) is flatter than and below its rigid counterpart (defined by equation 9.10'), and its asymptote is for a larger value of λ_1. In other words, firms are more willing to hire type 2 workers because they now make use of the option of replacing them; hence they require a lower arrival rate to post type 2 vacancies.

If there are no firing costs, (9.28) implies that AA collapses to a straight line DD defined by $\lambda_2 = \lambda_1/\rho$. In that case there is no option value of waiting for a type 1 worker rather than hiring a type 2 worker, since these can be replaced with skilled workers at no cost. As F increases, the option value increases, which raises the relative demand for skilled labor. As shown in figure 9.6, the contribution of the option value to the arbitrage condition is given by the vertical distance between AA and DD. This contribution accounts for all of the convexity of AA and its asymptote. The higher λ_1 is (the more abundant skilled workers), the higher is the

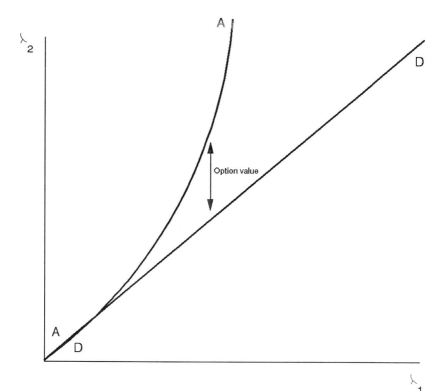

Figure 9.6
Effect of irreversibility on the shape of the arbitrage condition

contribution of the option value to the arbitrage condition. At $\lambda_1 = 0$ the two curves cross and are tangent to each other: The option value goes to zero, since skilled workers become infinitely scarce.

How is the flow equilibrium locus modified in the flexible regime? Equations (9.12) and (9.13) are still valid, but (9.14) is now valid only for type 1 workers. The separation rate for type 2 workers is now $s + \lambda_1$ instead of s: In addition to exogenous quits, there are now the layoffs due to those unskilled workers who are replaced with skilled workers. We will call this the *replacement effect*. Therefore for unskilled workers (9.14) has to be replaced by

$$\frac{dL_2}{dt} = -(s + \lambda_1)L_2 + m(V_2, U_2) = -(s + \lambda_1)L_2 + \lambda_2 V_2. \tag{9.30}$$

Equation (9.5) is also changed: Vacancies are now the sum of vacant jobs and type 2 jobs, since those are posted as vacancies in market 1. Therefore

$$V_1 + V_2 = K - L_1. \tag{9.31}$$

While the formulas for u_1 and v_1 are unchanged, (9.13) and (9.30) imply that

$$v_2 = \frac{1}{\lambda_2/(s + \lambda_1) + h(\lambda_2)}, \tag{9.32}$$

$$u_2 = \frac{h(\lambda_2)}{\lambda_2/(s + \lambda_1) + h(\lambda_2)}. \tag{9.33}$$

The replacement effect therefore induces a linkage between the two markets at this level: An increase in λ_1 increases the separation rate for market 2, thus increasing the unemployment and vacancy rates for these workers.

Plugging these equations into (9.31), we see that the new equation for the BB locus is

$$x\frac{1 + \lambda_1/s}{\lambda_1/s + h(\lambda_1)} + (1 - x)\frac{1}{\lambda_2/(s + \lambda_1) + h(\lambda_2)} = K. \tag{9.34}$$

The symmetry in (9.22) is now broken for two reasons: the replacement effect, and the fact that type 2 jobs contribute to vacancies for type 1 workers.

The form of equation (9.34) suggests that for low values of x, BB may have upward-sloping portions. We will ignore this possibility in the rest of the chapter.[7] This being ruled out, the new BB locus is quite similar to the rigid one, with asymptotes at $\bar{\lambda}_1$ and $\bar{\lambda}'_2 = h^{-1}((1 - x)/K)$.

The comparative statics with respect to x and ρ are comparable to the rigid case, as far as λ_1 and λ_2 are concerned. When ρ declines, AA shifts upward. As a result λ_1 declines, and λ_2 increases. Hence type 1 unemployment goes down. The only difference with the rigid regime is that the effect on type 2 unemployment is now ambiguous: The direct effect of λ_2 tends to increase u_2 but the replacement effect tends to lower it. Since λ_1 goes down, unskilled workers are less often replaced with skilled workers, which tends to raise their steady-state employment level. This suggests that the effects of a decline in ρ on unskilled and aggregate unemployment may be weaker in the flexible regime than in the rigid regime. This may be checked by numerical simulations. Figure 9.7 shows how the unskilled and aggregate unemployment rates vary along the portion of BB that is above the 45-degree line.[8] The pattern is U-shaped. An increase in ρ first lowers and then increases aggregate (or unskilled) unemployment. Therefore in the flexible regime an increase in ρ may well increase unemployment. Since skilled workers are less desired, firms find more of them to replace unskilled workers, and unskilled unemployment increases.[9]

The direct effect of F on unemployment is quite similar to the effect of ρ, since both shift the AA curve. A decline in F shifts the AA curve downward, as does a rise in ρ. Skilled unemployment unambiguously increases; unskilled and/or aggregate unemployment may either decrease or increase. Typically they will decrease if the replacement effect is not too strong, as suggested by figure 9.7, that is, if the economy starts from a

---

7. In other words, we will assume that BB is downward sloping above the 45-degree line. Because of the complexity of the expression in (7.34), it is difficult to make analytical statements about this possibility. Numerical simulations, however, show that λ_2 goes down and then up when λ_1 increases, for low enough values of x. As x rises, the range over which λ_2 goes down increases until x passes a threshold value above which λ_2 always decreases. If BB is upward sloping over some range, there may be multiple equilibria: If the replacement effect is strong enough, a high turnover equilibrium where unskilled workers are often replaced with (abundant) skilled workers may coexist with a low turnover equilibrium where unskilled workers are rarely replaced due to the scarcity of skilled workers. The simulations, however, indicate that when it is upward sloping, BB is quite flat, implying that multiplicity is unlikely.

8. The x-axis is the inverse of the slope of a ray from the origin to the corresponding point on BB; that is, it is the inverse of the slope of the corresponding AA curve for $F = 0$, which is the corresponding value of ρ. Therefore the rightmost values of u and u_2 are for a point on BB that is almost on the 45-degree line ($\rho = 0.99$), while the leftmost values are for a point of BB very remote from the 45-degree line ($\rho = 0.01$).

9. When F increases, the range of values of ρ over which unemployment increases is truncated, since the economy shifts to the rigid regime when ρ exceeds $1 - (r + s)F$.

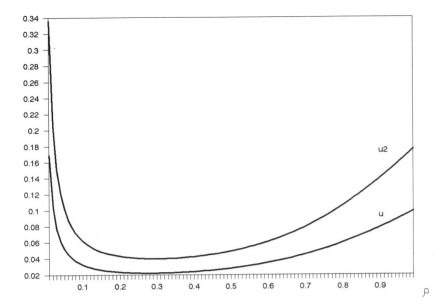

Figure 9.7
Evolution of u and u_2 along BB

point on BB is far enough from the 45-degree line, i.e. if F is large or ρ is small.

An increase in firing costs therefore reduces the relative demand for unskilled labor. Because of the replacement effect, however, the net effect on unskilled unemployment is ambiguous. This ambiguity is to some extent the same as the one typically found in the literature on labor demand and adjustment costs (see chapters 1 and 6). However, the mechanism is totally different. In the labor demand literature, firing costs may raise aggregate labor demand because they directly reduce firing. Here they reduce firing for a very different reason, namely that skilled workers are scarcer because the demand for them has increased.

Concerning the impact of an increase in x, it is apparent from equation (9.34) that BB now rotates clockwise around a point P in the (λ_1, λ_2) locus, which is no longer on the 45-degree line. More precisely, this point is defined by

$$\frac{1 + \lambda_1/s}{\lambda_1/s + h(\lambda_1)} = \frac{1}{\lambda_2/(s + \lambda_1) + h(\lambda_2)} = K.$$

This expression implies that point P is below the 45-degree line (see the appendix for a proof). Since AA is still above the 45-degree degree line,

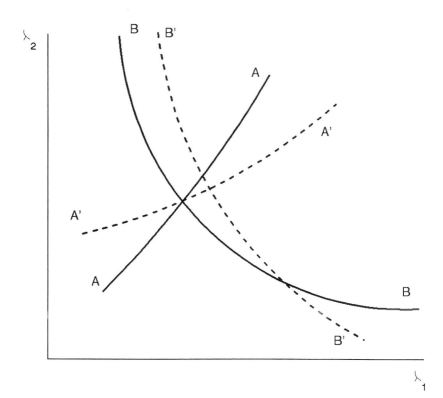

Figure 9.8
Cross-effect of F and x

the conclusion that both λ_1 and λ_2 increase still holds. As a result u_1 and u_2 unambiguously increase: The replacement effect now reinforces the direct effect, so u_2 rises unambiguously. Unskilled workers are not only less demanded, but there are now more skilled workers around to replace them. Concerning the aggregate unemployment rate, numerical simulations suggest a behavior similar to the previous section.

How do firing costs affect this analysis? Suppose that firing costs go down. As shown by (9.28), AA shifts downward and becomes flatter. Since we are interested in the cross-effect of F and x, we can neutralize the downward shift by assuming that ρ is changed so as to maintain the initial value of (λ_1, λ_2) unchanged. This implies a flatter AA locus going through the initial point (figure 9.8). It is then clear from figure 9.8 that at lower firing costs, an increase in x has a smaller effect on λ_2 and a larger effect on λ_1. Therefore the unskilled labor market is less slackened. This exercise highlights how the depressing effect of the supply of educated workers on

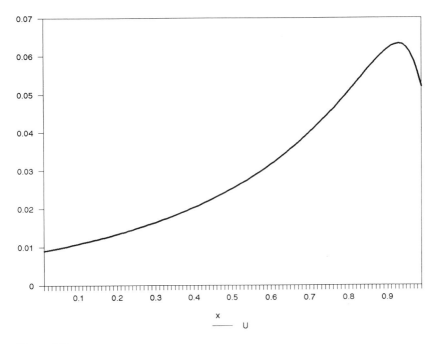

Figure 9.9
Effect of x on unemployment ($F = 0.5$)

the demand for unskilled workers is due to irreversibility: When hiring decisions are less irreversible, this effect is less strong.[10] Conversely, type 1 workers now benefit less from the reluctance to hire type 2 workers, so u_1 and λ_1 rise. Whether u_2 rises more or less compared to the high firing cost case is, however, ambiguous because the replacement effect runs counter to the direct effect.[11]

Figures 9.9 and 9.10 present numerical simulations of the response of aggregate unemployment to x under two values of the firing cost. They confirm the intuition developed in the previous paragraph, namely that the effect is less strong when firing costs are lower: The unemployment rate varies between 0.01 and 0.06 for $F = 0.5$, whereas it ranges from 0.01 to 0.08 when $F = 0.8$.

---

10. These effects do not disappear when F goes to zero for two reasons: First, there is some irreversibility left, associated with the constraint that the firm must choose ex ante the market to which any given vacancy should be directed. Second, x has mechanical effects on λ_1 and λ_2 due to the replacement effect.

11. λ_2 rises less when F is lower, but λ_1 rises more, and so does the separation rate for unskilled workers. The first effect makes u_2 rise less in response to an increase in x, and the second more.

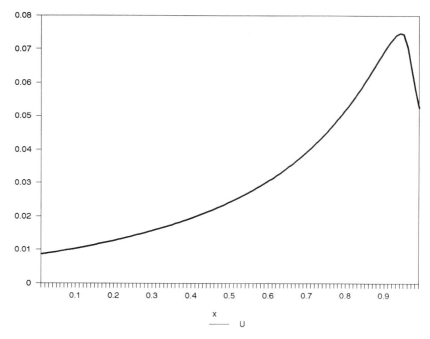

Figure 9.10
Effect of x on unemployment ($F = 0.8$)

What do we conclude from this section? First, the analysis is quite similar when one allows firms to replace unskilled workers with skilled workers. The replacement effect, however, tends to counteract the direct effect of λ_2 on u_2 when the AA curve shifts. This renders ambiguous some of the previous results: In particular, an increase in ρ may increase type 2 and aggregate unemployment. Second, a decrease in the firing cost improves the arbitrage condition for unskilled workers, thus working in a way quite similar to an increase in their relative productivity. Third, the negative effects of an increase in the supply of skilled labor on the market for unskilled workers are smaller when firing costs are smaller; the effects on aggregate unemployment are also smaller.

Last, we have seen that while a reduction in firing costs increases the relative demand for unskilled labor, the net effect on unskilled and aggregate employment is ambiguous because of the replacement effect.

9.4   Conclusion

It is widely recognized that unemployment is essentially a problem of the unskilled. The model I have just developed sheds light on two leading policy proposals to cure the unskilled unemployment problem: labor market flexibility and training programs.

Concerning the former, the model suggests that restrictions such as firing costs do reduce the relative demand for unskilled labor and make it more reactive to increases in the proportion of skilled workers. However, the conclusion that reducing firing costs would reduce unskilled unemployment is not warranted because of the replacement effect.

The model also sheds light on the effect of training programs on unemployment. The model suggests that the effect of these programs depend on how they are implemented and may indeed be quite perverse. If a training program works in such a way that it turns a fraction of the unskilled population into skilled workers, (i.e., if it increases x), it will make the economy move up the AA curve: The unemployment rate will increase both for the skilled and the unskilled, and the aggregate unemployment rate may well increase. It is true that those who benefited from the program will on average have lower unemployment rates, but the rest of the labor force will lose. If on the contrary, the productivity of the *whole* of the unskilled labor force is increased (i.e., ρ increases), then their unemployment rate will go down, and there are good chances that aggregate unemployment will also go down.[12] This suggests that an improvement in the quality of the schooling system has better chances to reduce unemployment than the limited training programs that are often implemented.[13]

One obvious extension is to endogenize x, the proportion of skilled workers. This issue is tackled in the next chapter, along with the more general one of the interaction between labor market institutions and human capital accumulation.

9.5   Appendix

Proof of Proposition 9.1

We have to prove that $du/d\rho > 0$. The aggregate unemployment rate is

$$u = x\frac{h(\lambda_1)}{\lambda_1/s + h(\lambda_1)} + (1 - x)\frac{h(\lambda_2)}{\lambda_2/s + h(\lambda_2)}. \tag{A9.1}$$

We want to analyze how u varies when ρ changes, that is, when one moves along the BB curves. Differentiating (A9.1), we get

---

12. Again, in the flexible regime the replacement effect may make the overall result perverse.

13. For the analysis of the impact of active labor market policy on unemployment in general equilibrium, see Calmfors (1993).

$$du = x\mu(\lambda_1)d\lambda_1 + (1 - x)\mu(\lambda_2)d\lambda_2, \qquad (A9.2)$$

where μ is defined by

$$\mu(\lambda) = \frac{(\lambda h'(\lambda) - h(\lambda))/s}{(\lambda/s + h(\lambda))^2}.$$

Differentiating the equation for BB yields a relationship between $d\lambda_1$ and $d\lambda_2$:

$$0 = x\varphi(\lambda_1)d\lambda_1 + (1 - x)\varphi(\lambda_2)d\lambda_2, \qquad (A9.3)$$

where φ is defined by

$$\varphi(\lambda) = \frac{(h(\lambda) - \lambda h'(\lambda))/s - (h'(\lambda) + 1/s)}{(\lambda/s + h(\lambda))^2}.$$

Plugging (A9.3) into (A9.2) one sees that

$$du = x\mu(\lambda_1)\left[1 - \frac{\mu(\lambda_2) \cdot \varphi(\lambda_1)}{\mu(\lambda_1)\varphi(\lambda_2)}\right]d\lambda_1. \qquad (A9.4)$$

Because of the convexity of h, $\mu(\cdot) > 0$. Since $d\lambda_1/d\rho > 0$, $du/d\rho$ has the sign of the term in brackets. It will be negative iff

$$\frac{\varphi(\lambda_1)}{\varphi(\lambda_2)} > \frac{\mu(\lambda_1)}{\mu(\lambda_2)}.$$

This is equivalent to

$$\frac{\lambda_1 h'(\lambda_1) - h(\lambda_1) + sh'(\lambda_1) + 1}{\lambda_2 h'(\lambda_2) - h(\lambda_2) + sh'(\lambda_2) + 1} > \frac{\lambda_1 h'(\lambda_1) - h(\lambda_1)}{\lambda_2 h'(\lambda_2) - h(\lambda_2)},$$

or rearranging, we get

$$\frac{\lambda_2 h'(\lambda_2) - h(\lambda_2)}{sh'(\lambda_2) + 1} > \frac{\lambda_1 h'(\lambda_1) - h(\lambda_1)}{sh'(\lambda_1) + 1}. \qquad (A9.5)$$

Differentiating this functional form with respect to λ, we see that it is increasing. Therefore (A9.5) is always true, since $\lambda_2 > \lambda_1$. This establishes the claim that $du/d\rho < 0$.   □

Proof That P Is Below the 45-Degree Line

The coordinates (λ_1, λ_2) of P are defined by

$$\frac{1 + \lambda_1/s}{\lambda_1/s + h(\lambda_1)} = \frac{1}{\lambda_2/(s + \lambda_1) + h(\lambda_2)} = K \qquad (A9.6)$$

We want to show that this implies that $\lambda_1 > \lambda_2$. To see this, we can rewrite (A9.6) as

$$\lambda_1 + sh(\lambda_1) = \lambda_2 + (s + \lambda_1)h(\lambda_2). \tag{A9.7}$$

This implies that

$$\lambda_1 + sh(\lambda_1) - [\lambda_2 + sh(\lambda_2)] = \lambda_1 h(\lambda_2) > 0.$$

Since $\lambda + sh(\lambda)$ is increasing in λ, it implies that $\lambda_1 > \lambda_2$. □

Derivation of the Results under Nash Bargaining

It can be shown that the results are qualitatively unaffected when wages are determined by Nash bargaining rather than the split-of-the-pie rule. Specifically the AA locus can be shown to have the same shape in the (λ_1, λ_2) plane. Clearly BB is unaffected by wage formation.

Let w_i be the bargained wage for type i worker. Then (9.2) and (9.3) are unaffected, but (9.6) and (9.7) become

$$0 = 2 - w_1 - (r + s)J_1 + \frac{dJ_1}{dt} + sVAC, \tag{9.6'}$$

$$0 = 2\rho - w_2 - (r + s)J_2 + \frac{dJ_2}{dt} + sVAC. \tag{9.7'}$$

Let PV_i (resp. PU_i) the value of being employed (resp. unemployed) for type i. Suppose that the unemployed of type i earn ωw_i, where ω is the replacement ratio, set by law. Then the Bellman equations for PU and PV are

$$0 = \omega w_i - (r + \mu_i)PU_i + \mu_i PV_i + \frac{dPU_i}{dt}, \tag{A9.8}$$

$$0 = w_i - (r + s)PV_i + sPU_i + \frac{dPV_i}{dt}. \tag{A9.9}$$

In (A9.8) μ_i is the flow probability of finding a job for an unemployed of type i. We have

$$\mu_i = \frac{m(v_i, u_i)}{u_i} = m\left(\frac{1}{h(\lambda_i)}, 1\right) = \frac{\lambda_i}{h(\lambda_i)} = g(\lambda_i).$$

Clearly $g' < 0$.

The employer's threat point is the value of a vacancy VAC, while the employed's threat point is the value of being unemployed PU_i. Consequently wage formation is determined by maximization at each instant of time of the following Nash product:

$$\varphi \log(J_i - \text{VAC}) + (1 - \varphi) \log(PV_i - PU_i), \qquad (A9.10)$$

where maximization takes place with respect to w_i. The first-order conditions are given by

$$\frac{\varphi}{J_1 - \text{VAC}} = \frac{1 - \varphi}{PV_i - PU_i}. \qquad (A9.11)$$

Now, subtracting (9.2) or (9.3) from (9.6'), or (9.7') and (A9.8) from (A9.9), and plugging the results on both sides of (A9.11) allows us to solve for w_1 and w_2 in steady state. This yields

$$w_1 = \frac{2(1 - \varphi)(r + s + \mu_1)}{\varphi(1 - \omega)(r + s + \lambda_1) + (1 - \varphi)(r + s + \mu_1)},$$

$$w_2 = \frac{2\rho(1 - \varphi)(r + s + \mu_2)}{\varphi(1 - \omega)(r + s + \lambda_2) + (1 - \varphi)(r + s + \mu_2)}.$$

It is then possible to substitute these expressions into (9.6') and (9.7') and to compute the equilibrium values of J_i. Next, plugging them into (9.2), (9.3), and (9.4) yields the new equation for AA:

$$\frac{\lambda_1}{\varphi(1 - \omega)(r + s + \lambda_1) + (1 - \varphi)(r + s + \mu_1)}$$

$$= \frac{\rho\lambda_2}{\varphi(1 - \omega)(r + s + \lambda_2) + (1 - \varphi)(r + s + \mu_2)} \qquad (A9.12)$$

Clearly (A9.12) is identical to (9.10) if $\varphi = 1$. It can be rewritten

$$\psi(\lambda_1) = \rho\psi(\lambda_2),$$

where $\psi(\lambda) = \lambda/(\varphi(1 - \omega)(r + s + \lambda) + (1 - \varphi)(r + s + g(\lambda)))$. ψ is strictly increasing and bounded from above. This in turns implies that AA has the same qualitative properties as in the text, namely that it is above the 45-degree line, it is increasing, and it has a vertical asymptote at λ_1^* such that $\psi(\lambda_1^*) = \rho \lim_{\lambda\infty} \psi(\lambda)$.

10   Human Capital Accumulation

Up to now we have considered the implications of labor rigidities for the structure and dynamics of unemployment. However, unemployment is not the only variable that one should be concerned with when discussing the implications of such rigidities. In particular, they may also affect productivity growth which is the most important determinant of welfare in the long run.

Growth and human capital accumulation are associated with a wide array of issues. We cannot tackle them all here. Rather, we will consider these factors insofar as they relate to our discussion in the preceding chapters. This chapter consists of two parts. In the first part, we consider the impact of rigidities on human capital accumulation in the framework of the model of chapter 9. The second part is a general discussion of the effect of two-tier systems on long-run growth. This way the chapter will shed some light on an important, but neglected topic: the impact of labor market institutions on long-run growth.

An important insight is that labor market rigidities may generate *increasing returns to education* through the supply effects highlighted in the previous chapter: An increase in the supply of skilled workers may increase the welfare gap between skilled and unskilled workers, in particular, by increasing the unskilled's likelihood of being unemployed relative to the skilled. This may be more than a theoretical possibility. The increase in the supply of educated workers in many European countries has not mitigated the unskilled unemployment problem, and growing numbers of people acquire skills to avoid unemployment.

10.1   The Simple Learning-by-Doing Model

In this section we extend the model of chapter 9 to take into account learning by doing. Our starting point is the flexible regimes where unskilled workers are employed until a skilled worker is found. What we are interested in in this chapter is endogenizing x, the proportion of skilled workers in the economy. We do so by assuming that skilled workers were once unskilled and become skilled on the job. We also assume that skilled workers may lose their skills during unemployment spells, thus becoming unskilled.[1] We thus embody within the model two very traditional arguments, namely that long spells of unemployment are associated with skill deterioration, while long job tenure improves skills.

The Markovian structure of the model is maintained by assuming that there is a flow probability α of an unskilled employed worker becoming skilled. Let β be the flow probability of a skilled unemployed worker becoming unskilled. Normalizing total labor force to 1, the proportion of skilled workers x is then governed by the following equation:

$$\dot{x} = \alpha(1 - x)(1 - u_2) - \beta x u_1. \tag{10.1}$$

We will call the first term at the right-hand side of (10.1) the *inflow* of skilled workers and the last term the *outflow* of skilled workers. Note that the likelihood of becoming skilled changes the arbitrage condition as compared to the previous chapter, since hiring an unskilled worker now embodies the likelihood of that worker becoming skilled. The appendix derives the new arbitrage condition.

In steady state the proportion of skilled workers is simply given by $x = \alpha(1 - u_2)/(\alpha(1 - u_2) + \beta u_1)$. It is essentially governed by the unemployment rates u_1 and u_2, and decreasing in both. Several other things should be noted: First, there exists a unique equilibrium value of x. This is because, as we have seen in the previous chapter, an increase in x raises both u_1 and u_2: The skilled are more abundant and so must be the unskilled for the arbitrage condition to be matched. The replacement effect reinforces the increase in u_2.

Uniqueness of equilibrium is illustrated in figure 10.1. An increase in x reduces the stock of unskilled employed workers, both because their supply falls and because their unemployment rate increases. This lowers the inflow of skilled workers. At the same time the outflow of skilled workers is increased, since there are more unemployed skilled workers. These two effects act as equilibrating mechanisms, pushing down the equilibrium value of x as driven by (10.1). This result contrasts sharply with the one obtained in the next section, where increasing returns to education and multiple equilibria are a pervasive phenomenon.

---

1. See Robinson (1993) for an analysis of the link between unemployment and human capital.

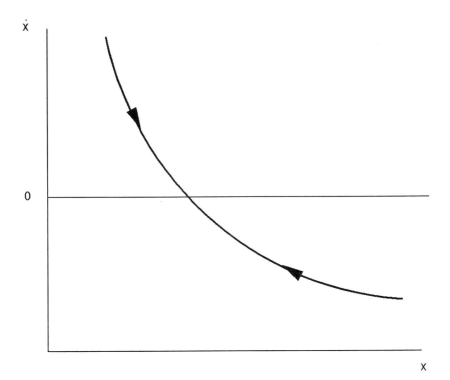

Figure 10.1
Evolution dynamics of x

Second, firing costs have an ambiguous impact on the equilibrium level of x. In the rigid regime lower firing costs increase unskilled employment but also skilled unemployment. Thus both the inflow and the outflow of skilled workers increase. The story is further complicated in the flexible regime. We know from the previous chapter that in the flexible regime a reduction in firing costs increases u_1, while it may either increase or reduce u_2. If it increases u_2, then the equilibrium value of x is clearly reduced. That is, even though the unskilled are more demanded by firms their higher turnover rate prevents them from acquiring skills on the job. At the same time the skilled are less demanded, so they lose their qualifications more often during their unemployment spells.[2] If on the contrary u_2 falls,

---

2. This effect would be even stronger if, instead of assuming a Poisson process for the transition from unskilled to skilled labor, one would assume a transition probability α that would be increasing with tenure. In that case a reduction in firing cost might lower the inflow of skilled workers even though it lowers u_2 because of higher turnover for unskilled workers.

the net effect on x is ambiguous and depends on whether the increase in the inflow of skilled workers is larger or smaller that the increase in the outflow.

We therefore have an example of increases in labor market flexibility that can have an adverse impact on the economy's stock of human capital. The mechanism we have here is based on turnover: When firing costs go down, the unskilled will stay in firms for shorter periods, which will hamper their ability for being trained. Note that this happens even though firms, when hiring an unskilled worker, fully take into account the fact that they become skilled with flow probability α.[3] However, there are two externalities that prevent firms from internalizing the full effect of tenure on human capital accumulation. First, they only reap half the benefits of the worker's skill improvement, since these benefits are split between firms and workers; second, they do not internalize the fact that the worker's skill level will benefit future matches between that worker and other employers.[4]

The effects just discussed have the flavor of an oft-heard argument about possible benefits, in terms of human capital accumulation, of regulations that restrict turnover. Remember, however, that such regulations are unlikely to be the most appropriate policy to increase the economy's human capital level (why not directly subsidize training). In the next section we will also obtain positive effects of firing costs on human capital, but through a very different mechanism: A rigid labor market increases the returns to education because it increases the demand for skilled relative to unskilled labor.

10.2 Labor Market Rigidities and the Returns to Education

We now consider how the equilibrium value of x is determined when workers acquire skills (at some cost) prior to entering the labor force. We can assume perfect borrowing and lending markets. During each time interval a proportion s of workers exits the labor force, and there is a matching inflow of new entrants. These new entrants choose between becoming skilled or becoming unskilled. If they become skilled, they have to incur an upfront cost C. We assume that C differs across individuals. Let $G(C)$, $G' = g$, be the cumulative distribution of C among new entrants. We assume that new entrants, once they have decided whether or not to

---

3. Note, however, that the flexible regime is less likely to occur, the higher is α.
4. See Acemoglu (1993) for an analysis of these issues.

acquire skills, enter the labor force as unemployed workers. Therefore an individual with acquisition cost C will become skilled if and only if

$$C < W_1 - W_2,$$ (10.2)

where W_i is the present discounted income from being unemployed in market i. To compute the equilibrium value of x, we have first to compute W_1 and W_2 in steady state. Let $g(\lambda_i)$ be an unemployed's flow probability of getting a job in market i. $g(\lambda_i)$ is the ratio of hirings over unemployment for market i. Formally we have $g(\lambda_i) = m(v_i, u_i)/u_i = m(1/h(\lambda_i), 1)$, where h is defined in (9.13). Clearly we have $g' < 0$.

To compute the equilibrium determination in the flexible regime where the unskilled are replaced with skilled workers, let us first consider market 1. Once a skilled worker is employed, he earns a wage equal to 1 and keeps his job until he retires, which happens with flow probability s. Retirement yields an income of 0 forever, implying that the present discounted value of being retired is also equal to 0. Consequently the present discounted value of being employed in market 1 is[5]

$$V_{e1} = \frac{1}{r + s}.$$ (10.3)

An unemployed worker in market 1 finds a job with probability $g(\lambda_1)$. This job yields a present discounted income flow equal to V_{e1}. Therefore the present discounted value of being unemployed in market 1 is

$$W_1 = \frac{g(\lambda_1) V_{e1}}{r + g(\lambda_1)} = \frac{g(\lambda_1)}{(r + s)(r + g(\lambda_1))} = W_1(\lambda_1).$$ (10.4)

Let us now turn to market 2. The present discounted value of being employed in market 2 satisfies

$$(r + s + \lambda_1) V_{e2} = \rho + \lambda_1 W_2.$$ (10.5)

Equation (10.5) states that a worker employed in market 2 earns a wage equal to ρ, retires with flow probability s, and is fired to be replaced with a skilled worker with flow probability λ_1. W_2 then satisfies

$$W_2 = \frac{g(\lambda_2) V_{2e}}{r + g(\lambda_2)}$$ (10.6)

Eliminating V_{2e} between (10.5) and (10.6), we get a formula for W_2:

---

5. Equations (10.3)–(10.7) can be obtained by writing the corresponding value functions recursively. For example, $V_{e1} = 1 \cdot dt + (1 - rdt)[(1 - sdt)V_{e1} + sdt \cdot 0]$.

$$W_2 = \frac{g(\lambda_2)\rho}{g(\lambda_2)(r+s) + r(r+s+\lambda_1)} = W_2(\lambda_1, \lambda_2). \qquad (10.7)$$

In steady state the equilibrium value of x is therefore given by

$$x = G(W_1 - W_2), \qquad (10.8)$$

where W_1 and W_2 are given by (10.4) and (10.7).

Let us first consider how firing costs affect the returns to education. As seen in the previous chapter, an increase in F reduces λ_1 and increases λ_2. Therefore it unambiguously raises W_1, while the effect on W_2 is ambiguous. On the one hand, the relative demand for unskilled workers deteriorates; on the other hand, they are replaced less often, since skilled workers are less available. This argument is very similar to the one on the effect of F on u_2 in chapter 9. Formally, if $R = W_1 - W_2 = W_1(\lambda_1) - W_2(\lambda_1, \lambda_2)$ is the return to education, we have

$$\frac{\partial R}{\partial F} = \left(W_1' - \frac{\partial W_2}{\partial \lambda_1} \right) \frac{d\lambda_1}{dF} - \frac{\partial W_2}{\partial \lambda_2} \frac{d\lambda_2}{dF}. \qquad (10.9)$$

$$\quad (-) \quad\quad (-) \quad (-) \quad\quad (-) \ (+)$$

The reduction in λ_1 makes it easier for the skilled to find jobs, thus increasing W_1 (first term in equation 10.9). The direct negative effect on unskilled labor demand (the increase in λ_2) tends to reduce W_2 (last term in equation 10.9). At the same time, however, the unskilled are fired less often because it is more difficult to fill the same job with a skilled worker (the replacement effect). This tends to push W_2 up (second term in equation 10.9). If the replacement effect is not too strong, an increase in firing costs will therefore increase the returns to education.

We now study the conditions under which an increase in x, the proportion of skilled workers, may increase the returns to education. We have seen in the previous chapter that whenever the arbitrage condition AA is steep enough, an increase in the proportion of skilled workers will have a large impact on the unskilled's unemployment rate. As a result the net return to becoming skilled may rise.[6]

This will actually be the case if when one moves to the right along AA, R increases. The corresponding condition is[7]

---

6. Fields (1993) has shown the possibility of increasing returns to education in a Harris and Todaro (1970) model of rationing, where wages fail to adjust to disequilibrium and applicants are ranked on the basis of their human capital.

7. This condition looks similar to (10.9), but is different. In (10.9) we consider shifts of AA, implying $d\lambda_2/d\lambda_1 < 0$. Here we consider shifts along AA, implying $d\lambda_2/d\lambda_1 > 0$.

$$\left(W_1' - \frac{\partial W_2}{\partial \lambda_1} \right) - \frac{\partial W_2}{\partial \lambda_2} \frac{d\lambda_2}{d\lambda_1} > 0. \tag{10.10}$$

$$(-) \quad (-) \qquad (-)\,(+)$$

The first term at the left-hand side of (10.10) is the reduction in the skilled's utility due to the increase in λ_1; this tends to reduce the returns to education. The second term is the reduction in the unskilled's utility due to the replacement effect: Unskilled workers are fired more often when λ_1 increases. This increases the returns to education. The third term is the direct effect on the unskilled's utility of a lower relative demand for them due to the increase in λ_1. This also tends to increase the returns to education.

When firing costs increase, $d\lambda_2/d\lambda_1$ increases, since one has $d\lambda_2/d\lambda_1 = \rho/(\rho - \lambda_1 F)^2$ (see equation 9.28). An increase in the skilled's arrival rate has stronger effects on the option value when there is more irreversibility in hirings. This tends to make (10.10) more likely. Therefore, *given* λ_1 and λ_2, increasing returns to education are more likely when firing costs are higher. However, firing costs will also affect the equilibrium values of λ_1 and λ_2. In particular, a higher firing cost makes λ_1 less reactive to x; therefore the replacement effect's contribution to the returns to education is smaller when x increases.

As a result one gets a rather complex interaction between labor market rigidities and the returns to education. First, while it seems plausible that firing costs increase the returns to acquiring skills, the replacement effect may potentially reverse this result. Second, increasing returns to education are a likely outcome of this model. Third, while it is plausible that a more rigid labor market makes increasing returns more likely, the replacement effect again tends to act in the opposite direction.

If there are increasing returns to education, then, as illustrated on figure 10.2, there may be multiple equilibria. In figure 10.2 the SS locus is the supply curve for human capital. It illustrates how x depends on R through (10.8), that is, through the skill acquisition decision. The DD locus is the demand curve, it tells us how, given x, the equilibrium value of R is determined. In the figure it is assumed that (10.10) holds over some range so that DD has an increasing portion. A high-skill equilibrium (point A) may coexist with a low-skill equilibrium (point B). At A the returns to education are high because the skilled have much better employment prospects than the unskilled. Because of the skilled's relative abundance, the option value of maintaining a vacancy idle rather than filling it with an unskilled is quite high, so the demand for unskilled labor is low.

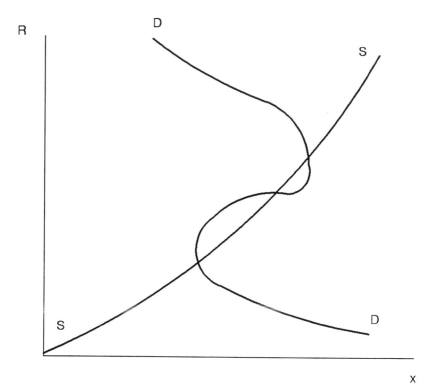

Figure 10.2
Increasing returns to education and multiple equilibria

Furthermore those unskilled workers who find jobs are quickly replaced, which further lowers the value of being unskilled. Therefore the returns to education are high, which tends to maintain x at a high level. The converse holds for the low-skill equilibrium B.

If firing costs are so high that the economy is in the rigid regime, it is very easy to compute the conditions under which there are increasing returns to education. Given that there is no replacement effect, (10.7) is now simply replaced with

$$W_2 = \frac{\rho g(\lambda_2)}{(r + s)(r + g(\lambda_2))}. \tag{10.11}$$

Equation (10.10) then becomes

$$\frac{g'(\lambda_1)}{(r + g(\lambda_1))^2} > \frac{g'(\lambda_2)d\lambda_2/d\lambda_1}{(r + g(\lambda_2))^2}, \tag{10.12}$$

where $d\lambda_2/d\lambda_1$ is now computed using the "rigid" arbitrage condition (9.10'), yielding

$$\frac{d\lambda_2}{d\lambda_1} = \frac{\rho}{(\rho - \lambda_1(1 - \rho)/(r + s))^2}. \tag{10.13}$$

Plugging (10.13) into (10.12), using $g(\lambda) = 1/\lambda$, and replacing λ_2 using (9.10'), we can see that after rearranging, (10.12) will hold if and only if

$$r(r + s) < 1. \tag{10.14}$$

Equation (10.14) suggests that low turnover (i.e., a low value of s) makes increasing returns more likely. A drop in s in the rigid regime is very similar to an increase in firing costs in the flexible regime, since it increases the option value of leaving a vacancy idle rather than filling it with an unskilled worker.[8] Similarly a drop in r increases the option value, since the future is less heavily discounted.

It is tempting to interpret this section's specification of human capital accumulation as a French model, the previous section being interpreted as a German model, since it is often argued that the German educational system is much more internal to the firm than the French one. If one were to fall into this temptation, one would conclude that the German model is more stable in the sense that it has a unique equilibrium. In the French model the economy can potentially move back and forth across equilibria; some generations may be underskilled, others overskilled, and so on.

Note that the high-skill equilibrium does not a priori dominate the low-skill one, since in the former the economy spends more resources in training costs. In related contributions (Saint-Paul 1994a, b), I have shown that under plausible assumptions "workers" prefer the low-skill equilibrium to the high-skill equilibrium. This is because in the latter they suffer from higher unemployment rates and higher real interest rates, since the higher demand for education puts a drain on national savings. For that same reason capitalists will prefer the high-skill equilibrium.

10.3   Perspectives on Labor Market Institutions and Economic Growth

The above discussion has brought the more general question of the interaction between labor market institutions and economic growth. In

---

8. Remember that the shadow firing cost in the rigid regime is simply $(1 - \rho)/(r + s)$. Here the analysis is unambiguous, since there is no longer a replacement effect.

particular, we have seen examples where labor market rigidities may be beneficial for human capital accumulation because they either increase the opportunities for on-the-job training or increase the returns to education.

This section takes a broader perspective and discusses how various approaches to growth affect the link between labor market institutions and productivity, with an emphasis on the role played by dual labor market.[9]

Learning by Doing

First, growth may be the result of a learning process that is internal to existing firms. In that case there will be a trade-off between labor market flexibility and economic growth. Increasing labor market flexibility may lead to excess turnover which will hamper the scope for productivity improvements within the firm; this is the logic that prevailed in section 10.2. However, there are several qualifications that apply to this argument.

First, for this argument to be potent, there must be a sense that the learning effects are not internalized by private agents. This is indeed the case in section 10.2, since the sharing rule prevents firms from fully taking into account the social gains from an unskilled worker becoming skilled while working for them. The economy may thus inadequately find itself in the flexible regime, whereas it would be better-off in the rigid regime. An increase in firing costs would then push the economy into the rigid regime, which could be beneficial for growth.

Second, one should refrain from drawing the simplistic policy implication that rigidity is good because it favors human capital accumulation. This argument holds only as long as an appropriate fiscal instrument such as a subsidy to training is not available. Obviously labor market rigidities are pretty far-fetched as an incentive for learning and innovation, and they are not meant, in general, to achieve that goal.

This being said, the two-tier systems that we have studied since the beginning of this book may well be a powerful instrument to get out of the trade-off between growth and flexibility. Assume that the learning that is made as a by-product of production is specific to the firm, but nonrival. That is, when a worker discovers a new way to produce more efficiently, it becomes embodied in the firm's organization and thus available to all other present and future workers. In that case flexibility could be reconciled with growth by having a core of permanent workers whose experience will serve as a basis for productivity improvements. Fluctuations in product

9. These issues have also been discussed by Ulph and Ulph (1993).

demand would be met through a buffer of flexible, temporary workers, so the marginal worker will have a very low firing cost. The core will be largely unaffected by these fluctuations. Of course, such form of organization is not an abstract view, since it sounds very much like the Japanese experience.

Schumpeterian Approaches

There is no unanimity about the view that the most important factor for economic growth is productivity improvement within existing firms. Many consider that the essence of the growth process is a continuous inflow of new firms making old firms obsolete, with the associated waves of job destruction and job creation.[10] Such Schumpeterian approaches offer a radically different perspective on the role of labor market institutions. According to the Schumpeterian view, labor mobility is a crucial instrument to promote growth. Rigidities such as turnover costs or insider power prevent labor from relocating from old to new industries.[11] Unemployment should not be a major concern, since it is essentially the sign of such productive reallocation, and an inevitable corollary of the large flows of job creation and job destruction implied by the growth process.[12]

Contrary to the learning-by-doing approach, the Schumpeterian view implies that there is no trade-off: More flexible economies will also grow faster. In fact, reducing growth rather than increasing unemployment may be the most important social cost of labor rigidities. A two-tier system has no particular virtues: It will improve over a one-tier, rigid labor market, but a move toward total flexibility would be even more desirable.

Fallick (1993) has provided empirical evidence that part-time work and precarious jobs are more widespread in fast growing industries. This evidence supports the Schumpeterian view that labor flexibility is an important component of growth.

10.4   Political and Distributional Issues

Labor market institutions may also indirectly affect economic growth through their impact on *income distribution*. High redistributive taxation

---

10. Recent growth theory has paid considerable attention to this view. See Aghion and Howitt (1992), Grossman and Helpman (1991), Caballero and Hammour (1994), and Cohen and Saint-Paul (1994).

11. This point has been developed in Bertola (1991) and Hopenhayn and Rogerson (1993).

12. See Lilien (1982), Davis and Haltiwanger (1990), and Aghion and Howitt (1994).

may discourage capital accumulation and reduce the rate of economic growth. To the extent that it is the outcome of a political conflict between rich and poor, inequality may exacerbate such conflict and lead to higher tax rates and lower growth.[13] This suggests that labor market institutions that are more egalitarian may, other things equal, generate more growth.[14]

How do then labor market institutions affect inequality? Given the book's focus on job security and two-tier systems, there are two points that should be made here.

First, job turnover is egalitarian.[15] A society where more jobs are destroyed also creates more jobs. There are less differences between being employed and being unemployed, since the employed often lose their jobs while the unemployed often find jobs. One should therefore expect labor market flexibility to alleviate redistributive conflicts, at least within the labor force. This should, all else equal, lead to less taxation and more growth. At the same time, however, the conflicts between labor and capital may be exacerbated to the extent that labor market flexibility reduces the rents that labor is able to appropriate.

Second, we expect two-tier systems to be harmful for growth by artificially creating redistributive conflicts between those who hold permanent jobs and those who do not. First, given wages, permanent income is higher when one holds a rigid contract, since one expects to spend less time in unemployment. Second, as we argued in chapters 4 and 7, there are reasons to believe that flexible workers will earn less than rigid workers. Flexible workers are therefore likely to support policies that tax the rich to subsidize the poor or that tax the employed to subsidize the unemployed. Such policies may reduce growth to the extent that they distort the incentives for physical and human capital accumulation. One may argue that flexible workers are less angry than if they were unemployed.

---

13. These issues have also generated considerable interests within the new growth literature. See Persson and Tabellini (1994), Alesina and Rodrik (1990), Perotti (1993), and Saint-Paul and Verdier (1993). Depending on the particular culture and institutions of the society one considers, taxation may take various forms: crime, political violence, corruption, and the like.

14. There are many qualifications that apply to these simple claims. First, labor market institutions may increase inequality by some measure and reduce it by others. For example, wage compression lowers inequality among wage earners but ·creates unemployment, which in itself tends to increase global inequality. The net effect is ambiguous. Second, the key issue for taxation is not inequality in general but how rich the decisive voter is relative to the mean. Third, redistribution may promote growth if it is in the form of productivity-enhancing public goods such as education. See Agell and Lommerund (1993), Saint-Paul (1996), and Saint-Paul and Verdier (1993, 1996).

15. This point is discussed further in chapter 11; see also Saint-Paul (1994c).

The key point, however, is that the unemployed will always remain a weak minority, while flexible workers can have a much larger impact on policy (see chapter 11). In the next chapter, we will study the role of another type of conflict between the two tiers of the labor market, different preferences about labor market institutions.

10.5 Summary

What lessons can we draw from this chapter?

First, labor market rigidities may have unexpected beneficial side-effects on human capital accumulation. In the model of section 10.2, firing costs may increase the proportion of skilled workers by inducing firms to keep unskilled workers longer, which favors their training. In the model of section 10.2, they depress the demand for unskilled labor relative to skilled labor, thus increasing the returns to education and the equilibrium level of skills. It is, however, unlikely that these side-effects be a justification *per se* for such rigidities, since other instruments are more appropriate to deal with learning externalities.

Second, labor market rigidities, in particular, firing costs, may generate increasing returns to education. An increased supply of skills may generate an increased *relative* demand for skills because of the option value and the replacement effects. The economy may be at an equilibrium where people acquire a lot of skills to escape unemployment and where the abundance of skills indeed raises the unskilled's unemployment rate.

Third, labor market institutions affect growth through various channels. While the learning-by-doing model suggests that a dual labor market may be a clever way of reconciling flexibility with growth, the Schumpeterian model predicts that complete flexibility would be even more desirable, while politicoeconomic models, which favor flexibility, also predict that two-tier systems may harm growth.

These lessons are preliminary. Much research remains to be done on these mechanisms.

10.6 Appendix

Labor Demand and On-the-Job Training

We derive the arbitrage condition AA, now taking into account the fact that firms expect workers to become skilled with flow probability α. We then derive the conditions under which the economy would be in the flexible regime.

Writing the value of a job held by an unskilled worker in a recursive way between t and $t + dt$, we get

$$J_2 = \rho dt + (1 - rdt)[\alpha dt J_1 + \lambda_1 dt(J_1 - F)$$

$$+ (1 - \alpha dt - \lambda_1 dt - sdt)J_2 + sdt\text{VAC}]. \tag{10.14}$$

The first term in brackets corresponds to the expected capital gain from the unskilled becoming skilled, the second term is the expected value from the unskilled being replaced with a skilled, the last term is the expected value from the worker leaving his job. Time indexes have been dropped, since we focus on steady states.

Equation (10.14) may simply be rewritten as

$$0 = \rho - (r + \alpha + \lambda_1 + s)J_2 - \lambda_1 F + (\alpha + \lambda_1)J_1 + s\text{VAC}. \tag{10.15}$$

The equation governing J_1 is unchanged:

$$0 = 1 - (r + s)J_1 + s\text{VAC}. \tag{10.16}$$

Finally, VAC is the value of a vacancy in either market, implying that

$$\text{VAC} = \frac{\lambda_1 J_1}{r + \lambda_1} = \frac{\lambda_2 J_2}{r + \lambda_2}. \tag{10.17}$$

The new arbitrage condition is simply obtained by eliminating J_1, J_2, and VAC in (10.15)–(10.17). We get

$$\lambda_2 = \frac{(r + s + \lambda_1 + \alpha)\lambda_1}{(r + s + \lambda_1)(\rho - \lambda_1 F) + \alpha} \tag{10.18}$$

This arbitrage condition has the same qualitative properties as (9.28). An increase in α clearly shifts AA down, while the asymptote shifts to the right.

The flexible regime will prevail whenever $J_2 < J_1 - F$. Subtracting (10.15) from (10.16), we see that $J_1 - J_2 = ((1 - \rho) + \lambda_1 F)/(r + s + \lambda_1 + \alpha)$. We will therefore be in the flexible regime if and only if

$$F < \frac{1 - \rho}{r + s + \alpha}. \tag{10.19}$$

Not surprisingly, a higher value of α makes it less likely that firms will replace unskilled workers with skilled workers. The α simply acts as an additional discount factor in valuing the difference between the value of a skilled job and that of an unskilled job.

11 The Political Economy of Two-Tier Systems

For years, reforming the labor market has been advocated by economists and policymakers as a prerequisite for curing the European unemployment problem. However, despite the magnitude of the problem, reform has been slow and cautious. The present chapter tries to understand the political constraints faced by labor market reforms and to relate these constraints to the economic structure of the labor market. The central idea is simple: Given that the unemployed are a minority, political decisions are likely to reflect the interests of the employed rather than the unemployed.[1] Hence a prerequisite for a government being able to fight unemployment is that unemployment reduces the welfare of the employed to a significant extent. Therefore measures against unemployment are politically viable in certain environments, but not others. This chapter identifies and characterizes these environments.

The discussion is centered around what is perceived to be a key issue in the debate over European unemployment: labor market flexibility. If unemployment is due to legal arrangements that limit the firms' freedom of choice over employment levels and wages, then getting rid of these arrangements is problematic, since they probably benefit the employed.[2]

This chapter is based on Saint-Paul (1993).

1. This logic is the same as that of the well known insider-outsider model of wage determination (Lindbeck and Snower 1988). However, the fact that it now works through the political system rather than firm-level wage bargaining radically changes the issues and the analysis. See Burda (1990) for a dynamic voting model of wage formation at the union level.

2. Otherwise, such limitations would not exist in the first place. It is possible to write models where the employed actually lose from such limitations (see Atkeson 1993). In partial equilibrium, the employed benefit from firing costs simply because they are fired less often, and these costs are typically payments from the firm to the worker. Also they are likely to increase their bargaining power. In general equilibrium, as long as labor is not the only factor of production, there is scope for the employed to increase their welfare at the expense of firm owners, and also at the expense of the unemployed. If labor is the only

The chapter first sets up a simplified model of the labor market under firing costs that gives formal content to this hypothesis. It then shows that a natural way to avoid this problem is by setting up a two-tier system, where flexible workers coexist with rigid workers. The main findings are as follows: First, two-tier systems may indeed generate a consensus between the employed and the unemployed over greater flexibility. Second, as the stock of flexible workers gradually builds up, there is increased political support for *further* increases in labor market flexibility. Two-tier systems may thus be used as an intermediate step toward a complete reform of the labor market.[3] Third, the very recognition of that by the employed may lead to ex ante rejection of the reform. As a result the reform that is ex ante politically viable may be limited. Fourth, one way to solve this problem is to embody in the reform a *commitment device* to postpone further reforms to a sufficiently remote date. The chapter shows that such a device may be a *conversion clause*, according to which flexible workers must eventually join the rigid labor force. As we have seen in chapter 6, most determined duration contracts in Europe are associated with conversion clauses. Fifth, *complementarities* are likely to arise between the initial flexibility of the labor market and the political support to fight unemployment. This is because in a more flexible labor market the employed are more affected by unemployment, both through lower wages and higher risk of becoming unemployed.[4] In the context of two-tier systems, it is shown that this complementarity may lead to multiple equilibria in the sense that if flexibility is low to start with, no two-tier system is politically viable, so it is impossible for the government to implement its reforms. If it is high enough, it is possible to increase it and to gradually reach a more flexible outcome.

Over recent years politicoeconomic models have come back into fashion, in part due to the influential work of Alesina (1987, 1988). This literature has insisted on the possibility of political business cycles (PBC) under rational expectations, and on various forms of redistributive taxation. The present chapter takes a rather different view: Contrary to the PBC litera-

---

factor of production, it is not possible for the employed to increase their welfare at the expense of firms, since they eventually get all the surplus from the match. This, however, may not hold under imperfect competition. Furthermore, in a renovating economy with costly labor reallocation, there is still scope for the employed to increase their welfare at the expense of the unemployed by reducing the turnover rate. Firing costs are the natural way of doing so, and it is precisely the mechanism studied in this chapter.

3. This result is in the spirit of the analysis of gradual reform in Dewatripont and Roland (1992).

4. Of course this story cannot go all the way through as flexibility increases, since in the limit there is no longer unemployment.

ture, it considers the problem of persistently high, rather than cyclical, unemployment, which is of especial relevance to Europe.[5] Also the redistributive aspects in the model of this chapter are of a special kind, since income differentials come from differences in labor market status that are transitory in essence (the unemployed find jobs; the employed lose them).

11.1 A Simple Model of the Labor Market

This section sets up the basic model that we will subsequently use to analyze the political support for fighting unemployment. It is a simplified description of the labor market with particular emphasis on flows, in the line of the matching approach already discussed in chapters 2 and 9.

At each instant of time, the hiring rate h_t, defined as the flow probability of an unemployed finding a job, is given by

$$h_t = \frac{m(u_t, v_t)}{u_t} = g(\theta_t),$$

where $m(.,.)$ is the constant returns matching function, u_t the unemployment rate, v_t the vacancy rate (in terms of the labor force), $\theta = v/u$ and $g(\theta) = m(1, \theta)$. The matching function (already used in chapter 9) only plays a minor role here.

Firms are subject to idiosyncratic shocks in the following manner: With some flow probability they experience a negative shock to their product demand such that it is no longer profitable to continue to operate.[6] They may, however, be prevented from closing due to labor market regulations (firing costs). The more rigid the labor market is, the lower is the proportion of firms that will actually close when hit by a shock. In addition to that, we assume another source of match dissolution, namely voluntary quits. These happen with constant exogenous flow probability ρ. As a result the rate of job destruction is equal to the sum of the quit rate and the firing rate:

$$v_t = s(F) + \rho, \qquad s' < 0, \tag{11.1}$$

where F is the firing cost. Note that s does not depend on time.

---

5. See Hibbs (1982) for the empirical analysis of unemployment and other macroeconomic issues of the PBC theories.

6. More specifically, we assume, as in Mortensen and Pissarides (1994), that there is a flow probability η of each firm being hit by a shock. Each time a firm is hit by a shock its marginal product q is drawn from some constant distribution with c.d.f. G. Typically it is optimal for the firm to close for $q \leq q^*$. q^* depends negatively on F. The firing rate is then $s(F) = \eta G(q^*)$.

Turning now to labor demand, it is very convenient to use the following result established by Pissarides (1990) and discussed in chapter 2: Under constant returns and a fixed flow cost of vacancies, it is optimal for firms to set the vacancy rate so that θ_t is *constant* and equal to its steady-state value all along the transition path. This in effect tells us that regardless of the initial level of unemployment, the hiring rate h_t will be constant.

How does labor market regulation affect h_t? Firms set vacancies so as to equate the cost of a vacancy with its expected return. The latter is equal to the flow probability of filling the vacancy $m(u, v)/v$ times the present discounted cash flow of a filled job. This PDV is lower, the more likely it is that the firm has to keep unprofitable workers and/or pay the firing cost when its product is no longer demanded. As a result, when the labor market is more rigid, the vacancy rate drops so as to induce an increase in the probability of filling a vacancy. To restore equilibrium, this increase must be proportional to the drop in the PDV of a job. This drop must be accompanied by more slack in the labor market, so that θ and h decline as well. Therefore

$$h_t = h(F), \qquad h' < 0. \tag{11.2}$$

To keep the analysis simple, we do not go further in explicitating the dependence of h on F: We would typically have to compute how the shadow cost of labor depends on F and then compute its impact on the PDV of a job.

Eliminating F between (11.1) and (11.2) yields a positive relationship between h and s:

$$h = h(s), \qquad h' > 0. \tag{11.3}$$

Increasing labor market flexibility therefore involves a trade-off between increased firings and increased hirings. The key assumption we make about this trade-off in this chapter is that h *is concave* (i.e., $h'' < 0$). That is, the marginal impact on the hiring rate of increasing the separation rate decreases as the labor market becomes more flexible. In other words, the gains from greater flexibility are larger when the labor market is more rigid to start with.[7]

It is now possible to derive the evolution equation for employment by writing that the change in employment equals inflows minus outflows:

---

7. More generally, it is reasonable to think that h is concave at least over some range. It may not, however, be concave everywhere. In that case the results are valid in the zone where it is concave.

$$\frac{dL}{dt} = h(s) \cdot (N - L) - (s + \rho) \cdot L, \tag{11.4}$$

where L is total employment and N total labor force. Equations (11.3) and (11.4) summarize the labor demand side of the model.

To analyze the political support for various measures it is necessary to compute the utility function of the different individuals in the labor market. Let us assume that agents are risk neutral (or equivalently have access to perfect financial markets) so that the utility function of any agent at time t is

$$V_t = E_t \int_t^{+\infty} (z_u - \varepsilon\xi(F))e^{-r(u-t)}du. \tag{11.5}$$

In (11.5), r is the discount rate, z_u is income at time u, ξ is an increasing function, and ε is a very small number. The term in $\varepsilon\xi(F)$ describes the resource cost of monitoring a regulated labor market, supposedly an increasing function of firing costs. Given that ε is small, equation (11.5) defines a lexicographic order: Agents first prefer income and then flexibility. Of two outcomes, the one that yields the highest expected present discounted income is preferred. In case of a tie, the one with the lowest F is preferred. In the sequel, we will ignore the monitoring cost except when it becomes relevant.

Let $V_e(t)$ be the utility of being employed at time t and $V_u(t)$ the utility of being unemployed. Let us assume that the employed earn a wage w and the unemployed a benefit $\overline{w} < w$. Both are assumed to be constant over time. Let us also assume that voluntary quits are into retirement, which yield no income forever. To keep the labor force constant, retirements are matched by a constant inflow ρN of new entrants into the labor force. The evolution equations of $V_e(t)$ and $V_u(t)$ can then be derived from (11.5):

$$\frac{dV_e}{dt} = (r + \rho + s)V_e - sV_u - w, \tag{11.6}$$

$$\frac{dV_u}{dt} = (r + \rho + h(s))V_u - h(s)V_e - \overline{w}. \tag{11.7}$$

Eliminating explosive solutions from (11.6) and (11.7), it follows that V_e and V_u are constant over time and given by

$$V_e = \frac{(r + \rho + h(s))w + s\overline{w}}{(r + \rho)(r + \rho + s + h(s))}, \tag{11.8}$$

$$V_u = \frac{h(s)w + (r + \rho + s)\overline{w}}{(r + \rho)(r + \rho + s + h(s))}. \tag{11.9}$$

We are now in a position to evaluate the political support for labor market flexibility. Suppose that the government wants to reduce F for all existing and future labor contracts, thus increasing both s and h. Will the majority support such a scheme? To answer that question, first consider whether the employed would support it. Differentiating (11.8) with respect to s yields

$$\frac{\partial V_e}{\partial s} = \frac{(w - \overline{w})(h'(s)s - r - \rho - h(s))}{(r + \rho)(r + \rho + s + h(s))^2}. \tag{11.10}$$

Now the numerator is negative because $sh'(s) < h(s)$ due to concavity. Therefore *the employed will oppose any increase in labor market flexibility.* This is easy to understand: Given that they are presently employed, they put more weight on the increase in the firing rate than on the increase in the hiring rate, which enters their utility only through the likelihood of becoming unemployed.

Turning now to the utility of the unemployed, we find that

$$\frac{\partial V_u}{\partial s} = \frac{(w - \overline{w})((r + \rho + s)h'(s) - h(s))}{r(r + \rho + s + h(s))^2}. \tag{11.11}$$

By concavity, the numerator is strictly decreasing in s. It is positive for s close enough to zero if $h(0)/h'(0) < r + \rho$. It eventually becomes negative when s increases beyond s_u, where s_u is defined by $h(s_u)/h'(s_u) - s_u = r + \rho$.

Therefore we see from (11.11) that the unemployed are likely to support the scheme if the labor market is initially rigid enough ($s < s_u$). In that case the direct gains from higher hirings outweigh the indirect losses from higher firings. This process has limits, however, since higher initial values of s imply lower marginal gains in terms of h. Thus, past a certain level of flexibility associated with turnover s_u, the unemployed also oppose any further increase in s.

For completeness, let us also consider the impact of increased flexibility on employment. Equation (11.4) tells us that the steady-state level of employment is given by

$$L^* = \frac{Nh(s)}{\rho + s + h(s)}. \tag{11.12}$$

Differentiating (11.12) with respect to s yields:[8]

$$\frac{\partial L}{\partial s} = \frac{-N[(\rho + s)h'(s) - h(s)]}{(\rho + s + h(s))^2}.$$

(11.13)

The analysis of (11.13) is formally similar to that of (11.11). Increased flexibility will benefit employment if and only if $s \in [0, s_e]$, with $h(s_e)/h'(s_e) - s_e = \rho$. A necessary condition for this interval to be nonempty is $h(0)/h'(0) < \rho$. Note that these conditions are more stringent than those necessary for the unemployed being better off. Therefore the unemployed will support all schemes that increase employment.[9]

The main message of this section is that there likely will be a conflict of interest between the employed and the unemployed. This conflict will harm the political viability of labor market flexibility. If the government wants to increase employment through greater flexibility, then the unemployed will support that reform, but the employed are likely to oppose it. Since the employed are presumably more numerous than the unemployed, the reform will never be implemented through majority voting.[10]

11.2 Two-Tier Systems as a Political Implementation Device

From the above analysis it is not surprising that there has been no attempt by European governments to increase flexibility in the whole labor market. Rather, what governments have tried to implement are *two-tier* systems according to which existing labor contracts are unchanged but the rules of the game are changed for future new hires. A typical example of this approach is the introduction of determined duration contracts (DDC) in various European countries, which we have studied in chapter 6.[11]

---

8. Note that the economy would reach the new value of L^* only gradually after the reform is implemented.

9. Due to discounting, however, there is more weight on hirings compared to firings in their utility function than in the expression for steady-state employment. Consequently they are likely to support some schemes that reduce employment. This is because flows, not stocks, enter people's utility function.

10. Note that formally, there is a majority of employed in the initial steady state iff $h(s) > \rho + s$.

11. Alternatively, we could examine the properties of two-tier *wage* systems, which would sound more natural to an American audience. There is some evidence that flexible workers also have lower wages, but it is quite weak. Also collective agreements tend to set wages in terms of skills and seniority regardless of contract duration. Therefore differences in firing costs seem more relevant to the European case than differences in wages. Anyway, the analysis of two-tier wage system would probably not be very different.

The rest of the chapter is devoted to the political analysis of such two-tier systems. We will consider the reform strategy of a government whose goal is to increase labor market flexibility (reducing F). The government faces a political constraint in that any reform must be preferred to the status quo by majority voting. We will not consider the reasons why a mandated government might have this priority rather than others;[12] nor will we consider all the possible alternative reforms or associated timings. In other words, no attempt will be made to characterize a dynamic voting equilibrium, the existence of which we know is problematic.[13] Rather, we will confine ourselves to simple strategies and discuss their viability and time consistency.

Let us first consider the impact of a once-and-for-all introduction of more flexible contracts. We will see that there is *consensus* over this reform: Both the employed and the unemployed will either support it or reject it. We will then deal with the support-building aspect of the two-tier system and the time consistency problem attached to it. It is shown that this problem puts limits over the extent of the reforms that can be achieved ex ante. Last, we will analyze the implications of one type of such limitation, namely *conversion clauses* that specify that temporary contracts can be renewed a limited number of times so that a given hire must be eventually converted into a permanent contract.

11.3 The Consensus Role of Two-Tier Systems

Suppose that at time $t = 0$, the government proposes the following reform: It is now allowed to sign new labor contracts that have a lower firing cost $F' < F$, while the terms of existing labor contracts are unaffected. This creates a two-tier system where workers performing the same tasks will have different employment security. As a result the separation rate for workers with flexible contracts becomes $s' > s$, while the separation rate for workers with rigid contracts stays equal to s.[14] For simplicity, we will

---

12. An important issue is why the same democracies that increased firing costs in the 1970s eventually changed their mind and wanted to reduce them in the 1980s, thus implementing two-tier systems. This is clearly compatible wi-th the model, since both a reduction in s in a one-tier system and an increase in s for flexible workers in a two-tier system are favored by the employed. However, the model offers no clue with respect to the particular timing of these reforms. A complex set of factors, including increased foreign competition and changes in popular attitudes toward unions, is probably at work.

13. For example, see Piketty (1992).

14. As in Mortensen and Pissarides (1994), we are assuming here that shocks are specific to each job/worker pair. Therefore, given constant returns, the introduction of flexible labor contracts does not affect the shadow marginal cost of labor for rigid labor contracts, nor does it affect the marginal product of labor for these matches.

assume that the new type of contract has no effect on the wage, which stays equal to w.

Flexible contracts have a lower shadow marginal cost of labor. As a result all new vacancies will be on this type of contracts.[15] Old contracts will progressively disappear at rate $\rho + s$ as quits or firings occur. The new hiring rate is exactly equal to the one associated with flexible contracts:[16]

$$h' = h(s').$$ (11.14)

Again, both θ and h are equal to their steady-state values from the onset. As a result at any time $t \geq 0$ the utility of an unemployed is determined by

$$V_u' = \frac{h(s')w + (r + \rho + s')\overline{w}}{(r + \rho)(r + \rho + s' + h(s'))}.$$ (11.15)

By the same token, the utility of a worker holding a flexible contract is

$$V_{ef}' = \frac{(r + \rho + h(s'))w + s'\overline{w}}{(r + \rho)(r + \rho + s' + h(s'))}.$$ (11.16)

Now for the reform to be passed at time $t = 0$, it has to increase the utility of the employed, who all hold rigid contracts at that time. After $t = 0$, the utility associated with holding a rigid contract evolves according to

$$\frac{dV_{er}'}{dt} = (r + \rho + s)V_{er}' - sV_u' - w.$$ (11.17)

The only difference between (11.17) and (11.6) is that V_u' appears instead of V_u: The holders of rigid contracts now recognize that if they become unemployed their next job will be on a flexible contract. By contrast, s is the same in (11.17) and (11.6). Contrary to the one-tier reform

---

15. Contrary to chapter 4, we now have constant returns firms with only one worker, so there is no scope for both types of contracts coexisting. Rigid contracts are still used only because they cannot be converted into flexible ones.

16. The stock of old contracts does not affect the marginal value of new vacancies, nor does it affect the nature of the input in the matching function. (Since those who hold rigid contracts would be worse off with a flexible one, they will not look for a job. Hence only the unemployed look for a job.) At any time t the stock of remaining rigid contracts affects the total stock of unemployed looking for jobs. But the great beauty of this model is that although the stock of unemployed is a state variable, under constant returns it does not affect *flow rates*. This is because only labor market *tightness* $\theta_t = v_t/u_t$ enters in the firm's value function (see chapter 2). Since v_t is non-predetermined if v_t is the saddle-path value associated with u_t, then λv_t is the value associated with λu_t. Hence the irrelevance of state variables for flow rates and value functions. As a result all flow rates are determined by their steady state value under F' from $t = 0$ on.

considered in the previous section, the firing rate is unaffected for those hired before $t = 0$.

Given that V_u' is constant from $t = 0$ on, elimination of explosive solutions from (11.17) yields

$$V_{er}' = \frac{w + sV_u'}{r + \rho + s} = \text{Constant} = V^\infty. \tag{11.18}$$

The consensus virtues of two-tier systems are now apparent from (11.18). Since $V_e = (w + sV_u)/(r + \rho + s)$, $V_{er}' > V_e$ if and only if $V_u' > V_u$. Therefore there will be *unanimity* among labor market participants over the reform. From the previous section's analysis we can conclude that if $s < s_u$ there exists a range of values of $s' > s$ such that the two-tier system will pass majority voting. This range is given by the interval $[s, \bar{s}(s)]$, where $\bar{s} > s_u$ is the maximum value of s' such that $V_u' \geq V_u$. Confronting (11.15) and (11.9), it is apparent that $\bar{s}$ is solution to

$$\frac{h(\bar{s})}{r + \rho + \bar{s}} = \frac{h(s)}{r + \rho + s}. \tag{11.19}$$

Hence $\bar{s}$ is decreasing in s and crosses the 45-degree line at $s = s_u$.

The intuition behind the consensus result is simple: The employed enjoy the best of both worlds, since they benefit from the high job protection associated with the old contracts and know that if they become unemployed, they will gain from the higher probability of finding a job associated with the new contracts.

11.4   Two-Tier Contracts as a Support-Building Device and the Associated Time-Consistency Problem

In the preceding section we neglected an important aspect of the two-tier system. As time passes, the stock of rigid contracts gradually erodes. After some date t^* those who hold rigid contracts will no longer be a majority in the labor force. At that date the government will have built a political support—essentially a coalition of unemployed and flexible workers—for further reforms toward more flexibility. For example, a majority is now in favor of converting all existing rigid contracts into flexible ones. This is because this reform does not affect the expected PDV of income streams of the unemployed, and those workers on flexible contracts, but reduces enforcement costs as represented by the term in $\varepsilon\xi(F)$ in (11.5).[17] There-

---

17. It is assumed that the F entering this term is the *average* in the economy. Therefore getting rid of permanent contracts will lower it.

fore at t^* the government will have exactly implemented the reform that was deemed impossible in the previous section: The conversion of *all* contracts into more flexible ones with lower firing costs. This is because the two-tier system, by making the reform *more gradual*, creates a *transitional phase* during which the political support in favor of flexibility is progressively built up.

Given that the government's objective is to increase labor market flexibility, we assume that it will indeed propose this reform as of t^*. The problem is now that *the mere recognition of that incentive by holders of rigid contracts may lead them to oppose the reform ex ante*. In other words the solution derived in the previous section is time-inconsistent.

The question is therefore the following: Suppose that at $t = 0$ the employed fully anticipate that at some future date t^* they will be a minority and that their privileges will be eliminated. Under what conditions will they nevertheless support the two-tier system at $t = 0$?

This question can be answered using the model. Those employed at $t = 0$ are likely to lose from the reform after $t = t^*$ and to benefit from it between 0 and t^*. For the scheme to be politically viable, the benefits must outweigh the costs. The benefits will be larger, the larger t^* (the slower the transition), the higher s (the more the employed are exposed to unemployment), and the higher $V'_u - V_u$ (the higher the gain to the unemployed generated by larger job creation). Since a higher s is itself associated with a lower t^*, and, past a certain level, a lower $V'_u - V_u$, the reform will be viable for *intermediate* values of s.

Let us now consider these issues from a more formal point of view. Suppose that flexible contracts are introduced at $t = 0$. First, consider the pace at which the stock of rigid contracts will go down. If L_{rt} is the number of employees with rigid contracts at some $t > 0$, then

$$\frac{dL_{rt}}{dt} = -(\rho + s)L_{rt}. \tag{11.20}$$

Equation (11.20) tells us that since no new rigid contracts are signed, the stock of rigid contracts goes down at a rate equal to the corresponding separation rate. Assuming the economy is in steady state before $t = 0$, according to (11.12) we must have $L_{r0} = Nh(s)/(\rho + s + h(s))$. Therefore, from (11.20),

$$L_{rt} = \frac{Nh(s)}{\rho + s + h(s)} e^{-(\rho+s)t}. \tag{11.21}$$

The critical time t^* is the one after which rigid employees are a minority (i.e., $L_{rt}^* = N/2$). From (11.21) we then have

$$t^* = \frac{\log 2 + \log h(s) - \log(\rho + s + h(s))}{\rho + s}. \tag{11.22}$$

Controlling for initial employment (i.e., the numerator of equation 11.22), a higher s implies a lower value of t^*. The transition is more rapid when the labor market is more flexible initially.

Let us now turn to the computation of the employed's initial utility. At t^* all contracts are converted into flexible ones. The corresponding utility of being employed is therefore $V_e' = V_{ef}'$ as defined by (11.16). This defines the terminal condition for equation (11.17):

$$V_{er}'(t^*) = V_{ef}'. \tag{11.23}$$

Integrating (11.17), we can then simply compute V_{er}' for any time $0 \leq t \leq t^*$:

$$V_{er}'(t) = V_{ef}' e^{-(r+\rho+s)(t^*-t)} + V^\infty (1 - e^{-(r+\rho+s)(t^*-t)}), \tag{11.24}$$

where V^∞ is defined in (11.18) and is the value of holding a rigid contract in a two-tier world where complete reform never occurs. Equation (11.24) must be substituted for (11.18) when complete reform occurs at t^*. It is easy to interpret: The value of holding a rigid job is a weighted average of the value of holding a flexible job and the value V^∞ of a rigid contract in a world where complete reform never occurs. The weight on V^∞ is larger, the longer the time to elapse before complete reform.

When will the two-tier system pass majority voting at $t = 0$? We know from section 11.3, that $V_e > V_{ef}'$, and from section 11.4, that $V^\infty > V_e$. Therefore the inequality $V_{er}'(0) > V_e$ is likely to be satisfied if the weight on V^∞ is large (t^* is large) or if $(V^\infty - V_e)$ is large compared to $(V_e - V_{ef}')$.

Formally, the condition that $V_{er}'(0) > V_e$ can be written

$$V_{ef}' e^{-(r+\rho+s)t^*} + \frac{w + sV_u'}{r + \rho + s}(1 - e^{-(r+\rho+s)t^*}) > V_e, \tag{11.25}$$

where V_e, V_{ef}', and V_u' are defined by (11.8), (11.16), and (11.15), respectively. Note that (11.25) ceases to be satisfied when s goes to 0, since when $s = 0$, $V^\infty = V_e$. Similarly, when s becomes large, (11.25) is not satisfied, since the weight on V^∞ becomes equal to zero as t^* goes to zero.

Substituting (11.8), (11.15), and (11.16) into (11.25), it is possible to obtain (after some computations) the *political viability condition*:

$$\frac{s[(r + \rho + s)h(s') - (r + \rho + s')h(s)]}{s' - s}$$

$$> (r + \rho)(r + \rho + s + h(s))e^{-(r+\rho+s)t^*}. \tag{11.26}$$

Equation (11.26) defines, for a given initial s, a range of values of s' that are politically implementable as a two-tier system at $t = 0$. This equation has a number of interesting properties:

PROPERTY 11.1   The left-hand side of (11.26) is decreasing in s'.

Proof   Compute the derivative and use the concavity of $h(.)$.   ∎

Given that s' does not intervene in the right-hand side of (11.26), property 11.1 implies that for each value of s there will be a maximum level of flexibility, associated with some $s' = \tilde{s}(s)$, which is politically implementable as a two-tier system.

PROPERTY 11.2 $\tilde{s}(s) < \bar{s}(s)$.

Proof   At $s' = \bar{s}(s)$ the left-hand side of (26) is equal to zero, due to (11.19). Therefore (11.26) cannot hold.   ∎

Property 11.2 tells us that the amount of flexibility that can be implemented is lower when the employed recognize that there will be further reforms at $t = t^*$. Therefore *the cost of the time-consistency problem is that it reduces the amount of flexibility that the government can implement through a two-tier system.*

Figure 11.1 illustrates the basic intuition behind property 11.2 by plotting the gain to rigid workers generated by the reform $((V^{\infty} - V_e)$ $(1 - \exp(-(r + \rho + s)t^*))$ and the losses $((V_e - V'_{ef}) \exp(-(r + \rho + s)t^*))$, as a function of s', the new level of flexibility. Since the losses come from higher firings and the gains from higher hirings, the concavity of h essentially implies that when s' rises the losses rise faster than the gains and eventually outweigh them. In the case of the previous section $(t^* = +\infty)$, the loss is zero. As t^* decreases, the maximum $\tilde{s}$ goes down, since the loss curve shifts upward and the gain curve downward.

PROPERTY 11.3   There exists some $s^+ < s_u$ such that no two-tier system with $s' > s$ is politically implementable if $s > s^+$.

Proof   This is a corollary of property 11.2 and of the fact that $\tilde{s}(s_u) = s_u$.   ∎

Property 11.3 is essentially another aspect of the limits to reform imposed by the time-consistency problem.

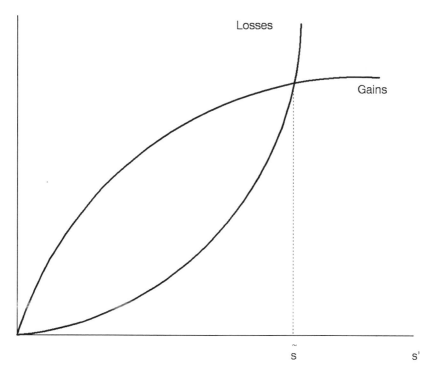

Figure 11.1
Gains and losses from flexibility to the employed

PROPERTY 11.4   There exists some value of initial flexibility s, denoted s^-, such that no two-tier system with $s' > s$ is politically viable if s is below s^-.

Proof   First, note that the right-hand side of (11.26) is bounded away from zero when s varies between 0 and some finite value. Second, note that the differentiability of $h(s)$ implies that the left-hand side is well defined at $s' = s$ and equal to $s((r + \rho + s)h'(s) - h(s))$. This can be made arbitrarily small as s goes to 0.   ∎

The intuition behind property 11.4 is that when the labor market is quite rigid to start with, the employed are so protected against unemployment that it is impossible to compensate them for the collapse of rigid contracts at $t = t^*$: The increase in the unemployed's utility generated by the two-tier system has only a very small effect on the employed's utility, since they heavily discount the possibility of being unemployed.

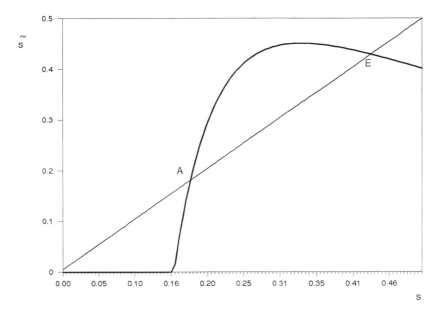

Figure 11.2
Maximum feasible reform as a function of initial flexibility, under a two-tier system

Consequently, *if the labor market is initially very rigid, the economy may be stuck at a "bad" equilibrium such that no reform is politically viable.* This phenomenon is also due to the time-consistency problem; If the government could commit on the value of t^*, the right-hand side of (11.26) could be made arbitrarily small in order to implement any reform such that $s' \leq \bar{s}(s)$. In that case we are essentially back to the analysis of the previous subsection.

To say more about the viability condition, it is necessary to specialize the assumptions about h. Figure 11.2 plots the numerical values of the $\bar{s}$ function associated with the following quadratic hiring function:[18]

$$h(s) = 0.1 + 5s - 0.1s^2.$$

The coefficients of h imply, for realistic firing rates, hiring rates of the same order of magnitude as observed in reality (see chapter 8).[19] For a two-tier system to be viable, the initial firing rate must be between 0.18 and 0.43. These restrictions illustrate the magnitude of the time-

---

18. In the quadratic case $\bar{s}$ has a closed-form solution.
19. Figure 11.2 was simulated with $\rho = 0.05$, $r = 0.05$. Note that neither $\bar{w}$ nor w enter in (11.26).

consistency problem: In the absence of this problem the corresponding interval is $[0, s_u]$. The value of s_u associated with this set of parameters is 2.

The above analysis is consistent with the real world observation that at the time temporary contracts are implemented, they are subject to various forms of limitations on applicability, renewal, firm size, or worker types. These clauses are equivalent, in terms of the above analysis, to reducing s'. They reflect the limits that ex ante recognition of future reforms puts on current reforms.

11.5   The Political Analysis of Conversion Clauses

One such limit that has been used in practice and can be analyzed with the present model is a conversion clause (CC), which, as was noted earlier, specifies that a temporary contract can be renewed, though only a limited amount of times. A temporary hire must therefore be eventually converted into a permanent one. Such a clause has obvious problems of enforcement, since there is an incentive to fire a temporary worker at the time his contract has to be converted, to replace him with a newly hired worker. We will nevertheless abstract from this issue in the sequel. The main questions we are interested in are the following: How do conversion clauses affect the dynamics of support for further reforms after the system is implemented, and do they increase the range of reforms that are ex ante politically viable?

CCs can be formally added to the model by assuming that there is a constant flow probability μ per unit of time that a temporary contract be turned into a permanent one. At $\mu = 0$, there is no conversion clause, so we are back to the previous section. At $\mu = +\infty$ conversion is instantaneous, and this is equivalent to no reform at all.

CCs modify the above analysis in several respects, all of them have important political implications. But, first, we should note that conversions increase the shadow cost of labor, so the hiring rate h is now

$$h_t = \hat{h}(s, s', \mu), \tag{11.27}$$

where s is the firing rate associated with rigid contracts and $s' > s$ the firing rate associated with flexible ones. In (11.27) we have $h_1' > 0$, $h_2' > 0$, and $h_3' < 0$, with $\hat{h}(s, s', 0) = h(s')$ and $\hat{h}(s, s', +\infty) = h(s)$. A convenient specification for $\hat{h}$ is the weighted average one:

$$\hat{h}(s, s', \mu) = \frac{\mu h(s) + \lambda h(s')}{\mu + \lambda}, \tag{11.28}$$

where λ is a constant. This we will use below. Let us now turn to the main effects of CCs.

First, the stock of employees in rigid contracts goes down more slowly under CCs and no longer goes asymptotically to zero, since there is a continuous inflow of new rigid contracts due to conversions. Specifically the joint dynamics of the stock of permanent employees L_r and of temporary employees L_f are now given by

$$\frac{dL_r}{dt} = -(\rho + s)L_r + \mu L_f,$$ (11.29)

$$\frac{dL_f}{dt} = \hat{h}(N - (L_f + L_r)) - (\mu + \rho + s')L_f.$$ (11.30)

Obviously the higher that μ is, the more slowly will L_r decline and the higher will be its asymptotical value. A necessary condition for the government to be able to implement the transition toward a fully flexible labor market is that rigid workers become a minority after some critical time t^*. Therefore, as long as rigid workers are a majority initially, there exists a maximum value of μ beyond which the holders of rigid contracts actually never become a minority. This value is the one such that the long-run level of L_r is just equal to $N/2$. According to (11.29) and (11.30), this long-run level is given by

$$\bar{L}_r = \frac{\mu \hat{h} N}{(\mu + \rho + s)\hat{h} + (\rho + s)(\mu + \rho + s)}.$$ (11.31)

The maximum value of μ for rigid workers to eventually lose their majority is therefore the one that satisfies $\bar{L}_R = 1/2$, which is equivalent to

$$\mu = \frac{(s + s' + \hat{h}(s, s', \mu))(s + \rho)}{\hat{h}(s, s', \mu) - \rho - s} = \mu_{\mathrm{maj}}(s, s').$$ (11.32)

Second, the incentives for holders of flexible contracts to support a suppression of rigid contracts at $t = t^*$ are quite different from the previous case. In the preceding subsection holders of flexible labor contracts were essentially indifferent about it, since it affected neither their hiring rate nor their firing rate; the only reason why they supported it was that it lowered the infinitesimal monitoring cost $\varepsilon\xi(F)$. Now the story is different: The suppression of rigid contracts is associated with both gains and losses for the holders of flexible contracts. The losses come from the fact that due to the conversion clause, flexible workers have a vested interest in maintaining rigid contracts, since they expect to get one at some point in the future. The gains come from the fact that getting rid of permanent contracts implies a de facto suppression of the conversion clause (μ becomes equal to 0), so the shadow marginal cost of labor goes down, which increases the hiring rate from $\hat{h}$ to $h(s')$. Therefore it is not obvious at all that the government will be able to pass its reform after t^*.

More formally, flexible workers will support total reform at t^* if it gives them a higher utility than the status quo. This utility is the one obtained by a worker if there are only flexible contracts. It has already been computed and is given by

$$V'_{ef} = \frac{(r + \rho + h(s'))w + s'\overline{w}}{(r + \rho)(r + \rho + s' + h(s'))}. \tag{11.16}$$

Let $\hat{V}_u(t)$, $\hat{V}_{ef}(t)$, and $\hat{V}_{er}(t)$ be the utility at time t of an unemployed, a flexible worker, and a rigid worker, respectively. The evolution equations of these three variables are

$$0 = w - (r + \rho + s)\hat{V}_{er}(t) + s\hat{V}_u(t) + \frac{d\hat{V}_{er}}{dt}, \tag{11.33}$$

$$0 = w - (r + \rho + s' + \mu)\hat{V}_{ef}(t) + s'\hat{V}_u(t) + \mu\hat{V}_{er}(t) + \frac{d\hat{V}_{ef}}{dt}, \tag{11.34}$$

$$0 = \overline{w} - (r + \rho + \hat{h})V_u(t) + \hat{h}V_{ef}(t) + \frac{d\hat{V}_u}{dt}. \tag{11.35}$$

If at t^* flexible workers do not support the conversion of rigid contracts, nothing changes at that date, and $\hat{V}_{ef}$, $\hat{V}_{er}$, and $\hat{V}_u$ must be equal to their steady state values from $t = 0$ on.[20] From (11.33)–(11.35) it is possible to compute the steady-state value of $\hat{V}_{ef}$:

$$\hat{V}_{ef}(t) = \frac{w(r + \rho + s + \mu)(r + \rho + \hat{h}) + \overline{w}(s'(r + \rho + s) + s\mu)}{(r + \rho + s)(r + \rho + s' + \mu) + \hat{h}(r + \rho + s + \mu)}. \tag{11.36}$$

Flexible workers will support total reform at t^* if $\hat{V}_{ef} \leq V'_{ef}$. After some computations using (11.16) and (11.36), we see that this is equivalent to

$$s'(h(s') - \hat{h})(r + \rho + s) + \mu[s(r + \rho + h(s')) - s'(r + \rho + \hat{h})] \geq 0 \tag{11.37}$$

---

20. The system (11.33)–(11.35) is clearly unstable.

Plugging (11.28) into (11.37), the condition can be rewritten:

$$\mu \leq \frac{(r + \rho + s)(h(s') - h(s)) - \lambda(r + \rho + h(s'))(s' - s)}{s'h(s) - sh(s') + (r + \rho)(s' - s)} = \mu_{\text{sup}}(s, s').$$

(11.38)

The implications of (11.38) are as follows. First, there exists a maximum level of the conversion clause $\mu_{\text{sup}}(s, s')$ beyond which flexible workers will prefer the status quo at t^*, in which case the transition toward full flexibility does not occur. This is easy to understand: At a high value of μ, the likelihood to get a permanent contract is high, so the losses from suppressing them are large. Second, the numerator of (11.38) may be negative, in which case there will never be scope for total reform regardless of the conversion clause. This happens, for instance, when λ is large; in that case $\hat{h}$ is close to $h(s')$, so total reform generates little gains in terms of additional hirings.

The third implication of CCs is that given that μ slows the transition (assuming that it occurs, i.e., $\mu \leq \min(\mu_{\text{maj}}, \mu_{\text{sup}})$), a higher μ alleviates the time consistency problem analyzed in the previous section: The critical time t^* at which rigid employees become a minority is more remote. They therefore reap the gains of flexible contracts over a longer time. A higher μ is then likely to increase the range of reforms that are implementable ex ante. The cost of it obviously is a loss of flexibility in one dimension. In principle, it is possible to compute, for any (μ, s, s'), whether the two-tier system is politically viable at $t = 0$ if total reform occurs at $t = t^*$. For this we have first to compute t^*, using (11.29) and (11.30), and then to integrate the system (11.33)–(11.35) to get the initial value $\hat{V}_{er}(0)$, given the terminal conditions at $t = t^*$.[21]

Since this is analytically tedious, we will use numerical computations. The main results from these simulations is that for any (s, s'), a two-tier reform with conversion clause is politically viable at $t = 0$ provided that μ is larger than some threshold $\mu_{\text{min}}(s, s')$. This confirms the intuition that CCs act as a commitment device to postpone the shift toward further reform; the higher the μ is, the more viable are reforms ex ante. μ_{min} may be equal to 0 if, as in the previous subsection, the reform is ex ante viable without CC.

To summarize, under CCs the political viability of the sequence of reforms considered here is subject to three constraints: ex ante acceptance of the two-tier system by the employed, reduction of rigid workers to a minority in finite time, and support of total reform by flexible workers.

---

21. These terminal conditions are given by $\hat{V}_u(t^*) = V'_u$, $\hat{V}_{er}(t^*) = \hat{V}_{ef}(t^*) = V'_{ef}$.

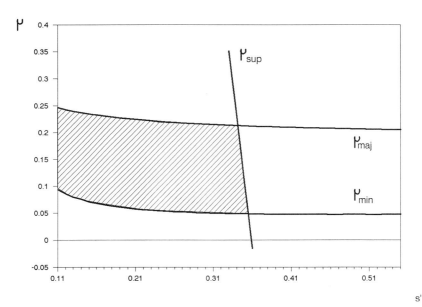

Figure 11.3
Politically viable reforms under a conversion clause ($s = 0.1$)

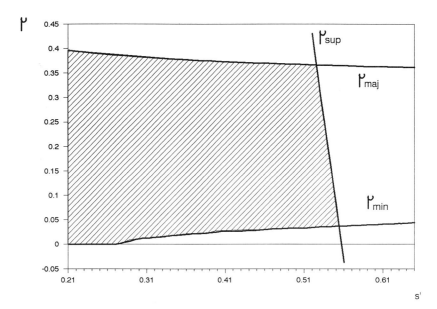

Figure 11.4
Politically viable reforms under a conversion clause ($s = 0.2$)

These three constraints are, respectively, represented by $\mu \geq \mu_{min}$, $\mu \leq \mu_{maj}$, and $\mu \leq \mu_{sup}$.

To get a firmer grasp on these constraints, figures 11.3 and 11.4 plot the three constraints as a function of the reform firing rate s' for two values of the initial firing rate s: $s = 0.1$ and $s = 0.2$. λ was chosen equal to 0.4, while all other parameters are the same as in figure 11.2.

At $s = 0.1$, μ_{min} is always strictly positive, so no reform is implementable without CCs. μ_{min} is, however, very small, so only a very limited conversion clause makes reform possible. Also μ_{min} is decreasing, suggesting that large increases in flexibility are more viable than small ones, at least over some range. Moreover μ_{maj} is smoothly decreasing with s', while μ_{sup} is steeply decreasing with s'. The set of viable reforms in the (s', μ) plane is given by the shaded area in figure 11.3. At $s = 0.2$, μ_{min} is initially equal to zero. As s' increases, μ_{min} becomes increasing contrary to the previous case. The shapes of μ_{maj} and μ_{sup} are qualitatively similar to the previous case. The set of viable reforms is again given by the shaded area in figure 11.4.

11.6   Empirical Evidence on the Political Aspects of Labor Market Flexibility

In Saint-Paul (1993), I have brought together some pieces of empirical evidence on the political support for labor market policies.

Various pieces of evidence corroborate the view that there will be more support for fighting unemployment when the employed are more exposed to it. First, in a pooling of election results for twenty-two OECD countries, the *level* of unemployment is not significantly positively correlated with the likelihood of the government's losing the election. By contrast, the *change* in unemployment is strongly positively correlated with that event. Clearly the employed's probability of losing one's job is much more correlated with the change than with the level.

Other dimensions of exposure are correlated with concern about fighting unemployment. For example, there is crosscountry evidence that active labor market policies are more likely to be adopted when real wages are more responsive to unemployment.

My study of the Spanish experience of two-tier reform, already discussed in previous chapters, from a political perspective, is broadly consistent with the above analysis in the following senses.[22] First, reform came

---

22. See Saint-Paul (1993), for details.

at relatively favorable times of very high unemployment and large re-allocative shocks, that is, both a larger rate of job destruction and job creation. Large job destruction meant that the employed were relatively exposed, while large job creation meant that there was a potential for flexible jobs to have large effects on employment. Second, labor unions were fully aware that flexible labor contracts would gradually undermine their support. This is why they managed to impose a conversion clause according to which a flexible contracts could only be renewed up to three years. They also insisted that their agreement over the reform was only temporary and that the reform will have to be removed in the future. Third, as the number of employees under flexible contracts grew, there was renewed political pressure in 1993 to further increase labor market flexibility with respect to existing rigid contracts. As a compensation for that, however, the government proposed that the flexible contracts be made more rigid.

11.7 Conclusion

Let us conclude with a summary of the main findings of this chapter.

Two-tier systems allow us to eventually increase the flexibility of the whole labor market by creating a transition phase during which the political support for further reforms gradually builds up as flexible workers become more numerous. The fact that this is ex ante recognized by the employed at the time they vote on the system creates a time-consistency problem, and it puts limits on the flexibility of new contracts. These limits are more stringent when the labor market is very rigid initially, since in this case the employed are so protected that they benefit very little from the introduction of flexible contracts.

One commitment device to solve the inconsistency problem is to have a conversion clause that slows down the erosion of rigid labor after the system is introduced. Some reforms that are rejected by the majority without a conversion clause can be accepted with a strong enough conversion clause. Flexible workers may reject extension of their contracts to the whole labor force because they have a vested interest in maintaining rigid contracts due to the conversion clause. As a result, for complete reform to be implemented in finite time, the conversion rate must not be too large.

The analysis of this chapter has focused on a peculiar type of policy measure, namely an increase in labor market flexibility through a reduction in firing costs. It has, however, pointed out to a principle that is more general: that in a world when the employed are a majority, there will be more political support for fighting unemployment when the employed are more vulnerable to it.[23] This in turn is likely to generate *complementarities* between the economic sphere and the political sphere. The more flexible the labor market, the more the employed are exposed to unemployment, and the greater is the political support to fight it.

Complementarities naturally arise in the analysis of two-tier systems as shown in figure 11.2. At least over some range, the maximum level of flexibility which is politically implementable is an increasing function of the initial level of flexibility. As a result, if the economy starts on the left of point *A*, it will be stuck at a low equilibrium where the very malfunctioning of the labor market makes any attempt to reform it politically unviable. By contrast, if the economy starts with a flexible enough labor market, it could eventually reach—through gradual two-tier reforms—an equilibrium like *E* where the market is more flexible and unemployment possibly lower.

The same principles can be applied to other types of measures, such as active labor market policies or direct employment subsidies; their support will be higher when the employed are more exposed to unemployment. They also can be applied to notions of "exposure" different from turnover, such as the effect of unemployment on the employed's wages through underbidding or discipline effects. As already mentioned above, there is some evidence that such complementarities do exist.

Last, note that the chapter has essentially analyzed the implications of conflicts of interests between the employed and unemployed. Such conflicts may or may not occur depending on the effects of reform. For example, we have seen in chapter 7 that the introduction of flexible contracts may lower the utility of both the employed and the unemployed because of its feedback on wage formation. Obviously, in that case, it would have very little political support.

---

23. For the application of such an argument to the political economy of unemployment insurance, see Wright (1986).

References

Abraham, K. 1988. Flexible staffing arrangements and employer's short-term adjustment strategies. In R. A. Hart, ed., *Employment, Unemployment and Labor Utilization*. Boston: Unwin Hyman, pp. 288–311.

Abraham, K., and L. Katz. 1986. Cyclical unemployment: Sectoral shifts or aggregate disturbances? *Journal of Political Economy* 94:507–22.

Acemoglu, D. 1993. Labor market imperfections, innovation incentives and the dynamics of innovation activity. Mimeo. Department of Economics, MIT.

Agell, J., and Lommerund, K. 1993. Egalitarian wage policies and long-run growth. *Scandinavian Journal of Economics* 95:559–80.

Aghion, P., and P. Howitt. 1992. A model of growth through creative destruction. *Econometrica* 60:323–51.

Aghion, P., and P. Howitt. 1994. Growth and unemployment. *Review of Economic Studies* 61:477–94.

Akerlof, G. 1982. Labor contracts as partial gift exchange. *Quarterly Journal of Economics* 97:543–69.

Akerlof, G., and J. Yellen. 1987. *Efficiency Wage Models of the Labor Market*. Cambridge: Cambridge University Press.

Akerlof, G., and J. Yellen. 1990. The fair-wage effort hypothesis and unemployment. *Quarterly Journal of Economics* 105:255–83.

Akerlof, G., and L. Katz. 1989. Worker's trust funds and the logic of wage profiles. *Quarterly Journal of Economics* 104:525–36.

Alba-Ramirez, A., and R. B. Freeman. 1990. Job finding and wages when long-run unemployment is really long: The case of Spain. NBER Working paper 3409. August.

Albrecht, J., and S. Vroman. 1992. Dual labor markets, efficiency wages and search. *Journal of Labor Economics* 10:438–61.

Alesina, A. 1987. Macroeconomic policy in a two-party system as a repeated game. *Quarterly Journal of Economics* 102:651–78.

Alesina, A. 1988. Macroeconomics and politics. *NBER Macroeconomics Annual*.

Alesina, A., and D. Rodrik. 1994. Distributive politics and long-run growth. *Quarterly Journal of Economics* 109:465–90.

Alogoskoufis, G., and A. Manning. 1988. On the persistence of unemployment. *Economic Policy* 7:427–69.

Alogoskoufis, G., C. Bean, G. Bertola, D. Cohen, J. Dolado, and G. Saint-Paul. 1995. *Unemployment: Choices for Europe*. London: CEPR.

Arai, M. 1994. An empirical analysis of wage dispersion and efficiency wages. *Scandinavian Journal of Economics* 96:31–50.

Atkeson, A. 1993. Comment on: On the Political Economy of Labor Market Flexibility. *NBER Macroeconomics Annual.*

Bean, C. R. 1994. European unemployment: A survey. *Journal of Economic Literature* 32:573–619.

Bentolila, S., and O. Blanchard. 1990. Spanish unemployment. *Economic Policy* 10:233–81.

Bentolila, S., and G. Bertola. 1990. Firing costs and labor demand: How bad is Eurosclerosis. *Review of Economic Studies* 57:191, 381–402.

Bentolila, S., and J. Dolado. 1992. Who are the insiders? Wage-setting and temporary contracts in Spanish manufacturing. Mimeo. Madrid: CEMFI.

Bentolila, S., and G. Saint-Paul. 1992. The macroeconomic impact of flexible labor contracts, with an application to Spain. *European Economic Review* 36:1013–53.

Bentolila, S., and G. Saint-Paul. 1994. A model of labor demand with linear adjustment costs. *Labour Economics* 1:303–26.

Berger, S., and M. Piore. 1980. *Dualism and discontinuity in Industrial society*. Cambridge: Cambridge University Press.

Bernanke, B. 1983. Irreversibility, uncertainty, and cyclical investment. *Quarterly Journal of Economics* 98:85–106.

Bertola, G. 1990. Job security, employment and wages. *European Economic Review* 34:851–86.

Bertola, G. 1991. Flexibility, investment, and growth. Mimeo. Princeton University.

Blackburn, M., and D. Neumark. 1992. Unobserved ability, efficiency wages and inter-industry wage differentials. *Quarterly Journal of Economics* 107:1421–36.

Blackwell, D. 1965. Discounted dynamic programming. *Annals of Statistics* 36:226–35.

Blanchard, O., and P. Diamond. 1989. The Beveridge curve. *Brookings Papers on Economic Activity* 1:1–76.

Blanchard, O., and P. Diamond. 1990. The cyclical behavior of labor markets flows in the U.S. *Brookings papers on Economic Activity* 2:85–155.

Blanchard, O., and P. Diamond. 1994. Ranking, unemployment duration, and wages. *Review of Economic Studies* 61:208, 417–34.

Blanchard, O., and L. Summers. 1986. Hysteresis and the European unemployment problem. *NBER Macroeconomics Annual.*

Bound, J., and G. Johnson. 1992. Changes in the structure of wages during the 1980s. An evaluation of alternative explanations. *American Economic Review* 82:371–92.

Brunello, G. 1993. Equilibrium unemployment with Internal labor markets. Mimeo. University of Venice. February.

Bulow, J., and L. Summers. 1986. A theory of dual labor markets with application to industrial policy, discrimination and Keynesian unemployment. *Journal of Labor Economics* 4:1, 376–414.

Burda, M. 1990. Membership, seniority and wage-setting in democratic labor unions. *Economica* 57:228, 455–66.

Burda, M. 1992. A note on employment determination in the presence of firing benefits. *Scandinavian Journal of Economics.*

Burda, M., and C. Wyplosz. 1994. Gross labor market flows in Europe: Some stylized facts. *European Economic Review* 38:1287–1325.

Caballero, R., and M. Hammour. 1994. On the timing and efficiency of creative destruction. Mimeo. MIT, *Quarterly Journal of Economics*, forthcoming.

Cain, G. 1976. The challenge of segmented labor market theories to orthodox theory: A survey. *Journal of Economic Literature* 14:1215–58.

Calmfors, L. Active labour market policy and unemployment—A framework for the analysis of crucial design features. Mimeo. Institute for International Economic Studies, Stockholm, 1993.

Calvo, G., and S. Wellisz. 1979. Hierarchy, ability and income distribution. *Journal of Political Economy* 87:991–1010.

Campbell, C. M., III. 1993. Do firms pay efficiency wages? Evidence with data at the firm level. *Journal of Labor Economics* 11:442–70.

Campbell, C. M., III. 1991. Tests of efficiency wage theories and contract theory with disaggregated data from the U.S. *Weltwirtschaftliches Archiv* 127:98–118.

Capelli, P., and K. Chauvin. 1991. An interplant test of the efficiency wage hypothesis. *Quarterly Journal of Economics* 106:769–88.

Card, D., and A. Krueger. 1993. Minimum wages and employment: A case study of the fast food industry in New Jersey and Pennsylvania. NBER Working paper 4509. October.

Carmichael, L. 1985. Can unemployment be involuntary? *American Economic Review* 75: 1213–14.

Cohen, D., and G. Saint-Paul. 1994. Uneven technical progress and job destruction. CEPR working paper.

Davis, S., and J. Haltiwanger. 1990. Job creation, job destrunction, and job reallocation over the cycle. *NBER Macroeconomics Annual.*

Davis, S., and J. Haltiwanger. 1992. Gross job creation, gross job destruction, and employment reallocation. *Quarterly Journal of Economics* 107:819–64.

Dewatripont, M., and G. Roland. 1992. Economic reform and dynamic political constraints. *Review of Economic Studies* 59:703–30.

Diamond, P. 1982. Aggregate demand management in search equilibrium. *Journal of Political Economy* 90:881–94.

Dickens, W., and L. Katz. 1987a. Interindustry wage differences and industry characteristics. In K. Lang and J. Leonard, eds., *Unemployment and the Structure of Labor Markets*. Oxford: Basil Blackwell.

Dickens, W., and L. Katz. 1987b. Industry wage differences and theories of wage determination. NBER Working paper 2271.

Dickens, W., and K. Lang. 1985. A test of dual labor market theory. *American Economic Review* 75:792–805.

Dickens, W., and K. Lang. 1992. Labor market segmentation theory: Reconsidering the evidence. NBER Working paper 4087.

Dickens, W., L. Katz, K. Lang, and L. Summers. 1989. Employee crime and the monitoring puzzle. *Journal of Labor Economics* 7:331–47.

Dixit, A. 1976. *Optimization in Economic Theory*. Oxford: Oxford University Press.

Doeringer, P., and Piore, M. 1971. *Internal Labor Markets and Manpower Analysis*. New York: Sharpe.

Drago, R., and J. S. Heywood. 1992. Is worker behaviour consistent with efficiency wages? *Scottish Journal of Political Economy* 39:141–53.

Drazen, A. 1986. Optimal Minimum wage legislation. *Economic Journal* 96:774–84.

Drèze, J., and H. Sneesens. 1994. Technical development, competition from low wage economies and low-skilled unemployment. Mimeo. CORE, Université Catholique de Louvain, Belgium.

Edin, P.-A., and J. Zetterberg. 1992. Inter-industry wage differentials: Evidence from Sweden and a comparison with the United States. *American Economic Review* 82:1341–49.

Fallick, B. 1993. The hiring of new labor by expanding industries. Mimeo. Federal Reserve Board, Washington.

Fehr, E., and G. Kirchsteiger. 1994. Insider power, wage discrimination and fairness. *Economic Journal* 104:424, 571–83.

Fields, G. 1993. Increasing private returns to education. Mimeo. DELTA. November.

Fougère, D. 1989. Recherche d'emploi en présence de contrats de travail de courte durée: modélisation et estimation sur données individuelles. *Annales d'Economie et de Statistique*.

Fougère, D., and T. Kamionka. 1992. Mobilité et précarisation sur le marché français du travail: une analyse longitudinale pour les années 1986–1988. *Economie et Prévision* 102/103:157–78.

Gibbons, R., and L. Katz. 1992. Does unmeasured ability explain inter-industry wage differentials? *Review of Economic Studies* 59:515–36.

Groshen, E., and A. Krueger. 1990. The structure of supervision and pay in hospitals. *Industrial and Labor Relations Review* 43:134S–146S.

Grossman, G., and H. Helpman. 1991. *Innovation and Growth in the Global Economy*. Cambridge: MIT Press.

Hall, R. E. 1982. The importance of lifetime jobs in the U.S. economy. *American Economic Review* 72:716–24.

Hammermesch, D., ed. 1988. *Labor Demand and the Structure of Adjustment Costs*. Cambridge, MA: NBER.

Harris, J. R., and M. P. Todaro. 1970. Migration, unemployment, and development: A two sector analysis. *American Economic Review* 60:126–42.

Helwege, J. 1987. Interindustry wage differentials. Mimeo. UCLA.

Hibbs, D. A. 1982. *The Political Economy of Industrial Democracy*. Cambridge: Harvard University Press.

Holzer, H., L. Katz, and A. Krueger. 1991. Job queues and wages. *Quarterly Journal of Economics* 106:739–68.

Hopenhayn, H., and R. Rogerson. 1993. Job turnover and policy evaluation: A general equilibrium analysis. *Journal of Political Economy* 101:915–38.

Ishikawa, T., and T. Rejima. 1993. Measuring the extent of duality in the Japanese labour market. University of Tokyo Working paper.

Jacobsen, H. J., and C. Schultz. 1992. Wage discrimination and unemployment. Mimeo. University of Copenhagen.

Jaslin, J. P., J. Loos, and M. Forse. 1988. Du dualisme à la flexibilité du travail. *Observations et Diagnostics Economiques* 23:105–22.

Jimeno, J. F., and L. Toharia. 1991. Productivity and wage effects of temporary employment: Evidence from Spain. Mimeo. London School of Economics.

Jones, S. 1987. Minimum wage legislation in a dual labor market. *European Economic Review* 31:1229–46.

Juhn, C., K. M. Murphy, and B. Pierce. 1993. Wage inequality and the rise in the returns to skill. *Journal of Political Economy* 101:410–42.

Katz, L. 1986. Efficiency wages: A partial evaluation. *NBER Macroeconomics Annual*.

Katz, L., and A. Krueger. 1992. The effect of the minimum wage on the fast food industry. NBER Working paper 3997. February.

Katz, L., and K. M. Murphy. 1992. Changes in relative wages, 1963–87: Supply and demand factors. *Quarterly Journal of Economics* 107:35–78.

Katz, L., and L. Summers. 1989. Industry rents: Evidence and implications. *Brookings Papers on Economic Activity*, pp. 209–75.

Keane, M. 1993. Individual heterogeneity and inter-industry wage differentials. *Journal of Human Resources* 28:134–61.

Krueger, A. 1988. Determinants of job queues for federal jobs. *Industrial and Labor Relations Review* 41:567–81.

Krueger, A. 1991. Ownership, agency, and wages: An examination of franchising in the fast-food industry. *Quarterly Journal of Economics* 106:75–102.

Krueger, A., and L. Summers. 1988. Efficiency wages and the inter-industry wage structure. *Econometrica* 56:259–93.

Lang, K. 1987. Job signaling and welfare improving minimum wage laws. *Economic Inquiry* 25:145–58.

Lazear, E. 1979. Why is there mandatory retirement? *Journal of Political Economy* 87:1261–84.

Lazear, E. 1988. Employment at will, job security, and work incentives. In R. A. Hart, ed., *Employment, Unemployment and Labor Utilization*. Boston: Unwin Hyman, pp. 39–63.

Lazear, E. 1990a. Job security provisions and employment. *Quarterly Journal of Economics* 105:699–726.

Lazear, E. 1990b. Pensions and deferred benefits as strategic compensation. *Industrial Relations* (spring) 29:263–80.

Layard, R., S. Nickell, and R. Jackman. 1991. *Unemployment*. Oxford: Oxford University Press.

Leigh, D. 1976. Occupational advancement in the late 60's: An indirect test of the dual labor market hypothesis. *Journal of Human Resources* 11:155–71.

Leonard, J. 1987. Carrots and sticks: Ray, supervision, and turnover. *Journal of Labor Economics* 5:S136–S152.

Lilien, D. 1982. Sectoral shocks and aggregate unemployment. *Journal of Political Economy* 90:777–93.

Lindbeck, A., and D. Snower. 1988. *The Insider-Outsider Theory of Employment*. Cambridge: MIT Press.

Lucas, R. E., and N. Stokey. 1989. *Recursive Methods in Economic Dynamics*. Cambridge: Harvard University Press.

Mangum, G., D. Mayall, and K. Nelson. 1985. The temporary help industry: A response to the dual internal labor market. *Industrial and Labor Relations Review* 38:599–611.

McLeod, W. B., and J. M. Malcolmson. 1989. Implicit contracts, incentive compatibility, and involuntary unemployment. *Econometrica* 57:447–80.

Macleod, W. B., and J. M. Malcomson. 1993. Motivation, markets, and dual economies. Discussion paper. Université de Montréal, Québec.

McNabb, R. 1987. Testing for labour market segmentation in Britain. *Manchester School of Economics and Social Studies* 55:257–73.

McNabb, R., and G. Psacharopoulos. 1981. Further evidence on the relevance of the dual labor market hypothesis for the U.K. *Journal of Human Resources* 16:442–48.

Millard, S., and D. Mortensen. 1995. The unemployment and welfare effect of labor market policy: A comparison of the U.S. and the U.K. Northwestern University Working paper.

Mincer, J. 1991. Education and Unemployment. NBER Working paper 3838.

Mortensen, D., and C. Pissarides. 1994. Job creation and job destruction in the theory of unemployment. *Review of Economic Studies* 61:397–415.

Murphy, K. M., and R. Topel. 1987. Unemployment, risk, and earnings: Testing for equalizing wage differences in the labor market. In K. Lang and J. Leonard, eds., *Unemployment and the Structure of Labor Markets*. Oxford: Basil Blackwell.

Neal, D. 1993. Supervision and wages across industries. *Review of Economics and Statistics* 75:409–17.

Neumann, S., and A. Ziderman. 1986. Testing the dual labor market hypothesis: Evidence from the Israel labor mobility survey. *Journal of Human Resources* 21:230–37.

Nickell, S. 1986. Dynamic models of labour demand. In O. Ashenfelter and R. Layard, eds., *Handbook of Labor Economics*. North Holland.

Nickell, S., and B. Bell. 1994. Would cutting payroll taxes on the unskilled have a significant impact of unemployment? Paper presented at the CEPR Conference on Unemployment Policy. Vigo, Spain, September 1994.

Organization for Economic Cooperation and Development. 1989. *Employment Outlook.* Paris: OECD.

Organization for Economic Cooperation and Development. 1995. *Jobs Study.* Paris: OECD.

Ortega, J. 1994. Membership rules, matching, and unemployment. Mimeo. DELTA.

Oi, W. (1962). Labor as a quasi-fixed factor. *Journal of Political Economy* 70:538–55.

Persson, T., and G. Tabellini. 1994. Is inequality harmful for growth? *American Economic Review* 84:600–21.

Perotti, R. 1993. Income distribution political equilibrium, and growth. *Review of Economic Studies* 60:755–76.

Piketty, T. 1992. Voting over redistributive tax schedules. Mimeo. DELTA.

Piore, M. 1980. Dualism as a response to flux and uncertainty. In S. Berger and M. Piore, eds., *Dualism and Discontinuity in Industrial Society*. Cambridge: Cambridge University Press.

Pissarides, C. 1990. *Equilibrium Unemployment Theory*. Oxford: Basil Blackwell.

Pissarides, C. 1992. Loss of skill during unemployment and the persistence of employment shocks. *Quarterly Journal of Economics* 107:1371–92.

Raff, D., and L. Summers. 1987. Did Henry Ford pay efficiency wages? *Journal of Labor Economics* 5:S57–S86.

Raff, D., and L. Summers. 1987. Unemployment, long-term employment relations, and productivity growth. *Review of Economics and Statistics* 69:627–35.

Rebitzer, J., and M. D. Robinson. 1991. Employer size and dual labor markets. NBER Working paper 3587. January.

Rebitzer, J., and L. Taylor. 1991a. A model of dual labor markets when product demand is uncertain. *Quarterly Journal of Economics* 106:1373–83.

Rebitzer, J., and L. Taylor. 1991b. The consequences of minimum wage laws: Some new theoretical ideas. NBER Working paper 3877, September.

Rebitzer, J., and L. Taylor. 1991c. Work incentives and the demand for primary and contingent labor. NBER Working paper 3647. March.

Ritter, J. A., and L. Taylor. 1994. Workers as creditors: Performance bonds and efficiency wages. *American Economic Review* 84:694–704.

Robinson, J. A. 1993. Unemployment and human capital formation. Mimeo. University of Melbourne. April.

Rosen, S. 1986. The theory of compensating differentials. In O. Ashenfelter and R. Layard, eds., *Handbook of Labor Economics*. Amsterdam: North-Holland.

Rosén, A. 1991. A matching model of discrimination. FIEF mimeo. Stockholm.

Rosenberg, S. 1980. Male occupational standing and the dual labor market. *Industrial Relations* 19:34–49.

Saint-Paul, G. 1990. Efficiency wage, duality, and the dynamics of labor demand. MIMEO. Department of Economics, MIT.

Saint-Paul, G. 1991. Dynamic labor demand with dual labor markets. *Economics Letters* 36:219–22.

Saint-Paul, G. 1992a. Understanding the cyclical behavior of labor market flows: A dual perspective. *Economics Letters* 39:339–43.

Saint-Paul, G. 1992b. Are the unemployed unemployable? CEPR Discussion paper 689. *European Economic Review*, forthcoming.

Saint-Paul, G. 1993. On the political economy of labor market flexibility. *NBER Macroeconomics Annual*.

Saint-Paul, G. 1994a. Unemployment and increasing private returns to human capital. CEPR Discussion paper, *Journal of Public Economics*, forthcoming.

Saint-Paul, G. 1994b. Unemployment, wage rigidity and the returns to education. *European Economic Review* 38:891–98.

Saint-Paul, G. 1994c. Searching for the virtues of the European model. *IMF Staff Papers* 41:624–42.

Saint-Paul, G. 1995a. Efficiency wages as a persistence mechanism. In H. Dixon and N. Rankin, eds., *The New Macroeconomics*. Cambridge: Cambridge University Press.

Saint-Paul, G. 1995b. Efficiency wage, commitment, and hysteresis. *Annales d'Economie et de Statistique* 37:39–53.

Saint-Paul, G. 1995c. The high unemployment trap. *Quarterly Journal of Economics* (2):527–50.

Saint-Paul, G. 1996. Labor market institutions and the cohesion of the middle class. *International Tax and Public Finance*.

Saint-Paul, G., and T. Verdier. 1993. Education, democracy, and growth. *Journal of Development Economics* (42):399–407.

Saint-Paul, G., and T. Verdier. 1996. Inequality and growth: A challenge to the traditional political economy view. *European Economic Review*.

Salop, S. 1979. A model of the natural rate of unemployment. *American Economic Review* 69:117–25.

Sargent, T. J. 1978. Estimation of dynamic labor demand schedules under rational expectations. *Journal of Political Economy* 86:1009–44.

Segura, J., F. Durán, L. Toharia, and S. Bentolila. 1991. *Analisis de la Contratacion temporal en Espana*. Ministerio de Trabajo, Madrid.

Shapiro, C., and Stiglitz, J. 1984. Equilibrium unemployment as a worker discipline device. *American Economic Review* 74:433–44.

Solow, R. M. 1979. Another possible source of wage rigidity. *Journal of Macroeconomics* 1:79–82.

Solow, R. M. 1986. Unemployment: Getting the questions right. In C. Bean, R. Layard and S. Nickell, eds., *The Rise in Unemployment*. Oxford: Basil Blackwell.

Strand, J. 1992. Business cycles with worker moral hazard. *European Economic Review* 36: 1291–1304.

Teulings, C. N. 1993. Experience in a shirking model with heterogeneous workers. Tinbergen Institute discussion paper.

Tilly, C. 1992. Dualism in part-time employment. *Industrial Relations* 31:330–47.

Ulph, A., and D. Ulph. 1993. Labor market institutions and innovative success. Paper presented at the Conference on Labour Market Institutions and Contracts, European University Institute, Florence, May 1994.

Wadwhani, S., and M. Wall. 1991. A direct test of the efficiency wage hypothesis. *Oxford Economic Papers* 43:529–48.

Weiss, A. A. 1991. *Efficiency Wages: Models of Unemployment, Layoffs and Wage Dispersion*. Oxford: Clarendon Press.

Wright, R. 1986. The redistributive roles of unemployment insurance and the dynamics of voting. *Journal of Public Economics* 31:377–99.

Index